Using the Law in Social Work

Sara Miller McCune founded SAGE Publishing in 1965 to support the dissemination of usable knowledge and educate a global community. SAGE publishes more than 1000 journals and over 800 new books each year, spanning a wide range of subject areas. Our growing selection of library products includes archives, data, case studies and video. SAGE remains majority owned by our founder and after her lifetime will become owned by a charitable trust that secures the company's continued independence.

Los Angeles | London | New Delhi | Singapore | Washington DC | Melbourne

7th Edition

Using the Law in Social Work

Robert Johns

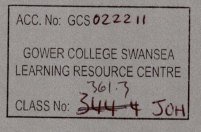

Learning Matters
An imprint of SAGE Publications Ltd
1 Oliver's Yard
55 City Road
London EC1Y 1SP

SAGE Publications Inc.
2455 Teller Road
Thousand Oaks, California 91320

SAGE Publications India Pvt Ltd
B 1/I 1 Mohan Cooperative Industrial Area
Mathura Road
New Delhi 110 044

SAGE Publications Asia-Pacific Pte Ltd
3 Church Street
#10-04 Samsung Hub
Singapore 049483

© 2017 Robert Johns

First published in 2003 by Learning Matters Ltd.
Reprinted in 2003 and 2004. Second edition published
in 2005. Reprinted in 2006. Third edition published
in 2007. Reprinted in 2008 (twice). Fourth edition
published in 2009. Fifth edition published in 2011. Sixth
edition published in 2014 by SAGE/Learning Matters.
Seventh edition published in 2017.

Editor: Kate Keers
Production controller: Chris Marke
Project management: Deer Park Productions,
Tavistock, Devon
Marketing manager: Camille Richmond
Cover design: Wendy Scott
Typeset by: C&M Digitals (P) Ltd, Chennai, India
Printed by CPI Group (UK) Ltd, Croydon, CR0 4YY

Library of Congress Control Number: 2017936984

British Library Cataloguing in Publication Data

A catalogue record for this book is available from the
British Library

ISBN 978-1-4739-7200-1 (pbk)
ISBN 978-1-4739-7199-8

At SAGE we take sustainability seriously. Most of our products are printed in the UK using FSC papers and boards.
When we print overseas we ensure sustainable papers are used as measured by the PREPS grading system.
We undertake an annual audit to monitor our sustainability.

Contents

Table of cases

Table of legislation

Primary legislation

Secondary legislation

Conventions

Guidance and Codes of Practice

Series Editor's Preface

We have witnessed significant changes and shocks in recent years. These have resulted in numerous challenges for the wider world, and for all four countries of the UK. These include political shifts to the 'popular' Right, a growing antipathy to care and support, and dealing with lies and 'alternative truths' in our daily lives. Alongside this, is the need to address the impact of an increasingly ageing population with its attendant social care needs and working with the financial implications that such a changing demography brings. At the other end of the lifespan the need for high quality childcare, welfare and safeguarding services has been highlighted as society develops and responds to the changing complexion. As demand rises so do the costs and the unquestioned assumption that austerity measures are necessary continues to create tensions in services, policies and expectations.

Migration has developed as a global phenomenon and we now live and work with the implications of international issues in our everyday and local lives. Often these issues influence how we construct our social services and determine what services we need to offer. It is likely that as a social worker you will work with a diverse range of people throughout your career, many of whom have experienced significant, even traumatic, events that require a professional and caring response. As well as working with individuals, however, you may be required to respond to the needs of a particular community disadvantaged by world events or excluded within local communities because of assumptions made about them.

The importance of high quality social work education remains if we are adequately to address the complexities of modern life. We should continually strive for excellence in education as this allows us to focus clearly on what knowledge it is useful to engage with when learning to be a social worker. Questioning everything, especially from a position of knowledge is central to social work.

The books in this series respond to the agendas driven by changes brought about by professional bodies, governments and disciplinary reviews. They aim to build on and offer introductory texts based on up-to-date knowledge and to help communicate this in an accessible way, so preparing the ground for future study and for encouraging good practice as you develop your social work career. The books are written by people passionate about social work and social services and aim to instil that passion in others. The current text represents an up-to-date edition of a key book in the series. It introduces you to core legislation and some of diverse ways in which law is interpreted in, for and by social work practice. The complexities of the law are presented in a clear, accessible way that sets the scene for exploring more specialised areas of law affecting practice.

Professor Jonathan Parker

Introduction to the seventh edition

This is the seventh edition of *Using the Law in Social Work*. There can now be no doubting the central role of law in qualifying programmes in social work. When the Department of Health set out regulations concerning the core curriculum for the first BA qualifying programmes in social work in 2002 (Department of Health, 2002) it specifically identified law as a distinct entity, which resulted in many social work programmes offering discrete modules in law at different levels. The changes instituted by the Social Work Reform Board reaffirmed the importance of social work law, with the Health and Care Professions Council (HCPC) Standards of Proficiency dedicating an entire set of proficiencies to it entitled 'be able to practise within the legal and ethical boundaries of their profession' (Standard of Proficiency 2 HCPC, 2012). It is not surprising, therefore, that this book has been widely used by students studying in the first and second years of undergraduate degrees, and in the first year of their Master's qualifying degree in social work. It is also widely used by practice educators as well as experienced practitioners.

The popularity of the book indicates that it meets a real need for an introductory text in law that prepares students for their first placements, and as essential grounding before being able to go on to tackle the more advanced, comprehensive and authoritative texts such as Brayne *et al.*, (2015) and Brammer (2015). The book was devised for student social workers who are beginning to develop their skills and understanding of the requirements for practice, particularly in statutory settings. While primarily aimed at students in the early stages of their degree courses, it is also designed to be useful for subsequent years depending on how programmes are formulated and at what stage students move into practice learning.

Requirements for social work education

Social work education has undergone a major transformation to ensure that qualified social workers are educated at least to honours degree level and develop knowledge, skills and values which are common and shared. A vision for social work operating in complex human situations has been adopted. This is reflected in the following definition from the International Association of Schools of Social Work and International Federation of Social Workers (IFSW, 2014):

> *Social work is a practice-based profession and an academic discipline that promotes social change, and development, social cohesion, and the empowerment and liberation of people. Principles of social justice, human rights, collective responsibility and respect*

for diversities are central to social work. Underpinned by theories of social work, social sciences, humanities and indigenous knowledge, social work engages people and structures to address life challenges and enhance wellbeing.

Human rights and justice are also fundamental to law. Law is a very important component of social work practice in Britain. The majority of social workers in Britain today are employed by statutory agencies — that is, organisations such as local authorities whose every action has to be based on some kind of legal power that authorises it. Even for social workers employed outside the statutory sector, the law provides the framework within which services are offered, and is crucial in areas such as child safeguarding, where inter-agency co-operation is essential and where every social worker has responsibilities. It is impossible to practise without coming up against the law; it is impossible to practise effectively without an in-depth understanding of how the law affects everyday social work practice. That is what this book is about.

This book has been carefully mapped to the new Professional Capabilities Framework for Social Workers in England and will help you to develop the appropriate standards at the right level. These standards are:

1. Professionalism

Identify and behave as a professional social worker committed to professional development.

2. Values and ethics

Apply social work ethical principles and values to guide professional practice.

3. Diversity

Recognise diversity and apply anti-discriminatory and anti-oppressive principles in practice.

4. Rights, justice and economic well-being

Advance human rights and promote social justice and economic well-being.

5. Knowledge

Apply knowledge of social sciences, law and social work practice theory.

6. Critical reflection and analysis

Apply critical reflection and analysis to inform and provide a rationale for professional decision-making.

7. Intervention and skills

Use judgement and authority to intervene with individuals, families and communities to promote independence, provide support and prevent harm, neglect and abuse.

8. Contexts and organisations

Engage with, inform and adapt to changing contexts that shape practice. Operate effectively within your own organisational frameworks and contribute to the development of services and organisations. Operate effectively within multi-agency and interprofessional settings.

9. Professional leadership

Take responsibility for the professional learning and development of others through supervision, mentoring, assessing, research, teaching, leadership and management.

References to these standards will be made throughout the text and you will find a diagram of the Professional Capabilities Framework in Appendix 1 on p192. In addition, reference will be made at the start of each chapter to the most relevant Standards of Proficiency (HCPC, 2012). The law is also directly relevant to a number of the National Occupational Standards for Social Work for Wales (Care Council for Wales, 2013), particularly:

SW 7 prepare professional reports and records relating to people;

SW 10 support people to participate in decision-making processes;

SW 11 advocacy;

SW 13 investigate harm or abuse.

As an academic text, this book is intended as an introduction to the study of social work law as a specific topic area. As such, the book relates to some key social work benchmarks (Quality Assurance Agency for Higher Education (QAA), 2016).

With regard to helping students to become accountable, reflective, critical and evaluative (section 4.7), this book helps readers think critically about the legal context in which social work is located and therefore:

- to work in a transparent and responsible way, balancing autonomy with complex, multiple and sometimes contradictory accountabilities;

- to exercise authority constructively within complex frameworks of accountability and ethical and legal boundaries.

With regard to Knowledge, Understanding and Skills (section 5), the book will assist in the following areas:

- the relationship between human rights enshrined in law and the moral and ethical rights determined theoretically, philosophically and by contemporary society (5.3 v);

- the complex relationships between justice, care and control in social welfare, and the practical and ethical implications of these, including their expression in roles as statutory agents in diverse practice settings and in upholding the law in respect of challenging discrimination and inequalities (5.3 vi);

- the importance of interventions that promote social justice, human rights, social cohesion, collective responsibility and respect for diversity and tackle inequalities (5.5 v);

- its delivery in a range of community-based and organisational settings spanning the statutory, voluntary and private sectors, and the changing nature of these service contexts (5.5 vi);

- the importance of social work's contribution to intervention across service user groups, settings and levels in terms of the profession's focus on social justice, human rights, social cohesion, collective responsibility and respect for diversities (5.5 viii);

- the leadership, organisation and delivery of social work services, which include:

  - the significance of legislative and legal frameworks and service delivery standards, including on core social work values and ethics in the delivery of services which support, enable and empower (5.6 vi).

With regard to the development of skills, the book will enhance your potential to:

- involve users of social work services in ways that increase their resources, capacity and power to influence factors affecting their lives (5.16 i);

- increase social justice by identifying and responding to prejudice, institutional discrimination and structural inequality (5.16 vi);

- operate within a framework of multiple accountability – for example, to agencies, the public, service users, carers and others (5.16 vii);

- observe the limits of professional and organisational responsibility, using supervision appropriately and referring to others when required (5.16 viii).

What's in this book?

Before launching into a summary of what is covered in each chapter, it may be worth saying something about the general approach of this book. It is part of a series that outlines and explores the knowledge base of social work as it applies to everyday practice. It is an example of applied theory and knowledge, with a strong emphasis on how knowledge underpins sound professional social work practice. It was written very much with the future needs of social work students in mind, in the sense that it places the application of law to everyday social work practice centre stage.

We begin in Chapter 1 with an overview of the purpose of law in social work, looking at the role of law, how it is made, different kinds of law and the purpose they serve.

In Chapter 2, there is a focus on basic human rights with an overview of the European Convention on Human Rights, the key legal benchmark, implemented in Britain through the

Human Rights Act 1998. By way of illustration, we look at the development of legislation that attempts to address the needs of people with serious mental health problems as a case example of how human rights legislation applies to social work. Key issues addressed in this example are as follows.

- Is it acceptable for people to be protected from themselves?

- To what extent can laws protect the public from people who might present an apparent threat?

- What is the extent of the responsibility of the state?

- To what extent do people have the right to determine their own future, even when their capacity to make judgements and decisions is seriously affected by mental health problems?

These are not just legal issues. They reflect fundamental debates about values and ethics in social work.

Chapters 3 and 4 explore the crucial issue of the relationship between social workers, the family and the state. In Chapter 3, the focus will be on children's basic needs and how these are provided for through legislative means. How does the state, Britain today, ensure that children have their basic needs met? What overall legal frameworks govern this? What measures does the law promote in relation to children's safety? What about their education? What about their care and support, especially where parents are not able to provide care themselves? Here the book explores the range of services available to support children, with social workers working in partnership with parents, and the provision of alternative accommodation when children cannot be cared for in their own homes.

Chapter 4 concentrates more specifically on various provisions in the Children Act 1989, the Children Act 2004, the Children and Young Persons Act 2008, and the Children and Families Act 2014. These are crucial Acts for any intending social worker to understand, regardless of whether they are employed in voluntary settings or the statutory sector. This chapter focuses on the principles underlying the Children Act 1989 in particular, especially working in partnership and ascertaining children's wishes and feelings. What happens when the law has to intervene directly in family life and sort out such matters as who cares for children after a divorce? What are the legal issues relevant to a social work assessment of children's needs? What happens when there is an allegation that a child is being harmed? When legal intervention is being considered on behalf of children, what do legal proceedings offer by way of offering a better future for certain children?

In Chapters 5 and 6, the focus switches to social workers' role in relation to adults, particularly those who may be in need of support services (Chapter 5) or, in extreme cases, protection from themselves or other people (Chapter 6). Here the book explores the issue of provision of services under various legal enactments that comprise what might loosely be called 'social care'. Chapter 5 offers an overview of the legal basis for adult care services, while the discussion in Chapter 6 is extended to measures by which local authorities, the voluntary sector and independent organisations can protect vulnerable adults who are at risk of various forms of harm. Included in this is consideration of the law relating to people's ability to make decisions for themselves, which the law terms 'capacity'.

Chapter 7 is a more specialist chapter, applicable to social workers who work in the field of youth justice. This book does not cover work with adult offenders, since in England and Wales this is the prerogative of the National Probation Service. However, social workers are employed in a nationwide network of Youth Offending Teams, multidisciplinary agencies that implement all aspects of youth justice legislation with a prime responsibility for preventing 'offending behaviour'.

Chapter 8 addresses the role of the courts as a key forum in which social workers are held publicly accountable. It focuses on practice issues that sometimes cause social workers anxiety: what actually happens in court, court's expectations, giving evidence in court, writing reports. This chapter highlights the main issues for social workers when they are called to account for their actions. Courts are the forum where the law is put into practice in the sense that cases are 'tried' or 'heard', and where independent decisions are made about social work practice or recommendations. It is therefore essential to understand the role that courts play in social work generally, but most especially in the fields of youth justice and child safeguarding.

Finally, Chapter 9 addresses a number of issues that are sometimes overlooked when social workers study the law, for this chapter is not about what social workers do, it is about who they are – their credibility and the standards of professional practice the public is entitled to expect. The emphasis in this chapter is on public accountability in the sense of ensuring that high standards of professional practice are maintained. What legal provisions exist to ensure that social workers are reliable and trustworthy? What standards apply to the kinds of services provided, especially in relation to residential care? How are social workers accountable to service users and employers?

The book concludes with an overview of its coverage, indicating areas for further study and urging a watching brief on the ever-changing world of social work law.

Learning features

The book is interactive. You are encouraged to work through the book as an active participant, taking responsibility for your learning, in order to increase your knowledge, understanding and ability to apply this learning to practice. The activities have been devised to encourage reflection and help you to incorporate the learning undertaken into practice. In this way, your knowledge will become deeply embedded as part of your development.

Each chapter begins with a reference to the relevant aspects of the Professional Capabilities Framework together with a summary of the chapter contents. The structure of each chapter varies, but in all cases there will be illustrative case material incorporated into the discussion. In keeping the discussion practical yet clarifying a number of complex issues, it is necessary to make some accommodation for readers' and social work practitioners' needs, so the following points need to be borne in mind.

- This book should not be treated as an authoritative statement of the law – it is intended as an introduction to relevant law, not an advanced legal textbook.

- Legislative sources will be cited as accurately as possible, but extensive quotation of legislation is avoided, so if you need to refer to specific sections of particular Acts you will need to use additional sources – for example, other textbooks or the Internet: see Further Reading and website addresses at the end of each chapter.

- Professional practice and decision-making should not be based solely on this book, which is intended as an introductory text for professional qualifying courses in social work (BA, BSc, MA or MSc in Social Work).

- This text does not cover every aspect of social work law, but should provide some indication of the areas which are of the most direct relevance to practice in England and Wales.

- There are major differences in the law in Scotland and Northern Ireland, and significant differences in relation to Wales. While every effort has been made to incorporate legislation and guidance in relation to Wales, practitioners may need to double-check on references to regulations and current policy. Practitioners in Scotland and Northern Ireland will need to consult reference sources for the law in those countries (see list at end of Chapter 1).

- Some important legislation was passed by Parliament in 2014. Most relevant here to Chapters 3 and 4 is the Children and Families Act 2014 (for Wales the Social Services and Well-being (Wales) Act 2014). In the field of adult care (covered in Chapters 5 and 6) the Care Act 2014 (and the Wales equivalent which is again the Social Services and Well-being (Wales) Act 2014) is of great wide-ranging significance. These stand along with developments in Wales (but only Wales) regarding a public body general well-being duty (Well-being of Future Generations (Wales) Act 2015) and changes in registration of social workers with the introduction of Regulation and Inspection of Social Care (Wales) Act 2016 and the establishment of Social Care Wales as a registration body. Several texts referred to in this book will not include references to these measures, so great care should be taken to ensure that any other textbooks or websites consulted are as up-to-date as possible.

While the book is as accurate as possible at the time of going to press, legislation and practice is constantly changing, so it is always important to check the latest legislation. For this purpose, each chapter concludes with a list of recommended websites and other resources that will help with this. The currency and validity of all these were checked when this book was prepared for publication.

1: But I Want to be a Social Worker, Not a Lawyer

In which case, this is the book for you. For this book is about social work practice, it is not a legal textbook. Yet it is about the law – the law that informs and underpins social work practice in England and Wales today.

Achieving a social work degree

This chapter will help you to develop the following capabilities from the **Professional Capabilities Framework:**

4. **Rights, justice and economic well-being**
    Advance human rights and promote social justice and economic well-being.

5. **Knowledge**
    Apply knowledge of social sciences, law and social work practice theory.

It is relevant to the following Standards of Proficiency:

1. Be able to practise safely and effectively within their scope of practice.
2. Be able to practise within the legal and ethical boundaries of their profession.

It will also introduce you to the following standards as set out in the 2016 Social Work Subject Benchmark Statement:

(Continued)

1

(Continued)

5.3 v   the relationship between human rights enshrined in law and the moral and ethical rights determined theoretically, philosophically and by contemporary society;

5.3 vi   the complex relationships between justice, care and control in social welfare and the practical and ethical implications of these;

5.6 vi   the significance of legislative and legal frameworks and service delivery standards.

Introduction

This chapter sets the scene by setting out a number of reasons as to why the law is an integral part of good social work practice. It is important to be clear about why the law is relevant, and how a detailed knowledge of what the law actually says is sometimes necessary for social work practitioners – this book sets out precisely those areas where social workers need to be thoroughly familiar with the law in everyday practice. The law is a major way in which people's rights are promoted, offering protection from discrimination, informing social workers and social work agencies of what they can and cannot do, and at a broader level clarifying the relationship between the state and the individual or family.

Social workers need to know about all of this. The majority of this chapter therefore is given over to a consideration of how the law sets the boundaries for social work practice. It does this through a 'case study' – not the usual kind of case study where we look at the needs of a family or individual, but a policy case study, an example of how the law has developed in relation to one area of social work practice. The case study examined centres on events that occurred in Cleveland in the mid-1980s that led to a highly influential government report. This report then became a blueprint for the relationship between the state, social work and the family. Do remember, though, when you read this case study that it is simply meant as an example of how changes in the law occur. It is the 'peg' on which to hang explanations of how the law changes and why. It is hoped that you will find this more interesting than simply reading a dry account of political and legal processes. By proceeding through this case example, you will encounter a number of terms which may be new to you; it may be helpful for you to note these as you proceed, so that you build up your own glossary of legal terms.

Why law?

In order to explain the importance of law to social work practice, it is necessary to reflect on the roles and responsibilities of social workers and how they might impinge on people's everyday lives.

The majority of social workers in Britain today are employed by publicly accountable organisations – local authorities or agencies directly commissioned by them. Much of social workers' professional lives are spent in providing services to people and, in some cases, intervening in people's lives in order to protect them from themselves or other people. Immediately it becomes obvious that social workers are deeply involved in issues to do with people's rights: rights of access to information, rights and entitlements to services, rights to be protected from harm. The extent to which social workers can offer services and can offer protection is bound to be determined by some kind of framework, and that framework is, of course, the law. So it is essential for social workers to know about the law.

Activity 1.1

Why else might social workers need to know about the law?

List as many reasons as you can for social workers learning about the law.

Comment

There are a number of reasons you could have listed and these are set out in the discussion below. Don't worry if what you have does not quite correspond to this; what matters is that you have begun to think about the role of law in social work. At the end of the chapter there are a couple of references for further reading on this topic. Chapter 1 of Braye and Preston-Shoot (2016) is particularly useful.

Generally, social workers need to know about the law because:

- it tells them what their powers and duties are;
- in some areas of practice it sets out what they have to do, what they have discretion to do, and what they may not do;
- it sets out clear lines of accountability which may include reference to bodies that adjudicate when necessary;
- it ensures that processes whereby decisions are made are fair and equitable;
- it may help clarify ethical practice issues;
- through the court system, the law makes or ratifies decisions made by social work agencies;
- it acts as a final arbiter between social workers and service users where there is a dispute that cannot be resolved by any other means.

It may also be worth mentioning some things that the law cannot do. The law cannot tell social workers what to do in every circumstance: it can only set out a framework. The law cannot resolve the everyday tensions and dilemmas of social work practice, since there is no ready prescription for resolving the complex problems that sometimes confront social workers. Above all, the law cannot be substituted for sound professional practice. Critically, social workers need to abide by a code of ethics and set of practice principles that are over and beyond what the law may offer. In this respect it is important to acknowledge that there may occasionally be a conflict between the law and social work values. For example, social work has a strong commitment to anti-oppressive practice. When it comes to counteracting discrimination in relation to race, the law supports and indeed encourages the anti-discriminatory approach of much social work practice (in particular the Equality Act 2010 directs local authorities to promote anti-racist policies). Yet until its repeal by the Local Government Act 2003, section 28 Local Government Act 1988 prohibited the promotion of homosexuality by local authorities, a law that clearly conflicted with social work values and principles which require people of different sexual orientations to be treated equitably. Furthermore, there is a danger that in seeing the law as the ultimate determinant of social work practice, the practitioner might then look to the law for 'easy' solutions to complex problems. For example, it is sometimes not easy to decide how exactly a child's cultural needs are to be met when it is necessary to provide a foster care placement outside that child's own family. It would be easy if the law said that children can be offered placements only with foster carers whose background matched the child's, yet the law does not say this. Instead, it declares the general principle that local authorities should take this factor into account when placing a child. Likewise, it is tempting to expect the law to determine when some child-rearing practices are abusive, yet the law cannot do this because so much depends on the context and the intention of those who are parenting the child. When you are more experienced as a practitioner, you will undoubtedly have to return to these sorts of dilemmas and may sometimes find the law frustrating where it does not apparently offer clear direction or watertight boundaries. For further examples and a broader discussion on this, see Johns (2016).

The whole issue of the extent to which the law should be involved in everyday social work decisions became headline news back in 1987. Social workers were accused of trammelling on parents' rights to look after their own children. The social services department was accused of outrageous, 'jack-boot' tactics in removing children thought to have been abused. Innocent families were 'made to feel like criminals', their pleas to be heard by professionals being 'ignored'. Social workers, police and doctors fell out with each other publicly. The tabloid press had a field day. Even the more respected newspapers such as *The Times* carried headlines such as *Wrong diagnosis toll in Cleveland reaches 30*; *Innocent parents in abuse cases losing children for a year*; *Polarised relations threat in Cleveland; Cleveland affair brought chaos to child care system* (*The Times*/NI Syndication: 5 August, 27 August, 3 September and 16 September 1987). Inevitably, this had to be sorted out, and it was – through a public inquiry. Although this may seem like history, the way in which the inquiry sought to address the controversy is really relevant to us at the initial stage of our study of social work law. So in this chapter we are going to start by devoting some space to an examination of the issues raised in Cleveland in 1987. For the inquiry itself and subsequent parliamentary debate said a great deal about the role of the law in social work, culminating in a framework outlining the relationship between the state (the Government) and families who justifiably claimed rights to determine their own lives, rights enshrined in Article 8 of the European Convention on Human Rights (see discussion in Chapter 2).

What went wrong in Cleveland?

The integration of social services through the amalgamation of former children's departments, welfare departments and certain health-related functions was brought about by the implementation of the Seebohm Report (1968) which was translated into law through the Local Authority Social Services Act 1970. Subsequently, a number of issues quickly emerged in relation to the protection of children, allegedly partially as a result of loss of specialisation due to the melding of these three disciplines. There followed what appeared to be an unending series of inquiries that started with the Colwell Inquiry in 1974 (DHSS, 1974), although this was not the first example of inquiries into child abuse (Packman, 1975, Chapter 8). These inquiries focused on the apparent lack of competence and professionalism in social workers who had 'failed' to protect children from death at the hands of a parent or carer, although there was also a feeling that social work itself was being undermined for political reasons (Parton, 1985 – for a broader discussion of this brought up-to-date see also Parton, 2014). The findings of these inquiries were brought together by the Department of Health (1991a) who drew lessons from them which, together with research-based findings (Aldgate, 2001), are important reading for intending practitioners in this field. In the majority of these cases social workers were criticised for their lack of action, whereas in Cleveland the issue was over-readiness, indeed alleged zealous enthusiasm, for intervening in families in order to 'protect' children.

The Cleveland Inquiry was instigated as a result of a large number of children being taken into care against the wishes of parents on the grounds that they were possibly sexually abused. The social services department and the local consultant paediatrician worked together in identifying what they thought were cases of serious abuse, but at that time the law afforded only limited provision for oversight of decisions to take children away from their parents by force. Furthermore, it appeared to be extraordinarily difficult for parents to challenge the diagnosis of the paediatrician and the professional practice of social workers. The following extracts from the Cleveland Report (the Butler-Sloss Inquiry) provide a flavour of the kind of issues confronting parents and children.

Case study

2.12   A number of parents complained that their consent was not sought or not obtained for medical examinations; or for the taking of photographs; or for disclosure work to be carried out with their children.

2.17   Grandparents, who were bringing up their 10-year-old grandson, told the Inquiry: We were simply told by a social worker [named] that [our grandson] had to be examined and our permission was not sought.

2.25   [.] received a letter from social worker which referred to children she (Mother) might have in the future and which included: 'there would be no guarantees from us that you would be entrusted to look after any children you may have.' The mother said she was pregnant at this time but as a consequence of receiving this letter the pregnancy was terminated.

2.34   The parents of three children aged 9, 7 and just under 2 years, described the total denial of access to their children both whilst in hospital and in foster care...

2.36   Many parents felt strongly that they should be heard at case conferences. A number told the Inquiry that they were informed that case conferences were to be held. Some said they were told they could not attend. Others said they were informed they could attend but would not be admitted or would not be heard whilst the meeting was in progress. Some said they were told the results of case conferences. Others complained they were told neither of case conferences nor of decisions reached there.

2.52   [.] The parents' complaints were threefold:

   1.   They were denied or unable to obtain information about their children or what was happening or what was planned for the future;
   2.   That social workers were not interested in and not enquiring into the family environment and history; and
   3.   That paediatricians and social workers had concluded that the parent (usually father) or parents were abusers and, until that was accepted by one or both, were indifferent, unresponsive and lacked compassion.

2.53   The father of one family referred to making numerous calls to social services but to being met with what can only be described as utter stonewalling.

(extracts from DHSS, 1988, pp38–44)

These are simply a few extracts that give a flavour of the issues at stake. It is easy to see straight away how parents saw themselves as being totally undermined and abused by professional action and the lack of legal safeguards. Critically, they were not afforded proper rights to present their views, a complaint echoed by service users in other areas of social work practice (Clarke, 1993, Chapter 5). Yet the Cleveland Report goes much further than this and acknowledges the underlying dilemma of child safeguarding work – namely, that social workers are *damned if they do, and damned if they don't* – pilloried if they fail to act when they should have done (with the benefit of hindsight), and castigated if they seemed to be too ready to remove children. The specific legal issues were that:

- the law as it then existed appeared to offer few avenues for parents to challenge social workers' or paediatricians' decisions;
- magistrates appeared to rubber stamp decisions and did not really call social workers or doctors to account for their actions;
- there appeared to be limited avenues of redress, with few appeal possibilities;
- children could be kept in care for some considerable time without anyone having to justify to the courts substantive reasons why they should be;
- the courts and the legal system generally appeared to be weighted against parents, in an adversarial system where the child's voice could not be heard;
- children were seen as objects of concern and not the central subjects of the court proceedings.

There was a whole host of other professional practice issues, not least of which was the relationship between different professionals, principally social workers and the police, but our concern here is to focus on the issue of rights and what this case demonstrates about the operation of the legal system.

It is apparent from the above that the legal system pre-Cleveland offered few safeguards for parents or children, and there was a lack of clarity about the role of the law and more specifically the courts. The public furore aroused by Cleveland led to Parliamentary debates and a clear commitment to change the law. The Butler-Sloss Inquiry (DHSS, 1988) promoted the idea that the law needed to be much clearer in establishing the boundaries between parents, children and social workers. In addition, the law needed to take a much more active role in regulating social work practice – not with a view to constraining it, but in order to clarify where and when social workers should intervene on children's behalf. The report also very strongly promoted the idea that the child should be the primary focus of the law's concern, and this particular area of the law needed far greater attention generally.

As a consequence, Parliament passed the Children Act 1989. This legislation addressed many of the issues highlighted by the Cleveland incident and in particular clarified the ways in which the law was to protect children. Chapter 4 will explain what the law now says and how it relates to current social work practice, but in this chapter we are going to explore how the Act reached the statute book, saying something about what kind of law it represents. This explanation will help you understand the process whereby laws are made and introduce you to a system of classifying legislation. The Children Act 1989 is a useful example, simply because you now know something about its origins. Other examples right across the range from adult care to education could have been used, so do remember that this is an exemplar of legislative process: all statute laws follow similar pathways and all of them can be categorised.

Let's begin this by asking a series of questions. Why was the law changed? How does a law get changed? What kind of law is the Children Act 1989 and what other kinds of laws are there? Developing this further, how does legislation such as the Children Act 1989 operate so as to set boundaries but without interfering too much in everyday practice? More generally, how can professional power be challenged and how does the law address infringements of people's rights?

We shall now address each of these questions in turn.

How and why is the law changed?

The formal mechanism whereby the law is changed is best demonstrated by a diagram (see Figure 1.1).

This is the process whereby the law is changed. Perhaps a more interesting question is why laws change. In this case example, why was the Children Act 1989 passed?

Activity 1.2

Why do you think the law changes? What reasons can you suggest for changes in legislation such as the Children Act 1989?

Spend a few moments reflecting on this. The answer is not quite as obvious as it may appear. Clearly, one could simply say that the law was changed because Parliament said so, but this task is asking you to think about why Parliament changed the law.

Who do you think may have exerted pressure on MPs? Whose interests were served by the introduction of the Children Act 1989? What are the wider and broader issues here?

If you have already studied some social policy, you may find it slightly easier to answer the question in a systematic way by looking at changes at different levels and related to different ideologies. Even if you have not done so, you should still be able to suggest people and institutions that were key agitators for change.

Comment

We are not going to stray too much into the area of social policy, which is the academic discipline that tries to explain developments in the welfare state and social welfare legislation, but listed below are some suggestions as to why this Act was introduced. They are issues to think about and consider; there are no right and wrong answers here, simply matters of opinion. You'll find academics divided about the role law plays in social work, and whether it is always positive or beneficial. Listed at the end of this chapter are some suggestions for further reading in the area of social policy.

Reasons for the introduction of the Children Act 1989

- Individual MPs took up the plight of parents in Cleveland who considered themselves falsely accused of child abuse, and pressed for a full investigation which eventually took the form of a judicial inquiry (DHSS, 1988). Those MPs then pressed for changes in the law along the lines recommended by the Inquiry Report.

- Lawyers acting for the parents and others involved in child care court proceedings seized on the events in Cleveland as a demonstration of the inadequacy of child care legislation. They influenced Parliament directly and indirectly through pressure groups such as the Law Society.

- Social workers and other child safeguarding professionals shared a common concern about the extent to which they are expected to intervene in families. They welcomed the Cleveland Report and the clarity that would be obtained by the Children Act 1989.

- Pressure groups representing the interests of children and families likewise seized the opportunity to press for 'reform' and they would have been able to provide other case illustrations of the need for change through the media and through contact with government departments and MPs.

All of these explanations – and there may well have been others that you could suggest – relate to people acting as individuals and groups. If we examine wider spheres of influences, it is possible to suggest additional factors operating.

- There was a broad ideological division between those who saw social workers and other child care professionals as always knowing what is in the best interests of the child, ranged against those who saw a need for the powers of professionals to be curtailed. The Children Act 1989 can be seen as part of the move to challenge professional power by involving the courts more in decision-making rights throughout the process of assessment.

- There may have been political differences between those who argue that it is a duty of the state to promote the welfare of children and therefore there ought to be extensive legal powers available to ensure this, contrasted with those who see the law as infringing parents' rights and duties to look after their own children. Those in the latter category see the law as relevant only in a very narrow range of cases where child abuse has clearly been proven.

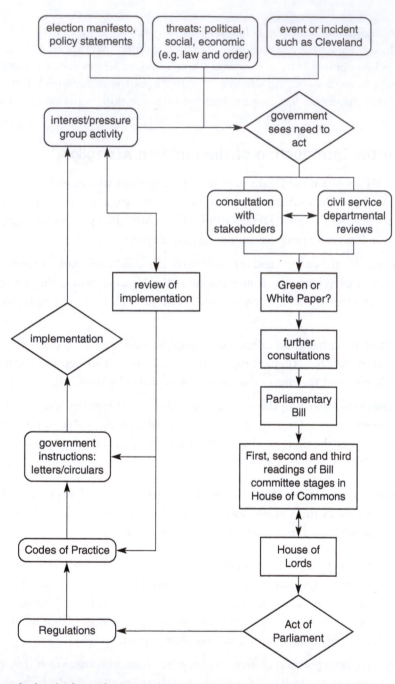

Figure 1.1 How the law is changed

At an even broader level, the Children Act 1989 may demonstrate something about the relationship between the family and the State. Some would interpret this as reflecting economic changes that require families to take greater responsibility for themselves with a diminution in the role of the State. According to this argument, curbing welfare professionals' power is necessary in order to reduce public expenditure and dependency on government officials such as local authority social workers (Clarke, 1993; Fox Harding, 1997). Debates about the welfare of children are complex and arouse deep feelings in people, as was seen spectacularly in the case of Peter Connelly, also known as 'Baby P' or 'Baby Peter', in late 2008 (Ofsted, 2008). Some believe that the extent of child abuse is grossly exaggerated and find it particularly difficult to accept that there is extensive sexual abuse of children. Conversely, some would argue that the extent of abuse is seriously underestimated. Media portrayals of social work tend to adopt one of these two extremes, whereas policymakers and legislators need to take a balanced view, and this is achieved through requiring courts to make the key decisions.

If you are unfamiliar with the broader explanations of law and social work, do look at the list under Further Reading at the end of this chapter for ways in which you can extend your knowledge and understanding.

A number of other potential explanations may have occurred to you. Do not worry if you failed to identify those enumerated here. What matters is not the number that you correctly 'guessed' but that you can now see why the law needs to be involved in social work and what it is anticipated that the law will achieve.

What kinds of laws are there?

What kind of law is the Children Act 1989 and what types of law are there?

The difference between criminal law and civil law is familiar to most people. Criminal law is the law that provides sanctions or penalties for 'breaking' the law. It proscribes (prohibits) certain behaviour. If you steal, you commit a criminal offence. If you evade paying tax by not declaring something you know you must by law declare, you commit a criminal offence. If you break the speed limit, you commit an offence. All will result in some kind of punishment (penalty or 'sentence') – assuming you get caught, of course.

Civil law is a means of arbitration when someone believes that they are 'in the right'. It may be about a legal wrong that results in harm to someone, for which they seek redress: recompense, compensation, matters put right, or some other course of action. It is not about punishment, so intention is often irrelevant. For example, you may unwittingly damage your neighbour's car when the tree in your garden falls on it. Or you may have caused injury to livestock by accidentally leaving a gate open, or failed to pay a debt. If you are libelled, you can claim for the damage done to your reputation and your career prospects. If you took lots of photocopies of this chapter without permission, you would be in breach of copyright and the publishers could sue you (so be warned). In the example of the Children Act 1989, the local authority believes it is right to protect the child, that the child is being subject to a 'wrong' – in this case, being harmed in some way. So, if parental action or inaction results in 'significant harm' to a child, the courts can take steps to address this – this is exactly what the Children Act 1989 says, so the Children Act 1989 is an excellent example of civil law. Another example relevant to social work would be that if central or local government fail to carry out their duties properly, the courts can declare them to be in error. Likewise, compensation can be ordered by the courts if an employer fails in their obligations to their employees or a trader sells faulty goods, and so on.

Table 1.1   Criminal law and civil law

	Criminal law	Civil law
Fundamental purpose	Prosecution	Redress
Referred to as	R v. Smith	Smith v. Smith Ayrshire v. Smith Re C.S. (a child), G (children)
Outcome	Sentence/punishment	Judgement or resolution by agreement
Essentially about	'Breaking the law', threat to society, intention (technically called *mens rea*) is important	Tort – legal wrong, no intent need be proved, protection of vulnerable, defence from actions of powerful bodies
Cases decided on (burden of proof)	Proof beyond reasonable doubt	Balance of probabilities

In social work much of the law is civil law, and often it is implemented through tribunals rather than courts themselves. Tribunals are in effect specialist courts, dedicated to a specific purpose. For example, there are tribunals that hear appeals concerning registration of residential homes, First-Tier Tribunals (Care Standards), and First-Tier Tribunals (Mental Health) that decide on detention of patients under the Mental Health Act 1983 (Tribunals, Courts and Enforcement Act 2007, Criminal Justice and Courts Act 2015). One other key difference between laws is a difference between what is written down – which is what

Table 1.2   Statute law and common law

Statute law	Common law
Written down laws: deal with specific topics (for example, local authority social services) or specific group of people (for example, the 'chronically sick and disabled'); can also be more general (for example, Equality Act 2010, Human Rights Act 1998)	General unwritten rules which are commonly understood to be the law of the land: for example, the limits of the role of local authorities, rights of courts to intervene in what a local authority does; can fill the gaps between statutes
Interpreted by reference to what the law actually says and how judges interpret what Parliament intended	Interpreted by judges' reference to long-established unwritten rules and what has happened before
Judges cannot change what statute law says but Parliament can	Judges can change common law but statute law always overrides common law so ultimately authority lies with Parliament

most people assume is 'the law' – and unwritten laws which are effectively principles and assumptions handed down over the years. These are the differences between statute law and common law.

Clearly, the Children Act 1989 is an example of statute law, as is any law that is an Act of Parliament.

Activity 1.3

Below is a list of criminal laws that are statute, criminal laws that are common law-based, civil laws that are statute and civil laws that are common law-based. They are all mixed up. Fit them into the matrix below so that you end up with examples of laws that fall into each of these categories.

Do bear in mind that statute laws sometimes fall into the categories of both criminal and civil law, since they can contain provision for criminal and civil offences. An example would be the Protection from Harassment Act 1997 which creates the offence of harassment (section 2) and potential for injunctions to prevent harassment (section 3). In this exercise opt for the category that primarily or mainly applies to that law.

Here is a list of laws to fit into the matrix below:

1 Children Act 1989.
2 Once found not guilty of an offence by the court a defendant cannot usually be retried.
3 People who are accused of crimes are assumed innocent until found guilty.
4 Crime and Disorder Act 1998.
5 Actively assisting someone to commit suicide is murder.
6 An employer's duty of care to employees.
7 Care Act 2014.
8 Failing to pay for a TV licence fee.
9 The Care Quality Commission (Registration) Regulations 2009.
10 Failing to pay rent.
11 All employees must be provided with a contract of employment.
12 Family Law Act 1996.
13 Spending money on a service which a local authority does not have statutory authority to provide means it is acting *ultra vires*.
14 Sexual Offences Act 2003.
15 Theft Act 1968.

(Continued)

(Continued)

Here is the matrix. Fit the laws listed above into the category of law that best fits or describes that kind of law.

	Statute law	Common law
Criminal law		
Civil law		

Comment

You will find the answers in Exercise Answers, p185.

How does the law operate to set boundaries but without interfering too much in everyday practice?

We now need to explain some of the ways in which the law achieves its aims on a day-to-day basis. If you look at the Children Act 1989 you will find the law set out in very broad terms, with procedures outlined and guidelines specified, such as criteria by which courts decide cases. For example, right at the start of the Act it tells us that in deciding children's cases the court must pay paramount consideration to the welfare of the child (section 1 Children Act 1989).

In this and other legislation, local authorities are given powers to provide services but the Act of Parliament itself does not necessarily say what those services should be. Part III of the Children Act 1989 empowers local authorities to provide services for children and parents, but does not make precise stipulations as to what the services might be. However, the Act does insist that certain categories of children are defined as being 'in need' – principally, children with disabilities.

There is a variety of mechanisms for putting the flesh on the bones, for providing instruction and guidance in addition to the Act, yet without telling social workers what to do in every single case. These mechanisms are Statutory Instruments, Circulars and Codes of Guidance.

Statutory instruments

This is the general term for a variety of means of implementing laws. One such Statutory Instrument is the Schedules or Rules linked to a specific Act. These set out how an Act is to be implemented and are compulsory. For example, a social worker writing a report for a court explaining how a child came to be placed for adoption would follow the Family

Procedure Rules 2010. Procedures adopted by tribunals about care standards in homes have to conform to the First-Tier Tribunal (Health, Education and Social Care Chamber) Rules 2008 (Care Standards Act 2000; Tribunals, Courts and Enforcement Act 2007). The terms Rules, Regulations and Directions may be regarded as roughly interchangeable. They are all in effect the means (instruments) of implementing statutes (Acts of Parliament) and therefore must be obeyed in the same way as the Act itself must be.

They can be very important indeed. For example, tribunal rules set out the procedures for hearing cases where people are detained in psychiatric hospital against their wishes and appeal for discharge. The Children Act 1989 Regulations cover a wide variety of matters, including placement of children and rules concerning allowing children on care orders to resume living at home with their parents (covered further in Chapter 4).

Circulars and Codes of Guidance

Implementation of an Act of Parliament can also be achieved through:

- Circulars from the relevant department which set out how legislation should be implemented: these do not have the full force of law;
- Codes of Guidance or Codes of Practice: these are likewise models of good practice rather than enforceable directions.

There is quite a large number of Circulars or Letters issued by the Department of Health – so many, in fact, that they are listed separately on the Department's website (their address is at the end of the chapter). Their main purpose is to set out arrangements whereby law and policy can be translated into practice – so much of it may be financial. However, their significance for social work practice must not be underestimated. In adult care a number of Circulars set out the precise kinds of services that local authorities may offer to individuals (see Chapter 5 for examples). Collaboration between health authorities and local authority departments is often facilitated and enabled by Circulars.

Some Codes of Practice give precise guidance regarding procedures to be adopted in certain kinds of circumstances. For example, the Mental Capacity Act 2005 delegates to the Code of Practice advice on procedures to follow regarding assessment of people who may lack the ability (capacity) to make decisions for themselves (see Chapter 6 for further discussion of capacity). Likewise, the Police and Criminal Evidence Act 1984 refers to a Code of Practice (section 66) which sets out procedures for interviewing suspects, detaining people, taking samples and the like. Social workers called to an interview at a police station would need to know what the Code of Practice says (see Chapter 7 for more on this). The advantage of a Code of Practice is that it can be amended from time to time without changing the Act of Parliament on which it is based and from which it derives its authority.

Whether a Code of Practice is obligatory depends on its status. Some are more compelling than others – for example, those specifically issued under the Local Authority Social Services Act 1970 are strongest. Section 7(1) of the 1970 Act states that local authorities shall *act under the general guidance of the Secretary of State*. This has been taken to mean that local authorities should not depart from the 'statutory' guidance (i.e. guidance issued under section 7(1) 1970 Act) without good reason. So it is important to be clear when looking at a Circular as to whether it is issued under the authority of this Act. It will usually say so right at the start.

Principles behind application of public law

- The law clearly cannot tell social workers what to do in every particular case. It is probably best to regard the law as a framework within which there may be a series of additional frameworks: Circulars, Codes of Practice or whatever. The social worker's employer may offer additional policy guidance, but inevitably much depends on the assessment of the individual circumstances and the social worker's professionalism. To clarify this, it may be worth setting out some key principles underlying the law and this relationship to social work. The group for whom services are provided needs to be identified, either specifically (for example, Chronically Sick and Disabled Persons Act 1970) or by interpretation. For example, the Care Act 2014 in practice applies to particular categories of adults in need and the Children Act 1989 focuses on specific groups of children.

- If Parliament says action must be taken, then the law applies to all, across the board. The duty cannot be refused on the grounds of difficulty, such as geographical isolation or lack of resources. The law also means what it says – for example, each local authority has to appoint a Director of Children's Services (section 18 Children Act 2004). Duties cannot be delegated to another department although, if the law allows, services may be provided by other agencies, including those in the independent sector.

- There is a very sharp distinction between mandatory and permissive powers. In everyday language mandatory means must, permissive means may. In fact, the law rarely makes the provision of specific services as such mandatory, preferring to make provision of information about services compulsory (as in section 4 Care Act 2014). Permissive powers are important since, without these, local authorities would not be able to do anything. A local authority needs to be empowered to act since local authorities can act only when and where the law says they can. This contrasts with the position of individuals, who are free to do whatever they wish unless the law says that they may not. In short, local authorities can do nothing unless the law says they can (otherwise they are acting *ultra vires*, beyond powers). Individuals can do what they want unless the law says they cannot.

- Furthermore, social work providers must offer services and exercise their powers (if they have powers established by law) in accordance with anti-discrimination legislation. In Britain, this legislation has until comparatively recently covered only three areas: gender or sex discrimination; racial discrimination; and disability discrimination. However, the Equality Act 2010 consolidated a host of regulations while extending the range of discriminations, referred to as 'protected characteristics' in the Act. These are: age; disability; gender reassignment; marriage and civil partnership; pregnancy and maternity; race; religion or belief; sex; sexual orientation (section 4 Equality Act 2010).

It is not intended to cover anti-discriminatory legislation in detail in this book. You may be surprised to learn that much of this does not directly address everyday social work practice. However, this is simply explained. Social work legislation is essentially positive action directed towards groups who are often disadvantaged or discriminated against, such as people with disabilities. By contrast, anti-discrimination legislation in Britain primarily provides for sanctions against people or bodies who 'unlawfully' discriminate against someone. This is rarely an issue in social work, although there have been isolated accusations of discrimination, such as in the case of selection of prospective adopters – for example, in relation to weight in a case cited in *The Yorkshire Post*, 12 January 2009. Anti-discrimination cases tend to be, with a few exceptions, confined to individual people who would claim to be the victims of discrimination. Employment has historically been the main focus. Legislation in Britain, in contrast to other countries, often places the responsibility on the claimant to prove they were discriminated against, rather than offering a general obligation on all employers – for example, to treat people fairly. However, in 2000, the tide began to turn. The Race Relations (Amendment) Act 2000 required public bodies to work towards the elimination of unlawful discrimination and promote equality of opportunity and good relations between different racial groups. Of major significance now is the Equality Act 2006 which established the Equality and Human Rights Commission to encourage and support the following:

- the development of a society in which people's ability to achieve their potential is not limited by prejudice or discrimination;

- there is respect for, and protection of, each individual's human rights;

- there is respect for the dignity and worth of each individual;

- each individual has an equal opportunity to participate in society;

- there is mutual respect between groups based on understanding and valuing of diversity and on shared respect for equality and human rights.

(section 3, Equality Act 2006)

Much of this accords with key principles and values of social work, with its emphasis on anti-discrimination principles and anti-oppressive practice (Dalrymple and Burke, 2006; Thompson, 2012). Furthermore, the Commission for Equality and Human Rights acts to promote these principles by engaging in wider education of the public, and to this end publishes a series of useful guides (see their website address at the end of the chapter).

Chapter summary

This chapter set out a number of reasons why the law is important in social work. It was suggested that the law should be seen in a positive light, setting the framework within which social work operates. It then offered a case example of a major legislative change that took place in Britain in the late 1980s – namely, the Children Act 1989. This resulted indirectly from the events in Cleveland where social workers were accused of acting overzealously. As a consequence, the judicial inquiry into events in Cleveland set out many of the key principles that are now enshrined in the Children Act 1989. Among these is the accountability of social workers to the law and, as you will see in Chapter 8, the courts play a key role in this.

The chapter then went on to consider the way in which laws are passed, and raised for consideration the issue of why the law changes. You may wish to read further on this, and will certainly be expected to do so if your social work programme includes social policy.

You were then introduced to different ways of categorising legislation, and the different ways in which legislation is enacted through statutory instruments and guidance. The chapter concluded with reference to the principles that underpin the operation of public law in Britain: public law meaning the law that concerns the operation of public bodies and the relationship between the state and the individual. This then brings us full square into the ambit of human rights, which is where the next chapter starts.

Further reading

To understand the purpose of law and law in context, it is essential to have some knowledge of social policy in relation to social work. One of the following will help.

Alcock, P, Erskine, A and May, M (eds) (2012) *The student's companion to social policy* (4th edn). Chichester: Wiley.

Bochel, H, and Daley, G (2014) *Social policy* (3rd edn). London: Routledge.

Cunningham, J and Cunningham, S (2017) *Social policy and social work: An introduction* (2nd edn). London: Sage.

The following texts complement and amplify the discussion here on the role of law in social work.

Braye, S and Preston-Shoot, M (2016) *Practising social work law* (4th edn). Basingstoke: Palgrave.

Long, L-A, Roche, J and Stringer, D (eds) (2010) *The law and social work* (2nd edn). Basingstoke: Palgrave.

Websites

To keep up to date with developments the following websites can be recommended.

Commission for Equality and Human Rights: www.equalityhumanrights.com

Department for Education: www.education.gov.uk/childrenandyoungpeople

Department of Health: www.doh.gov.uk

Legislation including statutory instruments: www.legislation.gov.uk/ukpga

Ministry of Justice: www.gov.uk/government/organisations/ministry-of-justice

2: Human Rights

It will also introduce you to the following standards as set out in the 2016 Social Work Subject Benchmark Statement:

5.3 v   the relationship between human rights enshrined in law and the moral and ethical rights determined theoretically, philosophically and by contemporary society;

5.3 vi   the complex relationships between justice, care and control in social welfare and the practical and ethical implications of these;

5.6 vi   the significance of legislative and legal frameworks and service delivery standards.

Introduction

This chapter explores the notion of rights as they apply to social work, focusing on 'human rights'. Here we will be primarily concerned with some very basic rights that have become adopted internationally and apply to the British legal and social welfare system. Leading on from this, the chapter summarises the various ways in which service users can challenge the decisions of social workers and local authorities in the courts. This is a key element in empowering individuals who feel they have not been fairly treated by people who are meant to be helping them or providing services for them. By reading this chapter and completing the associated exercises, you will be developing your basic understanding of how the law operates and what people's rights are.

In this chapter we will be looking at ways in which human rights are recognised by the law in Britain, focusing specifically on the impact of human rights-related legislation on social work. The scene is set by a discussion of human rights generally, distinguishing between the various United Nations conventions or declarations and the European Convention on Human Rights. Since before pursuing basic human rights cases applicants need to pursue legal remedies in the UK, there is then a discussion on rights of redress under UK law. This leads on to a consideration of the Human Rights Act 1998, setting out the rights of redress this offers. The discussion then ranges more widely into the relationship between social work service users and the law, using as an example the debate about mental health legislation. This raises major ethical questions concerning the right of the state to intervene in the personal lives of individuals perceived to be dangerous yet where no offence has been committed. The chapter concludes by illustrating other areas of social work where the European Convention may have some influence, highlighting cases that have already attracted attention.

What are human rights?

Any exposition of human rights has to start by posing the very basic question: what are human rights?

Activity 2.1

Either on your own or in a small group, answer the following questions:

What do we mean when we talk about human rights?

What are the most important human rights?

Comment

When asked to decide the most important human rights, people are unlikely to be in complete agreement. Nevertheless, most lists of basic human rights include reference to:

- some kind of right to life;
- some reference to personal respect (no arbitrary arrest, law applied equally to all, and associated rights);
- some basic legal rights, such as a fair trial, due legal process;
- prohibition on torture;
- prohibition on slavery;
- some kind of rights to freedom of expression and belief.

More generally, when we talk about 'human rights' there are a number of features that make them distinctive:

- they refer to basic, fundamental needs;
- they aim to be universal, that is they apply to everyone;
- they are essentially defensive, means through which individuals are shielded from excessive state power and protected from abuse by other citizens;
- they are quite general;
- yet they have to be attainable regardless of resources;
- they are unconditional, everyone gets them, they are not 'earned'.

Something you will have learned from this exercise is that it is not as easy as one might think. It is very tempting to talk about rights at a secondary level, such as entitlement to services and rights to participate in decision-making, and forget the prior requirement regarding the rights of people to participate in society more generally, and the rights to be treated equitably by the law. We take it for granted that people are no longer slaves, for example. Some of the difficulty may arise precisely from the fact that in Britain these basic rights are simply assumed – taken for granted and therefore unconsciously overlooked. However, there is no room for complacency and, as we shall see in this chapter, there are some fundamental principles concerning basic rights that may indeed conflict with current laws in the UK.

Before exploring this, we need to say a bit more about why we need human rights and where they come from.

The origins of human rights legislation lie in the aftermath of the Second World War. In order to prevent the recurrence of the atrocities that occurred during that war, countries of the world came together to form the United Nations and passed the Universal Convention on Human Rights in 1948, consisting of 30 Articles and a number of related subsequent covenants (Brayne and Broadbent, 2002, pp68–72). This has not been adopted by all countries and is not a code of law as such. Hence, it is not possible to complain to the courts that action in a particular case breaches the Declaration on Human Rights – it is not incorporated into the law in that sense. Instead, the Convention operates at a wider level. There are Conventions and Declarations made under the auspices of the United Nations that offer a kind of benchmark by which countries can be examined for the extent to which they comply with basic human rights.

One of the best known of these is the United Nations Convention on the Rights of the Child, dating from 1989 (the Convention can be found on the United Nations website; their address can be found at the end of the chapter).

There are certain other United Nations Declarations worth noting which operate in a similar fashion, covering areas relevant to social work. These include the Convention on the Rights of Persons with Disabilities (enacted 2008) and the Convention on the Elimination of All Forms of Discrimination against Women (enacted 1981).

Every five years there are reports on policy changes and practices in each country by an international team appointed by the UN. This may be very effective in focusing publicity on certain policies – for example, in the UK this has brought under scrutiny the policy of detaining 12–14-year-olds in custody (see Chapter 7), but it does not offer redress in individual cases.

Essentially, it is signing up to these Conventions and Declarations that is of significance, being in effect commitments of intent concerning legislation and policy. There are some other conventions that do have greater effect on individual cases – for example, there is a convention on torture that includes the power to investigate cases and, of course, there is a mechanism for hearing accusations of crimes against humanity in international courts at The Hague.

Of more immediate impact on individual cases is the European Convention on Human Rights. This was originally drawn up in 1950, but only in 1965 did Britain allow its citizens to petition the European Court. It is important to make one point absolutely clear here, since it is the cause of much confusion in the media. The European Convention on Human Rights is nothing to do directly with the European Union, although its 28 members are expected to share the same values. The European Union is essentially an economic partnership. Quite separately and apart from this economic partnership, a greater number of countries in Europe agreed to forge a political alliance, the Council of Europe, whereby they would agree that certain basic rights would be granted to all individuals in all member countries. There are currently 47 members of the Council of Europe. It is this Council of Europe that formulated the European Convention on Human Rights and implements it through the European Court.

Although the UK government agreed to acknowledge the principles of the European Convention on Human Rights, until October 2000 there was no possibility of arguing in UK courts that an individual case breached the Convention. Instead, having exhausted all legal remedies in the UK, individuals could then complain to the European Court – in effect taking THE UK government to court in Strasbourg. The position was changed by the Human Rights Act 1998 which incorporated the European Convention into UK law. It does this in two ways.

1. First, it declares that all laws passed from 1998 onwards will in principle comply with the European Convention on Human Rights, although there is provision for exemptions (for example, a partial opt-out to Article 5 to enable countermeasures in cases of alleged terrorism to be adopted).

2. Second, it gave the courts the power to adjudicate by reference to the Convention so that in individual cases people could argue that there had been a fundamental breach of their human rights. This naturally applies to decisions made in accordance with all legislation, including legislation that was passed prior to 1998; in this case, it may be that the court has to declare that part of the legislation itself is not compatible with the Convention.

Two limitations worth noting are that the Human Rights Act 1998 applies to public bodies, not to private individuals, or to all voluntary organisations. This may be a major obstacle in some cases, as we shall see in Chapter 5 (Cheshire Home case). The second limitation is that before appealing to the courts on European Convention on Human Rights grounds, applicants must attempt all other possible legal remedies. Only when someone has made every attempt to persuade the public body to their point of view can they then apply to the courts. The next section explains this in more detail.

How are infringements of people's rights challenged? How can decisions be challenged?

It is important to answer this in a general sense because it helps us to understand the role of courts in relation to local authorities and other service providers. In Chapter 1 we explored the differences between statute law and common law. One element of common law is the traditional role of the courts in protecting an individual against the arbitrary use of power, against the misapplication of the law by public bodies. The origins of this role are lost in the mists of time, yet they have great contemporary significance, for the High Court derives from common law its powers to overrule public bodies and tell them that their interpretation of the law is wrong.

However, before service users can rush to the courts they need to be aware of three key principles:

- courts will intervene only if there is evidence of unjust treatment or mistaken interpretation of statute law;

- generally, courts won't make decisions for local authorities or government – they will simply say that a decision is wrong in law for a particular reason, with the implication that the public bodies will then correct this;

- most important of all, complainants must explore *all other avenues* first.

What might these other avenues be?

Complaints procedures

The first obvious step, if someone is dissatisfied, is to complain. In the case of adult care, for example, the Care Act 2014 (section 72) makes provision for appeals and complaints which obliges local authorities to comply with the Local Authority Social Services and NHS Complaints Regulations 2009. Other service provision may not be regulated by specific Acts, but service providers will generally have to offer robust complaints procedures in order to comply with service level agreements – that is, a formal contract between the local authority and the provider, essential in order that the provider, acting as agent, delivers a service consistent with the commissioner's responsibilities.

Maladministration and injustice

In the case of public bodies complaints of maladministration may be referred to:

- the Parliamentary and Health Service Ombudsman for England (their website address can be found at the end of chapter), who deals with complaints about maladministration by government departments and the National Health Service, probably of most relevance to social work in hospitals and Care Trusts;

- the Local Government Ombudsman (Commissioner for Local Administration in England; their website address can be found at the end of the chapter) who deals with local authorities who employ social workers in their social services departments and children's services;

- in Wales, the Public Services Ombudsman for Wales (their website address can be found at the end of the chapter), who deals with all complaints regarding the work of public bodies (Public Services Ombudsman (Wales) Act 2005).

The ombudsman may investigate only injustice caused by maladministration. The complainant has to demonstrate that they suffered injustice through misapplication of procedures or lack of care over their application or something similar. Specifically *excluded* are matters of policy and allocation of resources. Inconsistency in the application of policy and procedures would be considered for adjudication, but not the actual principles and policies themselves. If the ombudsman's report goes against the local authority, the local authority has the power to pay compensation, but the commissioner's decision is *not* legally binding on the local authority.

Civil action for damages

If an individual has suffered damage or loss as a consequence of someone else's actions, they may wish to sue for damages in the civil court. To do this they would have to establish that some kind of civil legal wrong (technically a 'tort') occurred; for example, if a service user fell over an obstacle carelessly left around, or if someone alleged that they were injured or neglected as a result of the service provider failing to employ sufficient trained staff.

Having explored these remedies, what might service users expect of the courts?

Essentially, courts have powers of judicial review and are required to interpret the European Convention as it applies to UK law.

Judicial review

Courts might be invited to order local authorities or other bodies to act (*mandamus*) or not to act (prohibition) in certain ways, but note that judicial review concerns the process by which the local authority arrived at its decision, not the actual decision itself.

Judicial review can also consider the law itself as well as decisions made under the law and determine whether or not they comply with the European Convention on Human Rights. If the law and associated decisions are not compatible with the Convention, courts make a declaration of incompatibility and refer the matter back to Parliament. This obviously may offer little in the short term, but in the long run can have very considerable consequences. In the meantime, the assumption is that public bodies will offer some kind of compensation, recompense or redress.

European Court

Ultimately, having proceeded through all UK administrative procedures and through the courts, the applicant has the right to appeal to the European Court of Human Rights itself.

This can adjudicate when all UK procedures have been exhausted and when it is considered that there has been a specific breach of the European Convention on Human Rights.

However, it is no good having rights unless we know what they are, so in the next two sections we explore the kinds of basic rights implemented in Britain through the Human Rights Act 1998.

Human Rights Act 1998 and the European Convention on Human Rights

There are some misconceptions and misunderstandings about the Human Rights Act 1998. It does not provide a means for overriding existing legislation. It does not allow the courts to 'strike down' legislation in the way that the Supreme Court can in interpreting the US Constitution. It does not apply penalties to public bodies that breach the Convention, preferring compensation instead. It does not apply to everyone for, as we have already seen, it may not apply to voluntary organisations.

So what, then, are the principles underlying the Human Rights Act 1998?

- It provides an avenue for redress in the UK courts for an individual who believes that their Convention rights have been breached and they have been affected by this. The second statement is important as it prevents purely academic complaints. It also disallows 'class actions' whereby large groups of people as a body can complain and claim damages.

- It requires public bodies in all that they do to act in accordance with the Convention and face claims for compensation if they do not.

- It requires the courts to take heed of the Convention when interpreting legislation. This applies to all courts at all levels. If the legislation itself appears to be incompatible with the Convention, then courts refer this back to Parliament.

- Parliament committed itself to passing legislation after 1998 that was compatible with the Convention but the Convention is not absolute, and there may be occasions in which Parliament exempts parts of particular statutes from the Convention, knowing the consequences of this.

- Interpretation of law applies to all kinds of law, criminal and civil, and all aspects of work carried out by public authorities. So it could apply to someone accused of an offence, or someone asking for 'judicial review' of the decision by a public body.

From this, it would seem that the Human Rights Act is very wide-ranging, yet the Act itself is comparatively short. This is because it refers to the European Convention as the source of its authority.

Yet we still haven't answered the fundamental question: what are these Convention rights? Indeed, what are people's basic rights?

You may think you know some of the European Convention on Human Rights already, so now is the opportunity to put your knowledge to the test.

Activity 2.2

Either on your own or in a small group, answer the following questions:

- What areas do you think are covered by the European Convention on Human Rights?
- Which of the Convention Rights are most likely to be relevant to social work service users?

Comment

The answers to these questions are in Exercise Answers, pp185-6.

Applying the European Convention on Human Rights benchmark

Let's look at some influential cases where people have successfully used the Convention either in courts in Britain or in the European Court itself. The cases are illustrative in order to show the kinds of issues the courts have legitimately considered and are not meant to cover the whole range – that would be quite a task. Also, the law is constantly evolving in this area, so some of the cases discussed below may not be the last word (for most up-to-date law and cases, see the specialist chapters in this or other standard texts on social work law). Before looking at the examples, however, a word about citation of case law.

Where a case is reported, the convention is that the name of the person who initiated the legal action (the applicant, formerly referred to as the plaintiff) comes first followed by *v* for versus (often said as 'and' although it is actually Latin for 'against') and the name of the respondent (defendant), who in European court cases might be a national government. Then follows the source: the published law reports such as *All England Law Reports* (All ER), *Weekly Law Reports* (WLR), *Court of Appeal* (CA) and the number of the case. Instead of the law report reference, in the case of European Court cases (ECHR) there may be a specific date, so that the case can be accessed through the court's internet site, or it may simply be unreported, which means it is not published as such – although people who were there know what happened, of course. There are examples of each of these forms of citation in the following paragraphs, which provide brief summaries of cases that may be of general interest.

Case study

In January 2003 the European Court gave judgment about the use of public surveillance CCTV equipment in *Peck v United Kingdom* [2003]. The complainant, in a very depressed state of mind in the mid-1990s, had attempted suicide in a public place. His actions were filmed on closed-circuit television at the time and the police were called, took him for medical attention and he recovered. Subsequently, the videotape of the suicide attempt was used on television, broadcast regionally and nationally, to extol the effective use of closed-circuit TV in public places. A picture was also used in a newspaper. Advertising CCTV merits in this way was deemed objectionable since it was done without consent, and the complainant persuaded the European Court that this was a breach of Article 8, the right to privacy, going well beyond what can be justified in the public interest.

The Appeal Court confirmed a ruling that the UK government's policy, introduced in 2002, of denying benefits to those who failed to claim asylum as soon as practicable was a breach of the European Convention on Human Rights. The denial of state support to late applicants for asylum (section 55 of the Nationality, Immigration and Asylum Act 2002) would in effect leave them destitute, potentially damaging their health and safety, and was therefore incompatible with Convention Article 3 (inhuman treatment) (CA 18 March 2003).

In a European Court case, *O'Donoghue and others v UK* [2010], the Court found that UK rules that required foreigners to pay large fees to obtain permission from the Home Office to marry anywhere except in the Church of England had violated the right to marry (Article 12 of the Convention) and that it was discriminatory on the ground of religion (Articles 9 and 14). In 2010, the European Court in *JM v UK* [2010] also decided that a gay absent parent was unjustifiably discriminated against by being assessed to pay more child support than would have been the case if she had been heterosexual. This too contravened Article 14.

The tragic Bland case, *Airedale National Health Service Trust v Bland* [1993], concerned a victim of the Hillsborough disaster and whether life support equipment could be turned off where a person was in a vegetative state and unlikely to recover. Here the courts held that the obligation to preserve life is not absolute, and specifically in some circumstances it is acceptable to discontinue treatment.

In another tragic case, *Osman v United Kingdom* [2000], a teacher shot a school student's father. This followed a period of harassment which, it was argued, the police knew about, but from which they failed to protect the family. It was alleged that the police were negligent in this regard, and therefore the state had failed in its basic duty of protection of the right to life (Article 2). The court rejected this argument, referring to operational choices, priorities and resources that confronted the government and the police. However, although relying on this interpretation, in Savage v South Essex Partnership NHS Foundation Trust and *MIND (Intervener)* [2007] the Court of Appeal concluded that the mother of a mental health patient who committed suicide while detained under the Mental Health Act 1983 did not have to prove the health authorities to be

$\longrightarrow$

grossly negligent, yet acknowledged that the State had a particular responsibility to vulnerable people in the custody of the State.

Dianne Pretty wanted the courts in Britain to guarantee that her husband would not be prosecuted if he helped her to commit suicide. The courts in Britain refused to do this, arguing that assisting suicide was manslaughter and people did not have the right to die under the European Convention, a decision confirmed by the European Court in *Pretty v United Kingdom* [2002]. Likewise, in 2008 in the case of Debbie Purdy, *R (on the application of Purdy) v Director of Public Prosecutions* [2008], the UK courts refused to countenance advance immunity for assistance to terminally ill people who wanted to die, even if they went abroad to a country that allowed assisted suicide in order to do so.

In a case where a local authority took the serious step of removing a child from her mother shortly after birth, *P, C and S v the United Kingdom* [2002], the European Court ruled that this action was not justified by relevant and sufficient reasons. It could not be regarded as having been necessary in a democratic society for the purpose of safeguarding the child and therefore breached Article 8, right to family life.

The trial of two boys accused of the murder of James Bulger was held in an adult court and therefore, according to the European Court, in unsuitable surroundings where they were unable to participate effectively. Also in *V v United Kingdom* [1999] the European Court held that there was political interference in the sentence by the Home Secretary; sentences must be judicial. This case concerned interpretation of Article 6, the right to a fair trial, and has led to a major review of the trial setting for young people (see Chapter 7 for further discussion of this). It has also meant that the Lord Chief Justice will in future decide the actual length of time offenders remain in custody if this is indeterminate.

Two cases concerned the physical punishment of children. In the first, *Costello-Roberts v UK* [1993], corporal punishment of children in schools was held to be illegal (by 1993 it had been formally banned in State schools but permitted in independent schools). The second case concerned a stepfather who caned his stepson and was prosecuted, but escaped conviction in the UK criminal courts because he could argue, using case law interpretation of the Children and Young Persons Act 1933, that the assault was justified as reasonable chastisement. The European Court in *A v UK* [1998] rejected this and declared that in this instance the State had failed to protect a child from inhuman or degrading punishment (Article 3) by allowing the stepfather this defence. Subsequently, the Children Act 2004 (section 58) withdrew the defence on which the stepfather relied in this case, thereby implementing the European Court's decision.

A former resident of children's homes and community homes claimed the right of access to all records the local authority held about them, including adoption records. In *Gaskin v UK* [1986] this right was refuted by the courts which declared there had been no breach of Article 10. Since this case, there have been substantial amendments to the law, to such an extent that in effect service users do have the right to see written and electronic records (Data Protection Act 1998), but not adoption records (although there is provision even for this in the Adoption and Children Act 2002).

→

Of particular significance for social work is the 'Bedfordshire' case that proceeded over several years through different levels of courts in the UK (this case has different citations according to the court that heard it, but it's the same case). The case concerned the alleged lack of action by a local authority in protecting children. While there was no fundamental dispute that children in this case had been left too long with their family and should have been the subjects of care proceedings much earlier, the issue that the courts faced was whether this lack of action constituted a legitimate legal claim for compensation for the children arising from the local authority's failure to protect them. In 1995, the House of Lords in *X (minors) v Bedfordshire County Council* [1995] decided that local authorities should be immune from legal action since otherwise it would be an enormously difficult task for any local authority to carry out its child safeguarding functions without potentially being sued. However, the European Court disagreed, and awarded the children damages for the abuse. The court considered that there had been a breach of two Articles. The first is Article 3 – as a consequence of the local authority's failure the children had suffered inhuman treatment. The European Court in *Z and others v the United Kingdom* [2001] also declared the English legal system to be failing its obligations under Article 13 because it did not allow the children to sue the local authority, thereby denying them an effective remedy.

Comment

These summaries can do no more than give you a flavour of the kinds of issues raised in human rights cases that may have some relevance, directly or indirectly, to social work. If you are especially interested in this area, further cases relevant to health and social care may be found in Laird (2010).

At this point we turn to the use of the European Convention on Human Rights as a benchmark for legislation as there is an example that is of particular relevance for social work since it addresses the individual's ability to make decisions for themselves. The case example is the law relating to mental health and mental capacity, focusing in particular on amendments to mental health law. The aim here is twofold:

- to demonstrate how the principles underpinning the European Convention on Human Rights apply to one key issue, the liberty of the individual;

- to use this to facilitate an analysis of challenges posed by trying to balance people's rights to decide for themselves, and the need to protect them where they may be unable to make sound decisions.

When reviewing mental health legislation, the starting point was that Parliament now needs to ensure that any new legislation satisfies the requirements of the European Convention on Human Rights, so it is important to know what these are. The original proposals were set out in draft Mental Health Bills published in 2004 and 2006 (Department of Health, 2004a, 2006a), eventually culminating in the Mental Health Act 2007.

Mental health, the European Convention on Human Rights and persons of unsound mind

So what are the principles governing the way the European Convention on Human Rights addresses mental health laws?

First, we need to identify the relevant parts of the European Convention on Human Rights.

Article 5 covers rights to liberty, which has self-evident relevance to the detention of people with mental health problems.

Article 2, the right to life, is partially relevant as it requires governments to take appropriate steps to safeguard the lives of people within its jurisdiction.

Article 8 is relevant in respect of the rights of nearest relatives and access to information.

Article 3 concerns treatment, specifically stipulating that it must not be *inhuman or degrading*.

Article 5

Article 5(1) grants a general right to *liberty* and *security of person*. There are obvious exceptions to this as an absolute principle – for example, relating to people who are convicted of criminal offences, or are suspected of having done so. Exemption 5(1)(e), though, concerns the detention of *persons {.} of unsound mind*.

The European Court has considered a number of cases of people apparently of *unsound mind* and thereby established some general principles and safeguards. The key case concerned Dutch law and procedures for assessment and detention, *Winterwerp v The Netherlands* [1979]. Through this case, the European Court laid down that in order for detention to be lawful under Article 5(1)(e) three conditions must be met (except in emergency):

1. a true mental disorder must be established before a competent authority on the basis of objective medical expertise;

2. the mental disorder must be of a kind or degree warranting compulsory confinement;

3. the validity of continued confinement depends on the persistence of such a mental disorder.

The first principle clearly implies that there must be a prior medical assessment of mental disorder before someone can be detained.

The second principle has been clarified to refer to compulsory confinement somewhere which is appropriate for the detention and where treatment is offered. Detaining someone in a prison psychiatric wing for a lengthy period was considered in *Aerts v Belgium* [1998] to be a breach of the Convention as no medical or therapeutic treatment was offered.

Courts have also had to consider whether in order to qualify for detention the potential patient has to suffer from a condition that is *treatable*. Consideration of various cases has stretched the principle to encompass the need to protect the public even where it is unlikely that treatment will bring about any improvement, as in, for example, *Anderson and others v Scottish Ministers and another* [2000].

The third principle, validity of continued confinements, is relevant to tribunal discharges where someone is no longer mentally *disordered* to the extent that confinement is necessary. Article 5(4) is the right to challenge the lawfulness of detention. In practice this must mean a review of the decisions to detain within a reasonable period: in *E v Norway* [1994] two months was considered too long. The principles applicable here were brought together in a German case, *Megyeri v Germany* [1993]:

1. detainees are entitled to periodic reviews by court or tribunal;
2. procedures must be *of judicial character*;
3. detainees must either be present or speak through a representative, with special safeguards to protect people not capable of speaking for themselves;
4. detainees do not have to take the initiative.

Application of these principles led the British courts in *R (H) v London North and East Region Mental Health Review Tribunal* [2001] to conclude that sections 72 and 73 of the Mental Health Act 1983 were unlawful as they seemed to place the burden on the patient to prove that the conditions of detention were no longer met. Furthermore, in the Bournewood case, *HL v United Kingdom* [2004], using common law powers to detain someone was ruled contrary to the Convention, partly because it did not allow the potential for tribunal reviews (see further discussion below and in Chapter 6).

However, courts have taken the view that the periodic reviews by a tribunal do not imply an absolute right to be discharged if the tribunal agrees. In one case, *R v Mental Health Review Tribunal, Torfaen County Borough Council and Gwent Health Authority, ex parte Russell Hall* [2000], the tribunal ordered a patient's discharge from compulsory detention in hospital, but this could not be carried out because of lack of availability of discharge resources. The patient argued that this meant he had to stay in detention despite the tribunal ruling, and therefore his right to freedom had been curtailed. In *R v Camden and Islington Health Authority, ex parte K* [2001] the discharge plans were thwarted by the lack of availability of a forensic psychiatrist, but the patient failed to persuade the court that this violated the right to liberty principle.

Article 2

Article 2 states that everyone's right to life shall be protected by law. This is qualified by certain rights in relation to people who commit offences and in public order situations, but in mental health the European Court has emphasised that, in addition to refraining from the intentional and unlawful taking of life, governments are required to take appropriate steps to safeguard the lives of their citizens. This positive obligation is likely to apply to individuals who were receiving psychiatric services, particularly where detained in hospital under the Mental Health Act 1983 (as in the 2007 Savage case cited in the Case Study on p29). In Britain, the Department of Health and the Welsh Assembly have declared that they are taking steps to reduce the numbers of suicides by people with mental health problems by including them in audit procedures and targets: Department of Health Public Health Outcomes 4.10 (Department of Health online) and Together for Mental Health Delivery Plan 2.4 (Welsh Assembly Government, online).

Article 8

Article 8(2) states that there shall be no interference with the exercise of the right to privacy, family life, home and correspondence *except such as is in accordance with the law and is necessary in a democratic society in the interests of national security, public safety or the economic well-being of the country, for the prevention of disorder of crime, for the protection of health or morals, or for the protection of the rights and freedoms of others*.

Under this Article, Nearest Relative definitions (section 26 Mental Health Act 1983) were successfully challenged, since the Act allowed no leeway: Nearest Relative is defined by law not by the patient's choice, and the Nearest Relative has considerable power under the Act – for example, to order the patient's discharge). The impossibility in the Act of accommodating the patient's desire to change the identity of her Nearest Relative was considered a violation of Article 8 in *JT v United Kingdom* [2000].

Article 3

Article 3 outlaws inhuman or degrading treatment which must, according to the European Court, attain a *minimum level of severity*, dependent on the circumstances of the case.

Not surprisingly, there have been several complaints under this Article relating to the treatment of mental health patients. Forcible administration of food and medication, together with use of handcuffs and a security bed, were not considered a violation of Article 3 if they were a *therapeutic necessity* in *Herczegfalvy v Austria* [1992]. Likewise, the European Court will not concern itself with the side-effects of medication, refusing to accept in *Grare v France* [1993] that this is relevant to consideration of inhuman treatment. As long as the treatment is therapeutically necessary, the Convention is not considered to apply. However, a violation of Article 3 did occur in *Jean-Luc Rivière v France* [2006] when a prisoner suffering a diagnosed mental illness had his request to be released on licence refused yet continued to be detained without medical treatment or supervision.

The challenge of reviewing mental health legislation

Way back in June 2002, the Department of Health published a draft Mental Health Bill, proposals to 'reform' mental health law. This followed in the wake of publicity generated by cases where members of the public had been injured or, in isolated cases, killed by people with a history of mental health problems (the most well-known case being that of the murder of Jonathan Zito by Christopher Clunis, a man diagnosed with paranoid schizophrenia, in December 1992). The Mental Health Bill proved to be very controversial and did not become law. It was reintroduced for debate in the 2004–2005 parliamentary session, but ran into a great deal of difficulty, and again failed to become law. A revised Bill was then introduced in the 2006–2007 Parliamentary session.

For the purpose of providing an example of the kind of human rights issues that arise in this aspect of social work, we will focus on the key elements of legislation that was proposed at the time, particularly on the 2004 Bill. This will demonstrate what was so controversial (further details of what was covered in the 2004 proposals can be found on the Department of Health archived website; see the websites at the end of this chapter). The Mental Health Bill 2004 proposed:

*   compulsory treatment for some *mentally disordered* people in the community;
*   compulsory detention in hospital beyond 28 days to be authorised only by a tribunal;
*   safeguards for patients who do not have the capacity to understand or consent to treatment;
*   a broader definition of mental disorder, extended to learning disabilities and possibly personality disorders;
*   the social worker role in applying for admissions to be replaced by *approved mental health professional*;
*   patients' powers to nominate a person to represent their interests;
*   greater appeal rights to the Mental Health Tribunal;
*   formalised care plans;
*   changes in rules regarding discharge.

Activity 2.3

Looking back at the kinds of issues that have been brought before the European Court and bearing in mind these proposals, what general or specific objections do you think could be raised about the proposals? What does this demonstrate about the need to balance individual rights with the supposed duty of the state to protect vulnerable people?

(Continued)

(Continued)

You may wish to look at a number of websites to find out more information about the government's proposals and the points raised by various advocacy organisations and service user groups about them. You will find the list of websites at the end of the chapter.

Comment

There was no expectation that you would cover all the proposals. Indeed, there were such widespread objections to the proposals that it is difficult to be selective, but it would appear that the key areas where rights are most contentious and the debate most vigorous concerned compulsory treatment in the community, extension of the definition of mental disorder, capacity to understand and consent, the role of social workers and rights concerning nearest relatives. Each of these will now be amplified.

On the surface, it would appear that these proposals are well intentioned and conform to the European Convention on Human Rights (and the government has declared that the new legislation should be consistent with the Convention). However, a number of objections have been raised.

Compulsory treatment in the community

As we have seen, the European Court has not concerned itself with compulsory treatment in the community, leading to fears of a lack of court interest in this area.

Community treatment orders may mean that people are less inclined to accept any form of psychiatric treatment on the grounds that they are at risk of having this forced on them if they do not comply. There is, in addition, a large number of questions about the practicalities – for example, what happens if someone fails to turn up at a day centre? Who should force people to accept treatment or attend 'therapeutic' sessions? To what extent should the police be involved?

Role of tribunals

There would have to be more tribunals in order for UK procedures to conform to the principles laid down by the European Court (see discussion about Articles 5(1) and 5(4) above). This might divert financial and staff resources from frontline patient care.

Code of practice and principles for use of compulsion

There was very real concern that the principles for use of compulsion were much wider and therefore potentially open to abuse. Added to the broader definition of mental disorder, this might lead to a much more extensive use of compulsion. Some considered that the consequences would be increased and unwarranted use of compulsion. The Royal College of Psychiatrists believed that people should not be compelled into treatment or hospital solely in order to prevent criminal behaviour.

Capacity to understand and consent

Under the Mental Health Act 1983 people who lacked capacity to consent but did not actively resist admission to hospital or treatment were classified as 'informal' patients and therefore not protected by the same safeguards as detained patients. Such 'informal' patients could be treated and possibly kept in hospital under common law, or so it was thought, and the 2004 Bill continued with this presumption. For in 1998 a British court, in *R v Bournewood Community and Mental Health NHS Trust, ex parte L* [1998], decided that where someone does not have the capacity to agree or object to admission, but complies with being taken there, they may be kept in hospital 'informally' even if someone objects on their behalf.

However, the European Court in *HL v United Kingdom* [2004] ruled that this approach was not compatible with Article 5 of the Convention since using common law to detain someone in hospital was too arbitrary and lacked sufficient safeguards. This effectively compelled a rethink about core assumptions that underpinned mental health legislation and led to a new Mental Health Bill being put forward in 2006, together with amendments to the Mental Capacity Act 2005 (see Chapter 6).

Broader definition of mental disorder

There is very real concern here that people with learning disabilities will be brought into the ambit of mental health legislation. This extends the remit of mental health legislation quite considerably and may even challenge the European Convention principle that liberty should be restricted only where someone is proven to be of *unsound mind*. The same applies to the proposed extension of legislation to people with 'personality disorders', a move actively opposed by the British Medical Association and other professional and service user groups.

The social worker role

Both the 2004 and 2006 bills proposed substituting *approved mental health professionals* for social workers as approved applicants for patients' detention, thereby potentially broadening the scope for giving powers to non-social work professionals. Grave concern has been expressed at the lack of social care assessment as an integral part of the whole process and the significant reduction in the social work role generally.

Patients' powers to nominate advocates

This power had to be introduced to meet the objections to current legislation that arose in cases concerning definition of nearest relative (see discussion under Article 8 above) and also in the light of the passing of the Civil Partnership Act 2004. Generally, this move has been welcomed, and clearly offers patients potentially more say in who should represent them. Some reservations remain about exactly what powers advocates would have and how an advocacy system would be financed. Also, questions arise about advocates' rights of access to information.

More generally in relation to people's rights

Overall, there appears to be an underlying assumption that people with mental health problems are dangerous. Many organisations have pointed out that there is no service user right to an assessment, and no entitlement to services as such. If you look up the websites listed at the end of this chapter you will see that there remains a number of issues of concern to professional and service users, which primarily revolve around the overemphasis on control and compulsion, and disempowerment of service users themselves.

Conclusion

From this it will be seen that a number of important ethical and legal issues arise. They all centre on the issue of rights. To what extent should the State intervene in the lives of people who may not have committed a crime, yet may potentially pose a threat to themselves or to others? This is the crux of the matter. The European Convention offers some guidelines, yet we can identify some deficiencies, especially in relation to compulsory treatment in the community. At the same time, we can see that in trying to adhere to the Convention, there is a danger of overplaying the role of tribunals to the extent that resources for services may suffer. Yet we would have to concede that the Convention is important for, without it, there would be a real danger of the Government or State simply deciding who was dangerous without allowing any possibility of an independent review of such cases. The debate about the success of the Convention in promoting or constraining the rights of people with mental health problems is a very real and important one, which will continue for some time to come. The hope is that you can see how the Convention has an impact on UK law and social work practice, and also how it connects into major philosophical debates. At least by now you will understand how and why any new mental health legislation, such as the Mental Health Act 2007 which was the eventual outcome of all these processes, often represents a compromise path through a maze of controversial ethical issues. It may also explain why revisions of mental health legislation are infrequent. There has been no new legislation since 2007; the previous Act, much of which is still in force, being the Mental Health Act 1983.

Chapter summary

This chapter has explored the concept of rights in social work with special reference to the Human Rights Act 1998 that incorporates the European Convention on Human Rights into everyday social work law and practice. You were asked to identify the fundamental rights that human beings share, and were then presented with an overview of the forms of redress to which service users are entitled in UK. This started with a summary of the legal processes whereby decisions made by public bodies might be challenged. The ultimate test lies with interpretation of the European Convention either in UK courts or ultimately in Strasbourg at the European Court. To demonstrate the operation of human rights in practice, the chapter then highlighted some specific examples of decisions made about basic rights that may have relevance to social work. We then focused on the example of mental health law and the European Convention, specifically its provisions for detention and control of people (of unsound mind) perceived to be a danger to themselves or to others. This led to a discussion of the 2004–2006 contested proposals for changes in mental health legislation in England and Wales, and you were invited to assess these by reference to the European Convention. Some critical commentary made by a variety of organisations was then offered; this pointed to some key dilemmas in interpreting people's rights more generally.

Eventually, the Mental Health Act 2007 was deliberately framed in such a way that it complies with the requirements of the European Convention on Human Rights. This principle of compatibility with the European Convention applies to all laws currently enforced in the UK and, naturally, applies to all legislation and decision-making by public bodies in all other areas of social work. So do remember that mental health was just one example and that these principles apply equally to family law, adult care and youth justice.

The next chapter starts the specific examination of law as it relates to particular areas of social work, beginning with work with children and families. Yet again the issue of balancing people's rights with the obligations of the State will come to the fore, but now these will need to be examined in the context of children's rights.

Further reading

If you are particularly interested in the example of mental health cited here as a demonstration of the European Convention on Human Rights in practice, you may like to look at one of the following which explores the issues much further than space permits here.

Johns, R (2005) Of unsound mind? Mental health social work and the European Convention on Human Rights. *Practice*, 16(4): 247–59.

Richardson, G (2008) Coercion and human rights: A European perspective. *Journal of Mental Health*, 17(3): 245–54.

Websites

British Association of Social Workers: www.basw.co.uk

Department of Health: www.gov.uk/government/organisations/department-of-health

European Convention on Human Rights: conventions.coe.int/treaty/en/Treaties/Html/005.htm

European Court judgements: www.echr.coe.int/ECHR/EN/Header/Case-Law

King's Fund: Independent charity concerned with health and health information generally (lots of useful links to organisations and sources of information): www.kingsfund.org.uk

Local government ombudsman for England: www.lgo.org.uk

Mental Health Alliance, consortium of mental health voluntary organisations: www.mentalhealthalliance.org.uk

Mental Health Bill 2004: http://webarchive.nationalarchives.gov.uk/+/www.dh.gov.uk/en/Publicationsandstatistics/Publications/PublicationsLegislation/DH_4088910

Parliamentary Joint Committee on mental health: commentary on 2004 proposals: www.publications.parliament.uk/pa/jt/jtment.htm

Parliamentary and Health Service Ombudsman for England: www.ombudsman.org.uk/

Public Services Ombudsman for Wales: www.ombudsman-wales.org.uk/

Sainsbury Centre for Mental Health, a charity concerned with the quality of life of people with severe mental health problems: www.centreformentalhealth.org.uk/

SANE, mental health charity: www.sane.org.uk/home

United Nations Convention on the Rights of the Child: www.unicef.org.uk/Documents/Publication-pdfs/UNCRC_PRESS200910web.pdf

Welsh Assembly Government: www.wales.nhs.uk/documents/websiteEnglishNSFandActionPlan.pdf

3: Children's Rights and Needs

Achieving a social work degree

This and the next chapter will help you to develop the following capabilities from the **Professional Capabilities Framework**:

2. **Values and ethics**

   Apply social work ethical principles and values to guide professional practice.

4. **Rights, justice and economic well-being**

   Advance human rights and promote social justice and economic well-being.

5. **Knowledge**

   Apply knowledge of social sciences, law and social work practice theory.

7. **Intervention and skills**

   Use judgement and authority to intervene with individuals, families and communities to promote independence, provide support and prevent harm, neglect and abuse.

They are relevant to the following Standards of Proficiency:

1. Be able to practise safely and effectively within their scope of practice.
2. Be able to practise within the legal and ethical boundaries of their profession.

(Continued)

(Continued)

8. Be able to communicate effectively.

10. Be able to maintain records appropriately.

They will also introduce you to the following standards as set out in the 2016 Social Work Subject Benchmark Statement:

4.7 exercise authority constructively within complex frameworks of accountability and ethical and legal boundaries;

5.3 v the relationship between human rights enshrined in law and the moral and ethical rights determined theoretically, philosophically and by contemporary society

5.3 vi the complex relationships between justice, care and control in social welfare and the practical and ethical implications of these.

5.6 vi the significance of legislative and legal frameworks and service delivery standards.

Introduction

This chapter begins a two-part examination of the important relationship between children, their families, social work and the law. In this chapter, the focus is on children's basic needs and rights. This moves forward from the previous chapter where we looked at the basic human rights that everyone shares. Chief among these needs, specific to children, are education and the need to be looked after and supported during the process of growing up. One of the key concepts is that of working in partnership with parents. From the child's perspective, the law is important as it starts with their needs and then examines the most appropriate ways of meeting those needs, even if there is occasionally a conflict with some adults' perceptions of what those might be. In Chapter 4, we will be concentrating more closely on legal arrangements when things go wrong: when families have what appear to be irreconcilable disputes, or when children need protection from *significant harm*.

The lengthy list of relevant aspects of the Professional Capabilities Framework hints at the breadth of social work responsibilities in relation to children, as does the fact that there are two chapters devoted to this area. In this chapter we will be starting with some fundamental considerations of the position of children in society and within the legal system, before going on to consider some ways in which children's needs are met in the UK.

This chapter considers:

- the legal definition of childhood;
- the rights of children that are recognised internationally;

- meeting children's needs for education;

- supporting families and helping them to look after children;

- provision of substitute care when this is necessary for children;

- transition to adulthood.

What is a child?

You might think the answer to this question is pretty obvious, but bearing in mind that this is a book about the law and social work, how exactly would you define a child? After all, when we are talking about social arrangements to provide for the needs of children, we need to be clear from the outset exactly whose needs we are discussing. When we are talking about children's rights, we need to be able to say precisely to whom these rights apply.

Activity 3.1

If you were asked to come up with a definition of a child, what would you say? Bear in mind that the definition has to withstand legal tests: it has to be consistent, applicable to everyone, readily understandable and potentially enforceable – that is, someone should be able to come along and say quite definitively that that person is a child whereas another person is not.

You should spend about ten minutes on this activity.

Comment

You may have started to approach this from the perspective of the vulnerability or dependence of certain human beings, but there are problems in applying this in the legal context. No matter how you approach the issue of defining childhood, you will almost inevitably, for simplicity's sake, have ended up with a definition based on age.

A number of practitioners have pointed out that people with learning disabilities retain an apparently childlike capacity to conceptualise and relate to other people, which in some contexts makes them quite vulnerable. Nevertheless, the law cannot recognise this vulnerability since the law anchors its definitions solely on chronological age.

However, if childhood is defined by age, what age? Would you recognise, formally and legally, a transition stage between childhood and adulthood? If so, at what age does this transition start and when does it finish? It is tempting to answer this by reference to physical growth and development, perhaps using puberty – the biological transition from childhood to young adulthood – as the marker. However, this makes the issue more problematic, for puberty occurs at different ages in different young people, so the outcome would certainly not be consistent. Consistency will only really be achieved by using biological age, which is easy to check (through birth certificates and other formal documentation) and indisputable.

So if age is the key factor, what age marks the end of childhood? Do we still wish to incorporate a formal transition period – for the sake of argument, something akin to adolescence?

Sociologists and historians (principally Ariès, 1979) have pointed out that the age at which childhood ends varies considerably between different cultures and different time periods. Ariès points out that in France, along with a number of other European countries, for several centuries

Table 3.1   Age of criminal responsibility in other countries

Argentina	16
Austria	14
Czech Republic	15
England, Wales and Northern Ireland	10
France	13
Germany	14
India	7
Indonesia	8
Japan	14
Luxembourg	18
Portugal	16
Scotland	12 (s 52 Criminal Justice and Licensing (Scotland) Act 2010) technically this is the minimum age for prosecution not criminal responsibility
South Africa	7
Spain	14
Sweden	15
Thailand	7
Turkey	11
USA	Varies according to the state from 7 (Oklahoma) to 14 (California and others) although some have no minimum age

Source: UNICEF

the convention was that no gender distinctions were made between children until comparatively late, sometimes up to the age of seven, when children suddenly lost their 'innocence'. In Britain, children in the nineteenth century were held fully responsible under the criminal law from the time they attained their eighth birthday. The age of criminal responsibility is now ten in England and Wales, but this contrasts markedly with other countries.

Furthermore, if you look at the following table, you will see that there is not a great deal of consistency in ages at which children and young people are allowed to undertake certain activities in the UK.

You may think that these are simply anomalies, but in fact it reflects a difficulty in framing the law so that it protects the vulnerability of young people while not being too oppressive. One example of this may be the law regarding drinking alcohol: in many USA states, the minimum age for buying alcoholic drinks is 21, whereas in the UK there is a debate about whether it should be lowered from 18. It may be that this also reflects the fact that the law does not formally recognise adolescence. Adolescence is a psychological or sociological term, not a legal one. Where the law does make a distinction, most usually in criminal law, it uses the term *young persons* to refer to the in-between age, usually 14 to 17 (inclusive).

In the law which we are going to examine in this chapter and the next, the term 'children' has a slightly wider use than it does in everyday life. In the next section we look at the United Nations Convention on the Rights of the Child, which regards children as all people under the age of 18, unless the law of a particular country states otherwise. The law in Britain currently makes education compulsory up until the end of the academic term or year in which the young person attains the age of 16, the age having been raised to 14 in 1918, 15 in 1947 and 16 in 1972. However, the Education and Skills Act 2008 (sections 1 and 2) effectively made education or training obligatory up to age 18. So, 16 or 18? The Children Act 1989 has it both ways. In relation to 'private' proceedings – that is, court cases that do not concern local authorities or other public bodies – children are people under the age of 16. In relation to

Table 3.2   Ages at which activities become permissible (examples)

Age	Activity
13	Employment, although allowed at an even earlier age for theatrical performances and in agriculture
14	Hold a shotgun certificate
15	Watch 15 certificate films
16	Drive mopeds, consent to sexual activity, buy some alcohol to drink with meal, buy lottery tickets, join army or get married with parental consent
17	Drive car, purchase shotguns and firearms
18	Vote, marry, purchase alcohol, buy fireworks, use betting shop, be elected to Parliament
21	Drive bus, adopt (an unrelated child), get an airline pilot's licence

'public' law and social services departments'/children's services authorities' responsibilities for providing services to children, children are people under the age of 18.

Sometimes the law does not insist on a chronological age, but allows professionals to make a judgement. One sensible example of this relates to consent to medical treatment and respecting confidentiality. If the law insisted that children attained adult rights only on their eighteenth birthday, this would mean that parents had absolute rights to determine whether and how children accepted medical treatment. This issue came to the fore in the case of *Gillick v West Norfolk and Wisbech Area Health Authority* [1986] where a parent tried to stop a family GP giving contraceptive advice and medical treatment to anyone in the family under 18. The decision in that case confirmed that having arbitrary age limits was artificial and quite inappropriate since it ignored the level of understanding and competence of individuals concerned to give consent. Therefore, the judgment allows professionals to consider whether young people have sufficient competence to give informed consent, and if so, the young person's rights override those of the parent to object. In 2006, the courts confirmed this principle and extended it to young people's rights to confidentiality. In the Axon case, *R (on the application of Axon) v Secretary of State for Health* [2006], the court rejected a mother's contention that she had the right to know if health care professionals proposed giving her children advice on sexual matters, including abortion. Guidelines asserting young people's independent rights to confidentiality did not conflict with parental rights under Article 8 of the European Convention on Human Rights. These judgements are important and exert considerable influence on social work and medical practice, although confidentiality is not an absolute, and can be overridden in cases of risk to health, safety or welfare (see Chapter 4).

Children's rights

In Chapter 2 we examined some basic, fundamental human rights that people in the UK now expect to be respected through the operation of the Human Rights Act 1998. We are now going to consider the specific and additional rights that children ought to have, over and above the rights accorded to adults. The next activity asks you to consider what you think these should be, so it might be advisable to look again at Chapter 2 if you cannot recall what basic human rights are.

Activity 3.2

Think about children you know of different ages. Think about children in different parts of the world. Think about children from different cultures and diverse backgrounds. Then write down what you think are the basic needs of all children.

You should spend about 15 to 20 minutes on this exercise. It may be helpful to undertake the exercise in a small group where you can share ideas and challenge each other about whether identified needs apply to all children. You might also want to consider why it is not easy to come to an immediate consensus on this.

Comment

It is more difficult than you may have assumed to think about basic needs, since, especially in the West, it is so easy to take basic necessities for granted. Have a look and see if your list of needs can be fitted into the categories of physical, developmental and emotional.

Classifying children's basic needs in this way helps distinguish different kinds of needs:

- Physical: under this heading we might include shelter in the form of some kind of home in which to live, sufficient food and water to survive, access to primary medical care that ensures survival, protection from harm.

- Developmental: access to food and water of sufficient quality to provide for growth and development, access to medical care that prevents disease and promotes growth, literacy to a sufficient level that ensures participation in society.

- Emotional: security (in all its forms, including freedom from oppression and persecution and of identity), love and affection, respect as an individual.

The various countries of the world have attempted to codify children's basic needs and set out a charter of rights that is applicable to all countries. This codification is the United Nations Convention on the Rights of the Child. Before going any further, it is important to underline that this has not been adopted by the UK government as part of its legislative framework, so the United Nations Convention does not perform the same role as the European Convention on Human Rights in relation to the Human Rights Act 1998. Furthermore, it should be noted that not all countries are signatories to the United Nations Convention, the most conspicuous non-signatory being the United States (the other is Somalia) (see the website list at the end of the chapter for access to the full Convention).

Nevertheless, the United Nations Convention is important for a number of reasons. First, it sets out benchmarks by which countries ought to judge their own legislative provision. Second, those countries that have signed the Convention are assessed at least once every five years on the extent to which their legal system and child care practices conform to the Convention. As you will see in Chapter 7, the United Nations has in the past expressed some concern about the high rate of imprisonment of young offenders in Britain and specifically has drawn attention to the practice of sending 12–14-year-olds into custody (Goldson, 2002). If you look at the 54 provisions of the Convention, you will see that, apart from the technical provisions concerning jurisdiction and implementation, there are some that seem particularly relevant to social work and the law in the UK. These are as follows.

Table 3.3 United Nations Convention on the Rights of the Child and links to UK law

Article	Focus	Links
2.2	No discrimination on account of what parents do or say	
3	Best interests of the child to be a primary consideration for courts and administrative bodies, child safeguarding provision, safety and health	Children Act 1989
5	Respect for rights and duties of parents	
6	Right to life and development	Human Rights Act 1998
7, 8	Right to identity	Birth registration provisions
9	Separation from parents to be exceptional, proper procedures to apply	Children Act 1989 including placement regulations; Adoption and Children Act 2002
12	Child's right to participate in decision-making	
18	Promotion of parental responsibility	
19	Protection from abuse or neglect	
21, 22	Special status of fostering and adoption	
23	Children with disabilities	
24	Right to health	Health-related legislation
26, 27	Right to social security and basic living standards	Social security legislation
28, 29	Right to education	Education Acts
30	Right to own culture	
31	Right to play and recreation	
32.9	Protection from exploitation, drugs, sexual abuse, abduction, inhuman treatment or punishment, deprivation of liberty without advocacy, participation in armed conflicts	Various, including criminal law, Human Rights Act 1998, youth justice legislation, Children Act 1989
39	Rehabilitation after armed conflict	
40	Due legal processes for children accused of committing offences	Youth justice legislation especially Powers of Criminal Courts (Sentencing) Act 2000 – see Chapter 7 for further discussion

How are these translated into UK law?

Given that they are not declared as overarching in the same way as the European Convention on Human Rights, this means that in order to answer the question we need to look at specific areas where Parliament has attempted to match UK law to the Convention. Table 3.3 has attempted to do this for you by indicating the areas of legislation or specific Acts of Parliament that are most relevant – you will also notice that there are some gaps where no specific legislation applies, although there may be other provision through regulations, codes of guidance or policy directives. The now superseded *Every Child Matters* initiative (Department for Education and Skills, 2004) was important for it declared an overall ambition that children in the UK should be healthy, stay safe, enjoy and achieve. make a positive contribution; and achieve economic well-being.

However, when it comes to the actual law itself, the two areas that most directly concern social workers are the Children Act 1989, which specifically facilitates support services for children in need and their parents, and the various provisions relating to education, principally the Education Act 1996. We start with education.

Meeting children's needs for education

Case study

Declan (aged 15) and his half-sister Clare (aged 4) live with their mother, Trisha, in a house on an estate where the majority of housing is rented from a housing association. The local schools do not have a very enviable reputation. They are low in the league tables of relative achievements in GCSEs and Standard Attainment Tests. Declan's experience of school has been wholly negative and he cannot wait to leave. He has been excluded from school twice in the last year for being abusive to teachers and thinks he was unfairly treated on the last occasion. Trisha is wondering whether there is anything she can do to avoid subjecting Clare to Declan's experience, especially as Clare has a hearing impairment.

The Education Act 1996 consolidates much of the legislation regarding provision of education, but for completeness we also need to look at the Special Educational Needs and Disability Act 2001 and Children and Families Act 2014 (Part 3), which both address the provision of education for children and students with special needs. There are also a number of significant general amendments introduced by successive governments. The Education Acts of 2002, 2005 and 2011 together with the Education and Inspections Act 2006 covered matters such as standards, discipline, school governance and budgeting. The Education and Skills Act 2008, supplemented by the Apprenticeships, Skills, Children and Learning Act 2009 makes education or training compulsory up to 18 from 2015. The Academies Act 2010 enables all maintained schools to apply to the Secretary of State for Education to become Academies – that is, state-funded schools independent of local authority control and governance. The Children and Families Act 2014 (sections 37–51) introduces birth-to-25 Education, Health and Care plans for everyone under 25 with special education needs, principally disability, in order to provide a better co-ordinated and more consistent system of planning across education, health and social care. The Education and Adoption Act 2016 adds ministerial powers to intervene where schools are considered to be 'coasting' or failing to maintain standards. There is now a duty (under section 7) to convert a school requiring 'significant improvement' or 'special measures' to an Academy.

While children are entitled to start schooling only during the first term after their fifth birthday, in practice many start earlier than this. The Sure Start scheme, introduced in 1998 in order to address social exclusion and social deprivation through early access to education and related support, facilitated the inclusion of many 4-year-olds in mainstream education. So it may be possible for Clare to be involved in the school now. Declan, meanwhile, is obliged to wait until the official school leaving date. However, much depends on the availability of school places in the family's particular locality.

It is a popular misconception that school attendance is compulsory, whereas in fact it is education that has to be provided by parents. In the vast majority of cases parents will choose to ensure that children receive education by sending them to school, but this is not compulsory. However, if parents choose to have children educated at home (*or otherwise* – section 7 Education Act 1996) they must satisfy the local authority that this is satisfactory. If school attendance is preferred, parents have the right to express a preference for schooling, but do not have an absolute right of choice. They cannot insist that their children attend a particular school; schools have the right to refuse if they are oversubscribed and their admissions policies, when fairly applied, give priority to other children, although there is a right of appeal to an adjudicator (School Admissions (Admission Arrangements and Co-ordination of Admission Arrangements) (England) Regulations 2012 as amended by the Amendment Regulations of 2014; Welsh Government Schools Admissions Code 2013). So in this case Trisha can decide that local schools are not good enough for Clare, and so send her to another school (maintained, academy or independent) in a different area. Whichever is chosen, the additional costs in terms of fares and/or fees are, of course, the parents' responsibility.

Responsibility for ensuring that children receive full-time education lies with the local authority. This duty is carried out primarily through schools checking registers of attendance and reporting to education social workers (education welfare officers), who deal with more than just attendance issues. They are often referred cases where children have special needs and act as advisers where difficulties at home are having an effect on schooling, or even in some cases where there is abuse. Truancy can result in a parent being prosecuted, or in the child being placed under the supervision of the local authority where the court, applying the Children Act 1989 principles (see next chapter), is satisfied that the child is not being properly educated. In these cases, an education supervision order can be made for up to one year, with possible extensions up to three years (section 36 Children Act 1989).

Education legislation in the UK goes beyond the basics required in the United Nations Convention on the Rights of the Child. Not only is education compulsory, but in state-funded (or partially state-funded) schools, education must be offered in a specific way. There is a national curriculum of core subjects, together with an obligation to provide religious education, although parents have the right to withdraw children from this and from any specifically religious-based assemblies (Education Act 2002), a right which section 55 of the Education and Inspections Act 2006 extended to sixth-formers in England. There is also a national code of discipline in the sense that exclusion from school, which is the ultimate penalty, can be used only following the application of certain procedures, and within certain limits (Education Act 2002 as amended by Education Act 2011). Exclusion, unless permanent, can total no more than 45 days in any one school year, and is subject to appeal to the school governing body (School Discipline (Pupil Exclusions and Reviews) (England) Regulations 2012; Education (Pupil Exclusions and Appeals) (Maintained Schools) (Wales) Regulations 2003) as amended by Education (Pupil Exclusions and Appeals) (Wales) (Miscellaneous Amendments) Regulations 2004 and Education (Reintegration Interview) (Wales) Regulations 2010. The head teacher has the right to exclude (section 52 Education Act 2002, governors can override this and parents have the right to appeal against the governors' decision (section 88 Education and Inspections Act 2006; Education and Skills Act 2008).

The general principle is that all children should be educated in mainstream schooling unless they have special educational needs and their parents wish them to be educated outside the mainstream system (Part 3 Children and Families Act 2014). In this case, Clare would be entitled to an assessment to determine whether she has any learning difficulties arising from her disability (section 312 Education Act 1996). If a statement is issued confirming that she has special needs, then the local authority is under a duty to arrange for those needs to be met. If a statement is refused, parents have the right to appeal to the Special Educational Needs and Disability Tribunal (Section 51 Children and Families Act 2014). Note that it is the parents' right to appeal; although Clare is obviously too young to participate, it is worth noting that in England there is no provision for the child or young person to participate, which likewise appears to be contrary to the principles declared in the United Nations Convention. In Wales, comprehensive reform of the statementing and declaration of special educational needs system is planned with the implementation of new legislation when the Additional Learning Needs Bill 2016 is passed by the Welsh Assembly.

Supporting families and helping them to look after children

Case study

Trisha (whom you met in the previous case study) wants to know what support services are available for her and her family. Declan has no idea what he wants to do when he leaves school, and Trisha is worried that Clare is isolated in their community, with few friends of her own age and with what appears to be an increasingly serious disability.

In this section we examine support services available through a variety of initiatives but primarily through provisions in the Children Act 1989. Before outlining these provisions, we need to say something about the values which the Children Act 1989 promotes. Summarising the various sets of guidance and regulations (Department of Health, 1991b) it is possible to discern a number of key principles that underpin the Children Act 1989 and thereby set out the framework for social work with children and families. As we saw in Chapter 1, the Children Act 1989 drew its key concepts and principles from the Cleveland Report (DHSS, 1988), especially in relation to the boundaries between the family, the state and social work agencies, which was why it was important for you to know something of the background to this important piece of legislation. The key principles with regard to supporting families are set out in the official Introduction to the Children Act 1989 (Department of Health, 1989):

- children should usually be brought up in their own family;
- local authorities, working in conjunction with voluntary agencies, should aim to support families, offering a range of services appropriate to children's needs;
- services are best delivered by working in partnership with parents;
- parents and, commensurate with their ability to understand, children, should express their wishes and feelings and participate in decision-making.

This is underpinned by some specific requirements in the Children Act 1989 itself. The local authority must safeguard and promote the welfare of children in their area who are in need and promote the upbringing of such children by their families by providing a range and level of services appropriate to those children's needs (section 17 Children Act 1989). Furthermore, the Secretary of State is now under a statutory duty to promote the well-being of all children and young people and, by extension, their families and those who care for them (section 7 Children and Young Persons Act 2008). The Childcare Act 2006 (section 6 in England, section 22 in Wales) additionally requires local authorities to ensure that there is sufficient child care for parents who are working or are planning to work. In England, parents of 'qualifying children' (generally those under five) have the right to 30 hours of free childcare in 38 weeks of the year (Childcare Act 2016 section 1).

Logically, the tenor of these provisions implies that it is only in exceptional circumstances that social workers should directly intervene in families to the extent of making decisions that override the parents. It follows that court action should be a last resort; it is for this reason that principles relating to courts and statutory intervention are not addressed here but feature in Chapter 4. The main emphasis in social work ought to be on providing services to support children and their families. This immediately raises the question of what services and which children are defined as being 'in need'?

To take the second question first, the answer to this lies in section 17(10) of the Children Act 1989 that offers a list more or less consistent with the United Nations Convention: children who fail to achieve or maintain a reasonable standard of health or development, whose health or development is significantly impaired, or who are disabled. There is a definition of disability in this section and a local authority has a duty to maintain a register of disabled children under Schedule 2(2) of the Act, although both have been the subject of some criticism (Corker and Davis, 2000). So there is no doubt about it: Clare with her hearing impairment is definitely a child 'in need' and therefore entitled to services arranged through the local authority.

To answer the question about service provision, we need to look at Schedule 2 as well as the Children Act 1989 itself. Note that this now only applies to England (section 55 Social Services and Well-being (Wales) Act 2014 (Consequential Amendments) Regulations 2016); for Wales now see Part IV of the Social Services and Well-being (Wales) Act 2014 which is broadly similar. Schedules are mechanisms for providing detail that it would be inappropriate to include in the main body of the Act itself. They are similar to an appendix: important, yet containing material that would interfere with the main substance of a piece of work. Here we find that the Schedules to the Children Act 1989 provide considerable detail as to how the Act itself is to be implemented. It is important to recognise that, as the Schedule is attached to the Act, it does have the force of law. It is not like a Code of Practice which is open to interpretation. Social workers in all sectors of child care work ought therefore to be familiar with Schedule 2 of the Children Act 1989 as it sets out both additional principles and the mechanisms for achieving the Act's objectives. The Schedule covers a number of different areas and responsibilities. Local authorities are:

- to identify children in need and publish information about services;
- to act to prevent children suffering ill-treatment or neglect;
- at the same time to act to avoid children being involved in court proceedings;
- to take steps to enable children to live with their families and promote contact with them when they are separated from their families;
- to provide family centres, as appropriate, for needs identified by the local authority;
- to provide advice, guidance, counselling, activities, home help, and holidays for children and families where they think this is appropriate.

To this must be added services listed in section 18 of the Children Act 1989 itself:

- day care for children under five;
- out-of-school and holiday activities.

For the moment, we will set aside provision for children outside their own families where parents are unable to continue to look after them, as this is the topic for the next section.

Service provision may include in some exceptional circumstances local authorities offering financial support (section 17(6) Children Act 1989) and for children with disabilities this might include direct payments for services commissioned by the parent (section 49 Children and Families Act 2014).

Note that in Wales there are separate regulations enacted by the Children and Families (Wales) Measure 2010 concerning supportive children's services, including play opportunities, child minding and day care. Other provisions originally in this Measure, such as assessing the needs of children where their parents need care services, have been transferred to the Social Services and Well-being (Wales) Act 2014.

Given the range of different services potentially available, it is not surprising that some families find the range confusing and, more importantly, there are sometimes deficiencies. To counteract this, the law provides mechanisms to enhance service co-ordination. Specifically:

- providing information about services offered in the independent sector (Schedule 2);
- a duty to facilitate family support provision by non-statutory organisations (section 17 Children Act 1989);
- to seek help from other authorities in supporting children and families (section 27 Children Act 1989);
- a duty to co-operate in providing services for children with special educational needs (section 28 Children and Families Act 2014).

In order to bring all this together there is a duty to publish Children and Young People's Plans (section 194 Apprenticeships, Skills, Children and Learning Act 2009). These plans set out how children's services are to be organised and delivered so as to meet children's needs in a given area. Co-ordination has become a major issue, given the number of projects and initiatives that now exist to address general and specific needs in children. You may already know what some of these are, but if not, the following exercise will ask you to do some research on this.

Activity 3.3

Make a list of the initiatives that the government has promoted to enhance the well-being of all children under 16. If you can, find out how these schemes operate in your local area.

Comment

The government schemes are listed in the Exercise Answers, pp187–8.

Although this should mean that there will be a number of avenues of support for Trisha and Clare, it will be important for social workers to be aware of how all these services are integrated (or not, as the case may be) and how they relate to legislation and specific policy initiatives. Social workers should note in particular that, before deciding what services to provide, a local authority should ascertain the child's wishes and feelings and give due consideration to them (section 53 Children Act 2004). Also worth noting is the Childcare Act 2006 (sections 3 and 4 in England, sections 23 and 24 in Wales) which require early childhood services – early years provision, health services, social services and employment services – to be provided in an integrated manner.

Finally, let's not forget Declan. Although he may be nearly 16, he is still entitled to children's services, although it is questionable whether these would be suited to his age group. Rather, the expectation is that he will want to access services for young people (see the websites at the end of this chapter for what some of these might be). Section 68 of the Education and Skills Act 2008 makes encouraging the effective participation of young people in education or training the responsibility of local authorities.

Providing substitute care

Case study

Declan stops attending school and gets involved in a great deal of anti-social behaviour in the local community. Trisha is exasperated with him and is fearful of the bad effect she says he is having on Clare. She decides she does not want him living at home with her any more but has no alternative family members available to help her. In desperation, she turns to the local authority and asks them to take him 'into care'.

In responding to Trisha's request, we need to look closely at the Children Act 1989 and note the distinction made between two routes into 'care': being committed to care by courts under a care order (covered in Chapter 4) and responding to a voluntary parental request for 'care'. In fact, the term 'in care' is incorrect. The Children Act 1989 introduces the notion of children being *accommodated* or *looked after* rather than being 'in care'. This was deliberate. It was effected in order to make it very clear that a request by a parent for a local authority to look after a child is like any other request for services – that is, the parent still retains their full parental authority, still keeps all their rights and does not endanger them (as used to be the case under previous legislation) by asking for social work assistance.

Local authorities have a duty to provide accommodation for children in need (see above for an explanation of what 'in need' means) where there is no one who has parental responsibility for them, where they are lost or abandoned or, more usually, where the carer is unable to accommodate them (section 20 Children Act 1989, section 76 Social Services and Well-being (Wales) Act 2014). Given the voluntary basis of the request, section 20 also says that the local authority cannot accede to it if anyone with parental responsibility can offer care – and this may not necessarily be the parent who is currently looking after the child – or if the child themselves, if they are 16 or over, objects. So, in this case Declan would, once he attained the age of 16, acquire the right to veto his mother's request, although one wonders what he would suggest as an alternative. In making arrangements for accommodation local authorities must consider the child's wishes and feelings alongside those of people with parental responsibility and others of relevance to the child; give due consideration to religious persuasion, racial origin, cultural and linguistic background; explore potential placements in the child's family and networks; place close to home and with siblings if possible; continue to offer advice and if necessary financial assistance once the child ceases to be looked after (sections 22, 23 and 24 Children Act 1989; Part 6 Social Services and Well-being (Wales) Act 2014). Note that the Children and Young Persons Act 2008 (section 8) introduced detailed requirements as to how a local authority sets about providing appropriate accommodation and what factors it should take into account; these are added to section 22 of the Children Act 1989 to become sections 22A–22G.

Additionally, the placement of children in accommodation brings social workers into a whole welter of Regulations which practitioners will need to consult if they are directly involved in placement of children since they are essential guides to practice (a full list appears at the end of this chapter). These primarily concern arrangements for reviews, procedures for checking the suitability of foster carers, appointment of independent visitors (for children who have lost contact with their families of origin), regulations of children's homes and similar matters which are of great importance on a day-to-day basis for the quality of experience of children. Space does not permit a detailed consideration of these here, but there is one issue that does need to be addressed – namely, the special procedures that apply to children placed in secure accommodation.

Secure accommodation is defined as accommodation provided for the purpose of *restricting liberty* (section 25 Children Act 1989). Local authorities or voluntary organisations may not place the children they look after (those under a care order as well as those who are accommodated) in secure accommodation for more than 72 hours in any 28-day period without reference to a court (regulation 10 Children (Secure Accommodation) Regulations 1991). The purpose of secure accommodation is to deal with those children and young people who have a history of absconding or who are likely to injure themselves unless they can be kept in a restricted environment. A history of absconding has to include a likelihood of suffering significant harm in order to qualify for the provision of such accommodation (section 25 Children Act 1989). There must be an application to court for approval and once the local authority applies to court, an independent guardian will be appointed to look after the interests of the child or young person (for further information on guardians, see the 'Speaking up for children' section in Chapter 4). The court will then consider whether the criteria in section 25 are satisfied. If the court agrees to the order, its length should be determined by the welfare needs of the child (*Re M (a minor)* [1995] FLR 418), and in any case should not exceed three months (regulation 11 Children (Secure Accommodation) Regulations 1991). The order does not require the local authority or voluntary organisation to keep the child in secure accommodation, so is unlike orders that apply to criminal cases, but it grants them the power to do so if they deem it necessary. Do note that these procedures apply even if the child or young person is accommodated by a voluntary request by the parent, although obviously it is open to the parent in such cases to remove the child from local authority accommodation if they see fit.

Providing substitute care also encompasses adoption. This might be regarded as the ultimate request for parents to make of the local authority: to look after their child permanently and to give the child a new home and, in effect, a new identity. It is not proposed to cover adoption law in detail here, but you will find it covered in more comprehensive social work law texts (for example, Brammer, 2015, Chapter 11; Brayne *et al.*, 2015, pp. 320–34). Most current law derives from the Adoption and Children Act 2002. Requests to place children for adoption are quite specific and fall under separate legislation and rules – for example, governing adoption placement agencies and selection of adopters – foster carers are not considered automatically as potential adopters. Likewise, parental agreement can be withdrawn without implying that the parent wishes to withdraw arrangements for accommodation. Consent to an adoption order is a very serious matter and adoptions need to be ratified by a court process, even if full consent is given right the way through. Indeed, proceeding with an adoption order without both parents' full consent is wholly exceptional. UK legislation does allow for the courts to dispense with parental consent on certain grounds (section 52 Adoption and Children Act 2002), but it remains to be seen whether this fully complies with Article 8 of the European Convention on Human Rights concerning rights to family life. As an alternative, courts can now consider special guardianship, which does not involve a change of name and is not an order for life, but does provide security in placement (section 115 Adoption and Children Act 2002 as amended by Children and Adoption Act 2006 Schedule 2 and Children and Young Persons Act 2008 section 38).

Transition into adulthood

Transition to adulthood is particularly challenging for young people who have been accommodated by the local authority. Substantial research evidence has demonstrated that young people are especially vulnerable to homelessness and generally emerge from local authority accommodation with far fewer educational qualifications and employment prospects than the general population (Bhabra et al., 2002). This was recognised by the Children (Leaving Care) Act 2000 which made amendments to duties under the Children Act 1989. It focuses on the needs of 16- and 17-year-olds who were looked after by local authorities prior to that age – these are designated *eligible children* who, once they leave care, become *relevant children*. The duties towards these eligible children are to provide a personal adviser and to prepare a *pathway plan* for them, which must clearly identify needs and must involve the young person themselves (sections 23A–E Children Act 1989; *R (on the application of J) v Caerphilly County Borough Council* 2005). It is important not to confuse a pathway plan with a local authority review (*R (A) v London Borough of Lambeth* 2010). Pathway plans and the appointment of personal advisers are covered by the Care Leavers (England) Regulations 2010 and the Children (Leaving Care) (Wales) Regulations 2015.

There is an obligation to take steps to keep in contact with these young people until they attain the age of 21. They are to be offered support and material assistance, which can include financial support, and in certain circumstances, accommodation (*R (on the application of O) v Barking and Dagenham London Borough Council* 2010). In the case of those continuing to higher or further education, the local authority should offer vacation accommodation (section 4 Children (Leaving Care) Act 2000). The Children Act 2004 (section 9) extended the definition of a child to include any 18–20-year-old with learning disabilities who had been *looked after* by a local authority after the age of 16. Furthermore, the Children and Young Persons Act 2008 (section 22) requires local authorities to carry out an assessment of needs and prepare a pathway plan for *a former relevant child* who is pursuing or wishes to pursue education or training up to the age of 25. This can include assistance with expenses associated with the education or training. In addition, the Children and Families Act 2014 (section 98) requires local authorities to monitor and support *staying put* arrangements whereby *a former relevant child* remains with a foster carer after the age of 18.

Education is seen as key to making a success of transition to adulthood. Historically, looked after children have underperformed in education and government concern has been expressed about their lack of educational attainment and opportunities (Department for Education, 2011d). A specific requirement to promote the educational achievement of looked-after children was introduced by section 52 of the Children Act 2004, a provision strengthened by the Children and Young Persons Act 2008 (section 20 requirement to appoint nominated teacher in schools) and the Apprenticeships, Skills, Children and Learning Act 2009 (section 194 enhancement of Children and Young People's Plan). The Children and Families Act 2014 (section 99) requires the appointment of a local champion to *promote the educational achievement of looked after children*.

All of this both highlights and tries to address the disadvantage experienced by many young people that is made manifest by the experience of being looked after by local authorities. This raises an important question – and it is for reflection and consideration as it is a philosophical rather than a legal question – does the 'system' prevent children and young people achieving to the same level as the general population and make them particularly vulnerable, or is it that these children and young people have always been particularly vulnerable, having encountered a number of negative life experiences which no system can fully counteract?

What do you think?

Chapter summary

In this chapter, you were challenged to think about definitions of childhood and what ought to constitute children's rights. We then explored ways in which children's basic needs could be met, using as a benchmark the United Nations Convention on the Rights of the Child. In Britain, the two important areas that affect children's development are education and social care arrangements to support families. Having summarised what education legislation says about meeting the needs of all children, including those with special needs, we then went on to consider the ways in which social work legislation operates to support families. Here, by far the most important legislation is the Children Act 1989, although it is not the only relevant law, with parts of it being extended and complemented by the Children Act 2004, Children and Young Persons Act 2008 and the Children and Families Act 2014. Some space was given over to an outline of the principles behind the Children Act 1989 as they apply to parents who ask for assistance. We then examined some specifics in terms of the range of services available to children and families, and these were set in the context of other provisions made by a series of government schemes and initiatives. The last two sections examined the provision of substitute care for children where families cannot look after them, concluding with a consideration of the needs of young people leaving accommodation when they move to adulthood.

In the next chapter, we move on to consider the law as it applies to families when something goes wrong – when parents cannot agree about the care of their children, or where there are allegations that children are being abused and there is a need to safeguard them.

Further reading

Department for Education (2011a) *Children Act 1989 guidance and regulations. Volume 4: Fostering services.* Norwich: The Stationery Office.

Department for Education (2011b) *Children Act 1989 guidance and regulations. Volume 5: Children's homes.* Norwich: The Stationery Office.

Department for Education (2015a) *Children Act 1989 guidance and regulations. Volume 2: Care planning, placement and case review.* Norwich: The Stationery Office.

Department for Education (2015b) *Children Act 1989 guidance and regulations. Volume 3: Planning transition to adulthood for care leavers.* London: Department for Education.

Wilson, K, Ruch, G, Lymbery, M and Cooper, A (2011) *Social work: An introduction to contemporary practice* (2nd edn). London: Pearson.

Chapter 16 entitled Social Work with Children and Families is especially recommended since it includes a useful section on caring for looked-after children who cannot live at home.

Websites

Department for Education: www.gov.uk/government/organisations/department-for-education

Education Otherwise: charity concerned with the education of children outside the school system: www.educationotherwise.net

Office of the Children's Commissioner for England: www.childrenscommissioner.gov.uk

Office of the Children's Commissioner for Wales: www.childcom.org.uk

United Nations: www.ohchr.org/en/professionalinterest/pages/crc.aspx for Convention on the Rights of the Child in full, adopted by General Assembly resolution 44/25 of 20 November 1989

Welsh Assembly education website: http://gov.wales/newsroom/educationandskills/?lang=en

4: Meeting Children's Needs When Things Go Wrong

Introduction

This chapter is the second of the two-part examination of the law relating to social work with children and families. Leading from the previous discussion of children's basic needs and rights, and services available to promote their well-being, we now examine the arrangements made to address problems that might occur. The key areas are:

- action that families may take when they cannot agree about arrangements for children;
- what can be done in response to identified needs and shortcomings in meeting those needs;
- how social workers respond to allegations that children are being harmed.

Along the way we need to acknowledge what are probably the most disturbing aspects of social work: failure to protect children from death or serious harm, and the abuse of children and young people in placements where they were supposed to be protected and looked after.

As explained in Chapter 3, both these chapters together enable you to attain appropriate standards of the Professional Capabilities Framework and the 2016 Social Work Subject Benchmarks. These were clearly set out in the previous chapter and so are not repeated here.

Also outlined in the previous chapter was a number of core principles underpinning social work in this area, many of which are enshrined in the Children Act 1989. To remind you, the basic premise is that children's well-being is best promoted by encouraging and supporting them to live with their own families, and everything should be done to facilitate this. However, there are circumstances in which the advisability of children remaining with their own families becomes questionable, and the law sets out the criteria that need to be fulfilled for social workers or others to intervene directly in families' lives. Before we can consider these, there are two areas that need to be explored. First is the notion of parental responsibility, since it is crucial to understand this in order to be able to operate as a social worker under the Children Act 1989. Second, a number of additional principles come into play when the courts are involved in decision-making regarding children. In Chapter 8 we consider specifically the role of social workers in the court setting, so in this chapter we will be focusing on the powers of intervention in families and the kinds of cases where social workers need to refer cases to court.

Parenthood, parenting and parental responsibility

In this section, we start by drawing a distinction between parenthood, parenting and parental responsibility. The reasons for this will become clear when we discuss the outcome of the next exercise.

Acitivity 4.1

How would you distinguish between parenthood, parenting and parental responsibility?

In order to answer this question you may want to think about a number of subsidiary questions:

Is parenthood a legal term?

Who provides parenting? Are biological parents the only people who can offer this?

What are the expectations of parents? What are their responsibilities?

Is there a difference between parental responsibility and parental duties?

This activity should take about 40 minutes, and you may want to join together with others to help answer the questions.

Comment

Parenthood is not a legal term, although the law is quite strong on its insistence that those with parental responsibility (who in some circumstances are people other than the child's biological parents) have certain obligations as well as rights. The suggestion that there is a difference between parenthood and parenting is key to understanding law and social work practice in this area.

Parenthood might generally be understood to refer to motherhood and fatherhood, and therefore equated with those people who are the biological mothers and fathers of children. Interestingly, the law does not use the term parenthood, which is a concept rather than a legal status, but does concern itself very much with parental responsibility, which includes defining who might have this. You must not assume that the only people who have parental responsibility are the child's biological parents. This is far from the case. The law is also very clear that there is a difference between *parental duties* and *parental responsibility*. Those who are the child's biological parents clearly have obligations to the child, and the law tends to focus on these obligations as being primarily financial, a duty to *maintain*, enforced, if necessary, by child support legislation such as the Child Maintenance and Other Payments Act 2008 and associated regulations – an area not covered in this book. If we take parenting to refer to the process whereby a particular kind of nurturing and development is provided for children, then this kind of 'upbringing' does not necessarily or exclusively have to be provided by biological parents, but naturally if it is provided by someone else, those with parental duties would be expected to pay for it. Parental responsibility covers parental rights in areas such as deciding where a child should live, where they should go to school and how their other welfare needs should be met – protection, discipline, medical treatment, spirituality, property and so on (White *et al.*, 2008, Chapter 3). Crucially, this also affects status to participate in legal proceedings.

The people who are the child's biological mother and father are automatically people who have parental duties – that is, obligations to provide for the child, but may not automatically have parental responsibility – that is, all legal rights as parents. However, if the mother and father are married at the time of the child's birth, then they do both share parental responsibility automatically (section 2 Children Act 1989). If they are not married, the mother automatically has parental responsibility, as does the father if his name is registered on the birth certificate (section 111 Adoption and Children Act 2002). If the father's name was not so registered, it is possible for him to acquire parental responsibility either by marrying, by making a voluntary parental responsibility agreement, or by a court order – a parental responsibility order (section 4 Children Act 1989). In the case of children conceived through artificial insemination, special rules apply. These include strict requirements regarding applications for parental orders (section 54 Human Fertilisation and Embryology Act 2008).

However, parental responsibility is not the exclusive preserve of parents. Other people, such as grandparents or step-parents (which could include civil partners), might acquire parental responsibility by becoming the child's guardian, or by a Child Arrangement Order made by the court (see below for discussion of Child Arrangement Orders). If children are committed to care under a care order, local authorities also acquire and share parental responsibility, and in this case their right to determine where the child should live overrides that of the parents (section 33 Children Act 1989). Care orders and other court orders are discussed later in this chapter.

Principles that apply to court cases

Before beginning to explore how the law might apply to cases where families are in difficulties, we need to set out underlying principles that govern the way courts decide on disputes brought before them. We have already referred to the promotion of children's upbringing within their own families, but here we need to consider precise guiding principles set out in the Children Act 1989 itself.

First principle

The first principle is that when courts consider cases, the child's welfare is paramount (section 1 (1) Children Act 1989). This also applies to adoption cases by virtue of section 1 (2) Adoption and Children Act 2002. Note that this principle governs court considerations and does not apply to everything the local authority or parents might do to promote the welfare of children in terms of providing support, nor does it mean that it is the only consideration or that it always applies (White *et al.*, 2008; Brammer, 2015, p170; Brayne *et al.*, 2015, Chapter 5). Without going into too much detail about this, suffice it to say that this means, for example, that courts would not ignore concerns for public safety if anti-social behaviour issues were at stake and other legislation such as the Crime and Security Act 2010 applied. In a similar way, the courts in adoption cases might take a very long-term view which apparently ignored the immediate short-term welfare interests of the child.

Second principle

The second principle is that delay in hearing cases is deemed prejudicial to children's welfare. This is fairly self-explanatory, but clearly is of great concern when the courts themselves have a backlog of cases, or where there is a shortage of staff able to deal with them. Note that this does not mean that cases must be heard hastily or without proper assessment. Given the first principle it will always be the case that courts will give full consideration to the case and expect a comprehensive analysis of the child's needs and alternative courses of action; case law, for example *B (a minor)* [1994], suggests that courts will allow time to see if particular courses of action might be beneficial. However, the Children and Families Act 2014 (section 14(2)(ii)) now sets a time limit for care proceedings of 26 weeks.

Third principle

The third principle is that, in deciding disputed cases, courts should pay particular regard to the welfare checklist, namely:

• the ascertainable wishes and feelings of the child;
• physical, emotional and educational needs;

- likely effects of changing circumstances;
- age, sex, background and any other relevant characteristics;
- potential or actual harm;
- the capabilities of parents and others in meeting the child's needs;
- the range of powers available to the court.

There is clearly a major social work practice issue concerning how one determines the wishes and feelings of very young children. Ascertaining children's views is a core responsibility of children's guardians appointed in public law proceedings (see later in this chapter and Chapter 8). The list in the Children Act 1989 is often used by professionals as a reminder of the various aspects of children's welfare they need to take into consideration. It is a key element in the Department of Health guidance on assessment (Department of Health, 2000c) which is now partly superseded by *Working Together* (HM Government, 2015). It is not proposed to go through each aspect of the welfare checklist here, but they must be borne in mind when considering intervention in families, and social workers must consider the checklist most especially in cases involving allegations of abuse. It is self-evident that the list would be relevant where there are disputes between parents about arrangements for children. It may be worth noting, nevertheless, that in terms of background, attention must be paid to race, culture and religion. A number of cases in this area are summarised in the standard social work law texts (Brammer, 2015; Brayne *et al.*, 2015; Seymour and Seymour, 2013) and if you are practising in this area you will need to know what these are.

Fourth principle

The fourth principle is what some refer to as the *no order* principle – that is to say, generally speaking courts should avoid making any order at all unless it is considered that making an order is better for the child than not making one. There is much misunderstanding about this, with a belief in some quarters that this is some kind of legal presumption against making orders even where children have been demonstrated to be subjected to harm. This is not the case. It might be more accurate to say that this is a *no unnecessary order principle* (White *et al.*, 2008, Chapter 2; Brammer, 2015, p175). Two specific issues are relevant to social work practice. One is that social workers often assume that this means that if people can be persuaded to agree during court proceedings the court need not then make any kind of order. There may still be overriding reasons for rejecting this – for example, if making a child arrangements order is necessary in order to give a person looking after the child parental responsibility, as in the case of *G (children)* [2005]. The second issue is that where actions currently already comply with the likely court order – for example, contact already takes place – courts are unlikely to see the need to make an order. In fact, an order would secure existing arrangements and might also be what the child wants. The Children and Adoption Act 2006 extended this principle by enabling courts to make directions that facilitate contact without actually making a child arrangements order.

Disputes within families

Case study

Suzanne and Winston are unable to agree about who should look after their three children now that they have split up. Samuel (14) wants to go with his father. Jasmine (9) and Rebecca (6) want to stay with their mother. Suzanne wants all three children with her, arguing that she needs Samuel to look after the two girls. Winston wants all three children, arguing that by 'walking out' on the family, Suzanne has forfeited her right to look after any of them.

Cases such as this are regarded as 'private' law cases, since the dispute is within the family, not between the family and the local authority. All of the relevant orders will be found in section 8 Children Act 1989 and these comprise four kinds:

• child arrangements orders which concern where children will live;

• child arrangements orders which concern arrangements for children to keep in touch with others;

• prohibited steps orders which stop someone doing something;

• specific issue orders which compel someone to do something.

The orders are not exclusive to disputes within families; in some cases they may be appropriate in care proceedings as an alternative to care orders or supervision orders.

So, in this particular case study, mother and father would, if they cannot resolve their dispute, be applying for a child arrangements order. Note that if the parents are not married, Winston still has a legal right to make the application, a point established in *C (minors) (parent: residence order)* [1993]. The fourth principle set out above should impel parents and their solicitors to try to reach some kind of agreement if at all possible. Nevertheless, if it is irresolvable the courts will have to make some kind of decision. Clearly, in this case courts will be very exercised by what is in the overall interests of each child, and the third principle would direct them to be strongly influenced by the children's own individual wishes and feelings. Court practice would invariably follow the social work principle of according greater weight to older children's wishes, so it is very likely that Samuel's wishes would prevail over Suzanne's desire to have someone looking after her daughters. The court would certainly not be impressed by a desire to 'punish' one parent by denying them a child arrangements order. Once courts have decided about where children should live, the assumption is that there would then be an agreement about when the other parent could have contact with the child. It is not automatic that courts will make child arrangements orders concerning contact as well as orders regarding residence, but may do so if there is, again, failure to agree. As an alternative, courts might provide for joint care under a child arrangements order, where parents share decision-making more equitably, sometimes even if the parents' relationship is not totally harmonious as in *R (residence: shared care: children's views)* [2005] or in cases where they cannot agree on relocation as in *S (a child)* [2012].

It may be worth saying something about the effect of child arrangements orders. These do not divest the other parent of their parental rights and duties, but they do give the person looking after the child most of the time the right to say where the child will live and make day-to-day decisions about them. If a father, not married to the mother and not otherwise entitled to parental responsibility, is awarded a child arrangements order, he is automatically awarded a separate parental responsibility order (section 12 Children Act 1989). Child arrangements orders do not allow for a change of the child's name or identity, nor do they permit someone to take a child abroad, except for a holiday up to a month. An application for a child arrangements order is also one way of discharging a care order, but we will come to this point later.

It is not only parents who can apply for child arrangements orders. So can others who have an interest in the child, but in this case only with the permission of the court, although the Adoption and Children Act 2002 (section 112) strengthened the position of step-parents in this regard. This may be very useful in cases where, for example, grandparents end up caring for a child on a long-term basis, and courts may then reaffirm this as consistent with the welfare paramountcy principle even above the claims of the natural father, a point finally clarified by the *Supreme Court in B (a Child)* [2009]. Indeed, in such cases a child arrangements order is quite advisable as it clarifies the grandparents' legal rights and responsibilities. Where such residence is anticipated to last throughout childhood to adulthood – that is to age 18 – a special guardianship order may help to reinforce the child's security since such an order, while not removing parental responsibility from the child's birth parents, does limit this by transferring clear responsibility for decision-making to the special guardians (section 115 Adoption and Children Act 2002, Special Guardianship Regulations 2005 (as amended), Special Guardianship (Wales) Regulations 2005 (as amended). A relative with whom the child has lived for a period of at least one year can now apply for a special guardianship order (section 38 Children and Young Persons Act 2008).

Child arrangements orders may in effect compel someone to allow a child to communicate with, or even to stay temporarily with, someone else – for example, to go on holiday with the other parent. In effect, the court is ordering the person looking after the child to allow contact, and they must do so or risk some kind of penalty such as imprisonment or an unpaid work requirement or compensation (*M (contact order)* [2005]; section 4 Children and Adoption Act 2006). However, courts acknowledged in *L-W (Children)* [2010] that parents may not be able to force unwilling children to see the other parent. There have been a number of particularly contentious cases where courts have made orders even where there has been a record of violence. In *A v N (Refusal of Contact)* [1997] the court imprisoned a mother for six weeks for obstructing contact in these circumstances. In *M (Children)* [2013] a father appealed against an order refusing him contact with his three young sons. He had inflicted significant violence on his partner and had convictions for assault, for which he blamed her. As a consequence, a judge initially ordered no contact but the Appeal Court held that this breached Article 8 of the European Convention on Human Rights since the judge had not considered supervised contact. Here, the courts are persuaded by what is in the interests of the child – namely, that they should continue to see both parents, rather than using orders as a way of penalising parents who have been abusive. Only in serious cases where there is absolutely no alternative may courts stop contact altogether. In *H (termination of contact)* [2005] the court declared that it could not do this just because social workers are engaged in permanency planning for children.

A prohibited steps order is precisely what it says: it stops someone from doing something. In addition to denying an adult contact with the child, these orders have been used to prevent a change of school, a change in religion, a change of name and particular procedures such as circumcision where not medically justifiable as in *S (specific issue order: religion: circumcision)* [2004]. The converse to these orders are specific issue orders which have been made in cases where, for example, it is necessary to order that children should receive the MMR vaccine; where it was necessary to compel a mother to inform a child about the child's paternity and the existence of her father; to allow a 10-year-old to choose her own religion against her mother's wishes; or to resolve a dispute between parents about religious schooling. Relevant cases here are *F v F* [2013], *K (specific issue order* [1999], *C (a child) (child's religious choice)* [2012], and *G (children) (Education: Religious upbringing)* [2012].

However, these orders cannot be used as backdoor 'ouster' orders – that is, as ways of compelling someone to leave the home. Nor can they be used as a way of achieving the same ends as child arrangements orders.

These kinds of orders should not generally be made in relation to young people of the age of 16 or above (section 9 Children Act 1989) although section 114 Adoption and Children Act 2002 gives the courts discretion to extend the order to age 18. Apart from a child arrangements order, the courts cannot make these kinds of orders in relation to children who are subject to care orders. In addition to, or as an alternative to, these orders, courts may decide that it would be appropriate to offer advice or assistance through CAFCASS (Children and Family Court Advisory and Support Service) or the local authority, in which case it is open to them to make a Family Assistance Order (section 16 Children Act 1989). This is a short-term order, now lasting up to 12 months (section 6 Children and Adoption Act 2006), and is intended to try to resolve these issues without needing to make private law court orders.

Child safeguarding investigations

Activity 4.2

Look at the following brief scenarios and say whether you think in each case they are examples of abuse or not. Do not sit on the fence. You should try to make a definite yes or no decision. If you decide that they are examples of abuse, what kind of abuse would it be: physical, emotional, sexual or neglect? Obviously, in reality you would have far more information, but the point of this exercise is to get you thinking about definitions of abuse. You might like to try this exercise in a small group, in which case be prepared for a wide variety of opinion on some of the scenarios.

1. Children aged 5 and 3 who are left on their own for three or four hours every Friday evening.
2. A girl of 10 who is expected to spend an hour on household chores in the morning before going to school.
3. Children under 5 who have been punished by being shut in a cupboard for half an hour.
4. A 9-month-old child who has bite marks on her arm.
5. A 3-year-old who engages in highly sexualised play with his 14-year-old uncle.
6. Two boys aged 5 and 8 who are beaten by their father with a leather belt.

Comment

Having completed the exercise, you will no doubt have realised that part of its purpose is to demonstrate that deciding what constitutes abuse is not always easy. You will find commentary on the questions in the Exercise Answers, p188.

The exercise and commentary on the scenarios use the four categories (physical, emotional, sexual abuse, neglect) which are generally used when distinguishing various forms of abuse. The most important set of procedures and guidance relevant here is *Working together to safeguard children* (HM Government, 2015) which now incorporates a framework for assessment of children in need and their families (para. 35 et seq.). *Working together* sets out the ways in which local authorities and other agencies need to set about assessing and protecting children. We have already seen that local authorities have a duty to promote the welfare of children 'in need', which naturally includes assessing need, but in addition there is a specific responsibility for making inquiries in collaboration with other authorities in cases of alleged harm to a child (section 47 Children Act 1989). The Children Act 2004 (section 18) transferred responsibility for implementing the child safeguarding system from social services departments to directorates of children's services who must:

- consider whether it is necessary to apply to court for an order, especially if refused access to the child;

- see the child unless they already have sufficient information to make a decision;

- consider whether and when to review the case, if they decide not to apply for an order.

Furthermore, the local authority can be obliged by a court to instigate an investigation where a court is hearing a family proceedings case (broadly, the kind of cases we are considering in this chapter) and it appears to the court that a care or supervision order might be appropriate. The local authority must consider whether it should apply for a care or supervision order, whether it should provide services or take some other action. The local authority must, however, report to the court if it decides not to seek a care or supervision order, giving reasons and indicating other action taken or proposed (section 37 Children Act 1989).

All of this underlines the importance of the assessment process and the way in which investigations of alleged abuse are undertaken, taking all relevant factors into consideration. Assessment is an absolutely critical area of social work practice (see Parker and Bradley, 2014; Spray and Jowett, 2012). Leading on from this, we focus on how the law guides the assessment process, examining the various stages and highlighting the legal criteria that govern procedures.

So, first of all, what are we actually assessing, from a legal perspective? The short answer to this is *significant harm* (section 31 Children Act 1989). Is there evidence of a child possibly currently suffering significant harm? Is there evidence of the possibility of a child likely to be suffering significant harm in the future? The concept of significant harm is very important and was deliberately introduced into the Children Act 1989 following the Cleveland Report's recommendations (DHSS, 1988). It is not sufficient to prove just that a child as suffered some kind of harm: the harm has to be of a degree that indicates some impediment to the child's health, development or welfare. Ill-treatment would obviously be included, defined broadly enough so as to encompass sexual abuse and emotional abuse (acknowledging that all forms of abuse include an element of emotional harm). Health includes all those needs that we identified at the start of this chapter: physical, emotional, social, educational, and so on. The next section explores this in more detail as it is such a critical area, determining the extent to which the law authorises intervention in families, but for now we need simply to bear in mind that the assessment should be considering whether there is a possibility of significant harm, estimating the extent of it, and presenting a preliminary analysis of some of its causes. The outcomes of the assessment and the conclusions ultimately drawn from it might eventually need to be considered by the court under care proceedings.

The supervisory body for implementing child safeguarding procedures in each area is the Local Safeguarding Children Board. This is an inter-agency body charged with co-ordinating child protection or 'safeguarding' work and establishing procedures for agencies to follow, with appropriate representation to guarantee this (sections 13 and 14 Children Act 2004 as amended; for England, the Local Safeguarding Children Boards Regulations 2006 with 2010 and 2013 amendments; for Wales, the Social Services and Well-being (Wales) Act 2014). At the local level, individual cases are dealt with by child protection conferences, which bring professionals and family together following an initial assessment as to whether there is cause for concern in a particular case (a section 47 inquiry, as it is often called).

Working together (HM Government, 2015, pp43–8) itemises the responsibilities of the child protection conferences. These are to:

- bring together and analyse, in an inter-agency setting, all relevant information and plan how best to safeguard and promote the welfare of the child;

- make recommendations on how agencies work together to safeguard the child in future.

Conference tasks include:

- appoint a lead statutory body (either local authority children's social care or NSPCC) and a lead social worker, who should be a qualified, experienced social worker and an employee of the lead statutory body;

- identify membership of the core group of professionals and family members who will develop and implement the child protection plan;

- establish timescales for meetings of the core group, production of a child protection plan and for child protection review meetings;

- agree an outline child protection plan, with clear actions and timescales, including a clear sense of how much improvement is needed, by when, so that success can be judged clearly.

The aim of the child protection plan is to:

- ensure the child is safe from harm and prevent him or her from suffering further harm;

- promote the child's health and development; and

- support the family and wider family members to safeguard and promote the welfare of their child, provided it is in the best interests of the child.

One issue possibly unique to child safeguarding is the extent of joint investigation between the police and social workers. Not surprisingly, where there are allegations of abuse concerning a child, there are often allegations concerning who has caused the abuse. This means that the police may wish to conduct a criminal investigation. Home Office and Department of Health guidance points out that to obtain the best evidence in criminal proceedings the child should be interviewed jointly by a police officer and social worker, and this will be particularly important in cases of allegations of sexual abuse (Ministry of Justice, 2011). Not only will this be a joint interview, but good practice suggests that it should be recorded. In criminal trials, there is then the potential for the recording to be used to avoid the necessity of the child appearing in court in person. In care proceedings cases, the recording could potentially be used and case law, such as *B v Torbay Council* [2006] and *M (a child) (care proceedings: witness summons)* [2007], confirms that in some instances ought to be used. However, do remember that the burden of proof in care proceedings, which are civil cases, is not as stringent as that required in criminal cases (see Chapter 1, Table 1.1).

As to what happens after the investigation, there is a set procedure, summarised in diagrammatic form in *Working together* (HM Government, 2015, pp38, 48). An adapted version of part of this procedure, from the strategy discussion up to the development of the child protection plan, appears on p74. From this, it will be seen that much depends on decisions at various stages: not just child protection conferences, but also various strategy meetings held within the children's services authority.

What if people do not co-operate with the child protection investigation or assessment? One possibility then is a child assessment order under section 43 Children Act 1989. Its purpose is simply to allow an assessment of the child's needs, despite parental objections. It is not intended as an emergency order. It must be obtained by making application to a court, which may appoint a guardian to represent the child's interests (section 41 Children Act 1989). The grounds for the order set out in section 43 are:

- there is reasonable cause to suspect that the child is suffering or is likely to suffer significant harm;
- an assessment of the child's health or development is required to determine this;
- assessment is unlikely without an order.

A child assessment order, if granted, directs any person who can 'to produce the child' to the person named in the order; imposes duties to comply with court directions; and authorises assessment, subject to the child's consent. The order may not last more than seven days (section 43 Children Act 1989). A child assessment order is inappropriate if it is necessary to protect the child by removing them – a child assessment order does not convey this authority and here an emergency protection order would be more appropriate. This probably explains why in practice child assessment orders are quite rare and courts reluctant to grant them (Brayne *et al.*, 2015, p304).

If, in order to assess whether they need protection, it is necessary to remove children from home, this becomes direct intervention, raising fundamental questions about the rights of families and obligations on social workers and other agencies to separate children from their parents if need be.

Child safeguarding intervention

Case study

Megan, aged 5, and Michael, aged 3, are once again left on their own this Friday evening. The police are called by neighbours and they in turn contact the local authority children's services (Children's Social Care). By midnight, no adult has returned to the home.

You may well consider that in this situation the children should be taken to a safe place for the night, although this may not be the only alternative. If the police are to take action, this should be considered only as a very short-term measure, necessary in order to provide immediate safety and in order for the children's service authority to start an investigation.

The immediate challenge of the case, however, is for the police or the social worker to gain access to the children. The social worker may enter or search premises only with the permission of the owner or occupier, with the authority of an emergency protection order and then only if stipulated (section 48(3) Children Act 1989), with a warrant issued under specific provisions in the Children Act 1989 and then only when accompanied by a police officer, or under the authority of a recovery order issued where children go missing from care or a place of safety (section 50 Children Act 1989). The same provisions apply to the police, except that, in addition, the police may enter premises without a warrant to save or preserve life in a *life or limb* situation (section 17(1)(e) Police and Criminal Evidence Act 1984).

Having gained access to the home, what should happen then?

The police have powers to protect children without immediate reference to the court. The grounds are that there is reasonable cause to believe that the child would otherwise be likely to suffer significant harm (section 46 Children Act 1989). By removing the child under these powers, the police are to make arrangements for accommodation, detain children there and prevent their removal, and must appoint a designated officer to safeguard the welfare of the child. The police then have a duty to inform the local authority of the case, and must allow reasonable contact by relatives. The police child protection order lasts for an initial period of up to 72 hours and cannot be renewed. The next stage is for the police or local authority to apply to the court for an emergency protection order unless the order is allowed to lapse (section 46 Children Act 1989), although there are some circumstances in which police powers can be used even though an emergency protection order is in force, a point clarified in *Langley v Liverpool City Council* [2005].

Social workers do not have powers to protect children without reference to the court or to a magistrate. Any person (yes, literally *any* person) can apply for an emergency protection order for a child, but only the local authority or the National Society for the Prevention of Cruelty

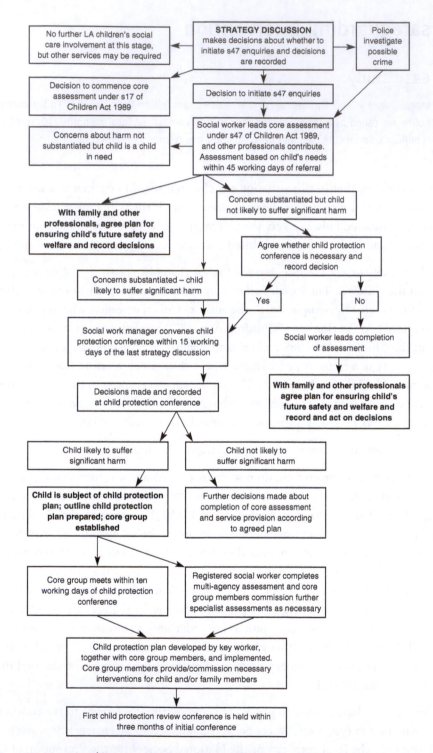

Figure 4.1 Working together (diagram adapted from official guidance: HM Government, 2015, pp38, 48)

to Children (NSPCC) can subsequently bring care proceedings. Applications can be made either *by summons* – that is, through the court having told people that you are intending to do this, or *ex parte* – that is, direct to a single magistrate and without the knowledge of parents – in which case, the decision can be challenged in court within 72 hours (section 45 Children Act 1989). The purpose of an emergency protection order is to permit removal of a child in an emergency, to prevent the removal of a child from accommodation or hospital, or to enable essential medical treatment to be authorised in an emergency. The grounds stipulated in section 44 Children Act 1989 are:

- there is reasonable cause to believe that the child is likely to suffer significant harm unless removed or detained;

- inquiries are being made by the local authority under section 47 as to whether the child is suffering, or is likely to suffer, significant harm;

- the local authority has reasonable cause to suspect significant harm and its investigation is being frustrated by unreasonable refusal of access to the child;

- the applicant has reasonable cause to believe that access is required as a matter of urgency.

The court has the power to appoint a guardian when it makes an emergency protection order unless it is satisfied that it is not necessary to do so (section 41 Children Act 1989).

The effect of an emergency protection order under section 44 Children Act 1989 is that it:

- directs any person who can to produce the child;

- authorises removal of the child where this is necessary for welfare;

- prevents removal of the child where this is necessary for welfare;

- for the duration of the order gives the applicant parental responsibility but only allows action which is reasonably required for the child's welfare – e.g. consent to urgent medical treatment (note this does not divest anyone of parental responsibility);

- may, if endorsed to this effect, authorise entry and search of premises;

- can limit or prevent contact with the child if the court so directs: the court must consider contact arrangements;

- can authorise assessment: the court should give directions about this.

It is also possible to include exclusion orders so that people who pose a risk to the child can be ordered to leave temporarily (section 44A Children Act 1989 inserted by Family Law Act 1996). The emergency protection order initially lasts up to eight days, and can be extended once for seven days, but the principle is to grant the order only until the first available date for consideration of an interim order or some other action (section 45 Children Act 1989).

So, in this case study, there are various possibilities, and which is pursued will probably depend on local arrangements, but it is quite likely that the case will be referred to court fairly swiftly for some kind of decision as to what should happen next.

Let us suppose that the police take action to protect the children, the local authority applies for, and is granted, an emergency protection order. What happens next to Megan and Michael?

By this time a guardian should have been appointed to look after the children's interests and ascertain their wishes and feelings. Clearly, a fair amount of work would have to be done in terms of finding out a great deal more about the family and the circumstances that led to the children being neglected. However, in order to think about what happens next, we need to think more widely about the overall plan for both children. It is tempting, far too tempting, to think in terms of punishing parents for allowing children to be exposed to potential harm and for considering family proceedings orders as being somehow proportionate to the degree of harm to which children have been exposed. Such thinking is, however, utterly wrong. Once the immediate situation has been addressed, social workers must consider very carefully what is in the best long-term interests of the children.

The preliminary consideration when intervening directly in families, especially when removing children from their parents' care, is the overall purpose of intervention. In cases of extreme abuse, it may be obvious that the child needs some kind of sanctuary, but if this is to be in the care system, how long should the child remain there? It is not axiomatic that the child should be taken into care and kept there for a lengthy period simply because the abuse was apparently severe. In the case of Megan and Michael, supposing that they were taken into care for a short period, at what point could they be returned to the parents? When the parents or parent understood how dangerous it was to leave children this young? When the parents changed their lifestyle? After they had attended parenting classes? These are all valid professional social work questions, and clearly much depends on the individual circumstances of the case and assessment of the parents' capabilities.

This kind of thinking lies behind the Children Act 1989, for it envisages emergency protection orders, interim care orders and care orders as being very much a last resort. Furthermore, even if a care order is made, parents do not lose their right to participate in children's lives. A care order is an order that transfers some parental responsibilities and rights, especially concerning where the child should live, to the local authority. It does not 'write off' the parents, and it certainly does not mean the child has to remain physically in care until they are 18, although that is when care orders formally end unless revoked earlier. There are provisions for children being returned to their families even while the care order continues to be in force (section 23 Children Act 1989; Care Planning, Placement and Case Review (England) Regulations 2010 with 2013 amendments; Care Planning, Placement and Case Review (Wales) Regulations 2015). Care orders can be discharged by the court (section 39 Children Act 1989). Local authorities, one parent or the young person themselves, if they are old enough to understand and give instructions to solicitors, can apply.

Furthermore, there are alternatives to care orders. The court might consider making a supervision order (see below), or might consider agreeing to the child living with another relative under a child arrangements order. The Children Act 1989 encourages courts and social workers to view statutory care as a last resort, although it should never be forgotten that for some children it is this last resort that has literally saved their lives. Unfortunately, however, even within the care system, there have been cases of children being abused (see the next section), so we should never assume that a care order is always the best option.

So, let us suppose that in this case study the parents are not co-operative and the local authority reluctantly concludes that they must take some action. While the case is being investigated and assessments are being formulated, the case will need to be adjourned for a few weeks. But if the children are in care, probably with foster carers, the court cannot just adjourn the case but must consider what interim measures to put in place. After an emergency protection order, the most likely step to be considered is an interim care order, or even a series of interim orders for there can be as many of them as are necessary before the case is fully heard. The criteria for interim orders differ from the grounds for an emergency protection order since now the court must decide that they have reasonable grounds for believing that there are grounds for the full care order (section 38 Children Act 1989) and this must, according to *GR (children) (care order)* [2010], be demonstrated in relation to each child. Furthermore, there is no expectation that just because the court grants an interim care order, it will eventually grant a full care order. In any case, there is a difference between declaring *reasonable grounds for believing* and concluding that the grounds for a care order are *satisfied*. Conversely, the case of *F (care proceedings: interim care order)* [2010] suggests that courts should not grant interim care orders even if other children in the family have previously been committed to local authority care.

The grounds for a full care order are the same as for those for making any order under care proceedings – namely, there must be proof that the child is suffering or is likely to suffer *significant harm*. Furthermore, the court has to be convinced that the significant harm can be attributed to the child being beyond parental control, or it can be attributed to the fact that the care which the child is receiving or is likely to receive differs from what it would be reasonable to expect parents to offer (section 31(2) Children Act 1989). Exposure to harm of itself is insufficient; there has to be evidence of its significance and likelihood means a real possibility of significant harm, as in the case of *A (children) (care proceedings: threshold criteria)* [2009]. The Supreme Court case of *J (Children)* [2013] established that likelihood of significant harm can only be established by reference to past facts that are proved on the balance of probabilities.

Having adjudicated on this threshold criteria, the court would then consider what kind of order would best meet the child's needs.

This all sounds very complicated, so let us take it stage by stage. Case law has established that in cases of alleged harm courts should consider two issues separately (*Humberside County Council v B* [1993]). First, it has to decide, factually, whether the child is being harmed or is in a situation where they are likely to be harmed unless the court takes some action. Harm is ill-treatment, which obviously includes sexual abuse, but may also extend to emotional abuse, or impairment of health or development. Health may include mental health, and development refers to all aspects of development (as discussed earlier in this chapter); the Adoption and Children Act 2002 (section 120) extended this to include *seeing or hearing the ill-treatment of another*. In order to assess impairment of health or development, the law says practitioners need to compare this child with what could reasonably be expected of a similar child (section 31(10) Children Act 1989). If the harm arises from the child's being beyond parental control, then the threshold criteria are met. Otherwise, the harm has to derive from parents failing to offer the level or quality of care which it would be reasonable to expect (section 31(2)(b)(i) Children Act 1989). Figure 4.2, adapted from White *et al.* (2008), may simplify this.

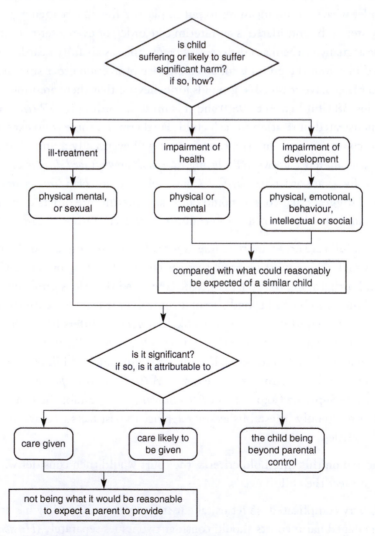

Figure 4.2 Significant harm threshold criteria

It may be worth adding that the significant harm grounds need to be interpreted within the wider ambit of the child needing care or supervision. If it is a specific issue which is of concern – for example, the parents refusing to co-operate with medical treatment – then courts would probably opt for other ways of addressing this.

Activity 4.3

What other ways are there for addressing this? Spend a few moments considering the problem.

Comment

Hopefully, the answer you gave would be to ask the court to make a Specific Issue Order under section 8 Children Act 1989, although there are other legal mechanisms such as Wardship and invoking the High Court's inherent jurisdiction (see Brammer, 2015, pp269–70).

Illustrations may be helpful here. In 2010 the courts were asked in *A Local Authority v SB, AB and MB* [2010] to make a care order on a child who had a serious medical condition which doctors considered could now only be treated by surgery to stop the very frequent epileptic fits which were risking the boy's life. The parents disagreed, preferring continued use of medication. The court declined to consider care proceedings since there were no wider concerns or considerations, inviting the hospital to take other action. The second example, about which students often ask questions, is what happens if parents, for religious or other reasons, refuse to allow blood transfusions for their child. Here the law is clear in that, if the child is unable to give their own consent and the condition they are suffering is life-threatening, hospitals can, under common law, proceed to save the child's life despite parental objections. However, where this is likely to be an issue in a particular case, hospitals would be well advised to apply to the courts for an order to this effect in advance. For our purposes, the point to note is that such cases are not 'care' cases.

Returning to our case study, it would be reasonable to expect parents to look after a 5-year-old and a 3-year-old directly themselves, or else to provide someone to carry out this task for them. Few would argue that to leave children of this age unattended and uncared for during the night would be reasonable. The harm, in terms of potential physical harm, is obvious, as is the actual emotional harm caused by fear and anxiety. So in this case, the threshold criteria might well be proven. Next, the court considers what to do about it, and here they look, separately, at the needs of each child and their welfare, and specifically the welfare checklist contained in section 1 of the Children Act 1989. At this second stage, the court considers whether or not to make an order. It is perfectly feasible for a court not to make an order even though the harm is proven: remember the *no order* principle? Courts may seriously want to consider this if, during the proceedings, the parents begin to realise the seriousness of what is at stake and agree that there are issues that they need to address. They might therefore reluctantly agree to the child being accommodated under section 20 of the Children Act 1989 and thereby avoid any further legal proceedings, but practitioners need to be alert to the dangers of coercive 'voluntary' agreements obtained in this fashion especially bearing in mind cases such as *Coventry City Council v C and others* [2013], where a parent was deemed not to have been able to give proper consent, rendering the section 20 application null and void. Do note, however, that withdrawal of proceedings once they have commenced requires the court's agreement, and this might be challenged if, as happened in *WSCC v M, F, W, X, Y and Z* [2011], the court-appointed guardian considered that the local authority plans after withdrawing the proceedings ought to include certain actions relating to the mother's mental health.

If it is considering making an order, the court then considers what kind of order to make. Is there a grandparent who can offer the children a home? If so, and they are willing and suitable to care for the children, why not make a child arrangements order stipulating this? Alternatively, why not avoid any order and ask the local authority to consider the child a 'looked after' child under section 20 of the Children Act 1989 (but they are *looked after*, not just a *kinship care* arrangement, if the local authority approaches the grandparents in the context of otherwise having to pursue care proceedings as happened in *SA v KCC (Child In Need)* [2010]).

If there really are no other alternatives, the court will need to consider supervision orders or care orders.

A supervision order gives the supervisor the duty to *advise, assist and befriend* the child (section 35 Children Act 1989). The child remains living at home, but the order might require the child to submit to some kind of medical examination, subject to the child's informed consent. There can be a requirement to participate in certain activities, and clearly there is an expectation that there would be regular visits, although there are no regulations about this. The supervision order lasts initially for up to one year, but can be extended for up to three years if the supervisor applies for this (Schedule 3 Children Act 1989); a judge has no discretion to make initial supervision orders for three years (*T (a child) (supervision order: duration)* [2008]).

Before making a care order, courts must consider two important issues. First is Article 8 of the European Convention on Human Rights (see Chapter 2), which implies that care orders should be regarded as temporary measures, and that the order must be proportionate and necessary (*B (a child) (care order: proportionality: criterion for review)* [2013]). Therefore, the local authority should consider alternative family placements, and might even consider placing the child at home under the aegis of the care order, since the care order still gives the authority the right to remove the child if need be. However, supervision orders should be made in preference to care orders if a child is allowed to return home and there is no strong, compelling reason to include a power to remove the child. A care order with the child placed with the parents would only be appropriate *where the local authority needed the power not only to remove the children instantly but also to plan for their long term placement outside the family without any prior judicial sanction (T (a child) (care order)* 2009). Critically, in this regard, the court must consider the local authority's intentions for the child before they can be awarded the care order (section 31(3A) Children Act 1989). This is the care plan, and that plan must be *viable (R (care: plan for adoption: best interest)* [2006]). The extent of courts' control and supervision of care plans is contentious following a House of Lords decision in *S (minors) (care order: implementation of care plan)* [2002] overruling an attempt to introduce a *starring system* whereby the courts could review the implementation of care plans once care orders were made. The Appeal Court had concluded they could do this because of their interpretation of the European Convention on Human Rights, but the position now is that once care orders are made, courts will not review them unless someone makes an application for a variation in contact or a discharge of the care order. However, section 25B Children Act 1989 now gives the Independent Reviewing Officer significant powers to monitor and review this including the right to refer the case to CAFCASS (section 10 Children and Young Persons Act 2008). Furthermore, local authorities must consider at every statutory review, chaired by the Independent Reviewing Officer, whether to discharge the care order (Arrangements for Placement of Children by Voluntary Organisations and Others (England) Regulations 2011; Review of Children's Cases (Wales) Regulations 2007 as amended by Social Services and Well-being (Wales) Act 2014).

The second issue the court must consider before making care orders are the arrangements for contact between the child and people of significance to the child. There is a presumption in favour of contact between the child and family members, so any restriction on contact must have a court order. If there is someone who poses a potential danger to the child, it is possible to order that contact be supervised, and also contact can be defined or even prohibited. If necessary, the local authority can make emergency arrangements to refuse contact for up to seven days where they believe this is consistent with the promotion of the child's welfare (section 34 Children Act 1989). Once the court hears the case, it may make any order it sees fit in relation to contact, and impose appropriate conditions, provided it is convinced that this is consistent with the promotion of the welfare of the child. Note that these are not the same as section 8 child arrangements orders made in private law cases.

Care orders have the effect of discharging any section 8 order. Once made, care orders can be discharged by application to the court by the local authority, the young person, or anyone who has parental responsibility (section 39 Children Act 1989). It is possible to appeal to the High Court against any order made or refused by a Family Proceedings Court. Appeals against orders made or refused by judges in county courts go to the Court of Appeal (Civil Division) (see diagram in Chapter 8, p154).

Naturally, given the requirements of the Children Act 1989, especially the welfare paramountcy principle, the child's wishes and feelings will be considered, usually interpreted to the court through the guardian represented by a legal advocate, although sometimes articulated on their behalf by a lawyer alone.

This appropriately brings us on to the issue of speaking on behalf of children and acting as their advocates.

Speaking up for children

Generally speaking, children are not expected to participate in court proceedings (Chapter 8 addresses court work in greater detail). They are, however, a party to the proceedings – that is, they have the right to address the court through a lawyer, and additionally children have a guardian allocated to them who will ascertain their wishes and feelings, and present them to the court through a comprehensive report and oral evidence. Children's guardians are appointed by the Children and Family Court Advisory and Support Service (CAFCASS or CAFCASS Cymru) (section 12 Criminal Justice and Court Services Act 2000 for England; Children Act 2004 Part 4 for Wales; Children and Adoption Act 2006). Guardians may compile reports for the court in private law family proceedings, but the bulk of their work is carried out in public law care proceedings where they furnish comprehensive reports to the court and also give evidence if required. They must be appointed where courts are considering a care or supervision order, section 37 directions (obliging local authorities to assess harm in private law cases), discharge of care orders or variation and discharge of supervision orders, section 34 Children Act contact orders, and in certain other proceedings (section 41 Children Act 1989).

In Chapter 8 we devote a section to user perspectives and experiences of the courts and advocacy, but suffice it to say here that the overall message from parents and children is a desire to take a greater part in the decision-making process. Lack of full consultation is a recurrent theme (see, for example, Cossar *et al*., 2014). For a complete summary of relevant research into the operation of the Children Act 1989, it is well worth consulting summaries of research which can be accessed through the government website (address at the end of the chapter).

System failure

What happens when the system appears to fail? At the first level, there are, of course, complaints procedures. In relation to the Children Act 1989, these are more formalised and run alongside the system for conducting regular reviews of cases (section 26 Children Act 1989). There is then the potential to apply to the local government ombudsman if there is an allegation of maladministration. Alternatively, or in addition, it is open for service users to apply to the courts under common law for judicial review of local authority decisions.

One example of this concerned the decision by a local authority to consider someone as posing a risk to children even though he had been acquitted on sexual abuse charges. In *R (on the application of S) v Swindon Borough Council* [2001] this was held to be lawful as section 47 of the Children Act 1989 concerned reasonable cause to suspect abuse, not a definite conclusion that there had been. Concerning a local authority's apparent failure to act, as was alleged in the Climbié case in 2000 and the case of Peter Connelly in 2008, there are the Secretary of State's default powers, powers of inspection and power to hold inquiries (section 84 Children Act 1989; Inquiries Act 2005). There is also a serious case review system (HM Government, 2015, Chapters 4 and 5) or, in Wales, child practice reviews (Welsh Assembly Government, 2013b). Sometimes these findings are made public. However, formal public inquiries as such are most often held where a child has been killed or seriously harmed and where it is considered action could have been taken to prevent this, but they may also be appropriate where children have been abused within the care system itself.

No summary of child safeguarding social work would be complete without reference, regrettably, to cases where things have gone badly wrong.

In the 1980s and 1990s a substantial number of inquiries took place after children had been killed or seriously injured. It is not proposed to summarise all of these. Instead, we shall highlight two fundamental areas: child safeguarding supervision failures, as demonstrated in the Victoria Climbié case, and institutional abuse, referring briefly to examples such as Staffordshire and North Wales. Although some time has passed since these cases occurred, the lessons are still valuable and echoes of these failings were apparent in subsequent cases.

Case study

The Victoria Climbié Case

At the post-mortem examination, Dr Carey recorded evidence of no fewer than 128 separate injuries to Victoria's body, saying, There really is not anywhere that is spared – there is scarring all over the body. Therefore, in the space of just a few months, Victoria had been transformed from a healthy, lively, and happy little girl, into a wretched and broken wreck of a human being. Perhaps the most painful of all the distressing events of Victoria's short life in this country is that even towards the end, she might have been saved. In the last few weeks before she died, a social worker called at her home several times. She got no reply when she knocked at the door and assumed that Victoria and Kouao [her aunt] had moved away. It is possible that at the time, Victoria was in fact lying just a few yards away, in the prison of the bath, desperately hoping someone might find her and come to her rescue before her life ebbed away.

(Department of Health and Home Office, 2003, 1.9–1.11)

So what went wrong? To answer that in terms of poor professional practice, you need to read the Victoria Climbié Inquiry Report in detail since this catalogues the failures on the part of social work, police and medical staff who should have acted to prevent the continuous persistent abuse. It is harrowing reading, but important lessons need to be drawn from it. The Inquiry Report does just this, setting out 108 recommendations for change. Lord Laming pledged that Victoria's suffering would mark an *enduring turning point in ensuring proper protection of children in this country*. The inquiry was extensive, costing £3.8 million and hearing from 158 witnesses and 121 child protection experts. The report concluded that the child safeguarding system failed as a result of a lamentable lack of *basic good practice* by frontline staff and, especially, senior managers failing to take responsibility for the failings of their organisations. Some recommendations applied to direct practice, so may be worth highlighting; in particular, see the following case study.

Case study

Recommendation 34

Social workers must not undertake home visits without being clear about the purpose of the visit, the information to be gathered during the course of it, and the steps to be taken if no one is at home [.]

Recommendation 35

Directors of social services must ensure that children who are the subject of allegations of deliberate harm are seen and spoken to within 24 hours of the allegation being communicated to social services [.]

Recommendation 36

No emergency action on a case concerning an allegation of deliberate harm to a child should be taken without first obtaining legal advice [.]

Recommendation 45

Directors of social services must ensure that the work of staff working directly with children is regularly supervised. This must include the supervisor reading, reviewing and signing the case file at regular intervals.

Recommendation 51

Directors of social services must ensure that all strategy meetings and discussions involve the following three basic steps:

→

- A list of action points must be drawn up, each with an agreed timescale and the identity of the person responsible for carrying it out.
- A clear record of the discussion or meeting must be circulated to all those present and all those with responsibility for an action point.
- A mechanism for reviewing completion of the agreed actions must be specified. The date upon which the first such review is to take place is to be agreed and documented.

The government's response was to issue a Green Paper outlining proposed changes to the organisation of services which culminated in the Children Act 2004, along with a number of publications under the heading of *Every child matters*. At the same time overall responsibility for child care social work services provided by local authorities in England was transferred from the Department of Health to the Department for Education and Skills, subsequently the Department for Children, Schools and Families, now the Department for Education. In Wales, child care social work is now the responsibility of the Welsh Government. In 2005 the first Children's Commissioner for England was appointed, the first Children's Commissioner (for Wales) having been appointed in 2001 under the Children's Commissioner for Wales Act 2001. The Commissioners' role is to champion the interests of children, compile reports and conduct general investigations. In both England and Wales, local authorities subsequently engaged in the task of integrating children's services and appointing the new hybrid education and social work Directors with 'lead members' of Children's Services as required by sections 18 and 19 of the Children Act 2004.

Other examples of inquiries of which practitioners ought to be aware include inappropriate restraint of young people in residential care in Staffordshire, the so-called Pindown Inquiry (Levy and Kahan, 1991; Brayne and Broadbent, 2002) and the systematic abuse of young men by a paedophile ring in the residential care system in North Wales investigated by the Waterhouse Inquiry (Department of Health, 2000d). Both raise very important and very different issues; in the North Wales case, the inquiry itself has been challenged as being inadequate, to the extent that, in 2012, the government ordered a judicial review which is considering the scope of the inquiry and whether it failed to investigate specific allegations of abuse.

Finally, of great significance for contemporary child safeguarding social work practice is the case of Peter Connelly, which occurred in 2007. This led to two serious case reviews, the controversial dismissal of the head of children's services in Haringey, and the commissioning of an important review of social work practice in child safeguarding, now generally referred to as the Munro Review (Department for Education 2010b and 2011c).

If you intend to practise in this area, it is important for you to be aware of the history of cases such as this, so that lessons can be learned for the future.

Chapter summary

This chapter offered you an overview of how the law can be used to promote children's welfare when things go wrong. We started by explaining the importance of the notion of parental responsibility, setting out the ways in which the law determines who has this, how they might share it and what it actually means. This may have seemed an odd starting point, but the law centres on the notion of parents taking responsibility for their children and social workers working in partnership with them, as you saw in the previous chapter. Therefore, it was crucial to know who can have parental responsibility and who has the right to participate in decision-making regarding children.

The chapter then summarised the position regarding disputes about the care of children, in what lawyers would call private law family proceedings. In practice, these are dominated by failures to agree over where children should live following the divorce of their parents. As we saw, however, court cases do not exclusively concern themselves with residence, but may also need to consider contact, and securing children's welfare by insisting that certain things be done, or else that they should not be done.

We then proceeded into one of the most demanding areas of professional social work practice: responding to allegations that children have been abused. The chapter considered the underlying principles of the Children Act 1989 as they relate to child safeguarding investigations, and also summarised the system that exists for ensuring that decisions are based on sound evidence and result from effective inter-agency working. A number of court orders that may have to be considered in the short term, and we looked at how these related to the final decision-making of the courts concerning care and supervision. In passing, some key principles were underlined in relation to proving the threshold criteria and applying the welfare principles enshrined in the legislation. Looking specifically at the court system, we saw that there is provision for separate representation and advocacy for children involved in public law proceedings, and Chapter 8 will say more about the social work role in court.

The chapter concluded by alerting you to examples where the system has, unfortunately, failed children. An extract from the Climbié Inquiry was quoted as it resulted in significant changes in the law and practice directions that guide child safeguarding social work.

It is important to state that in some respects we have only been able to scratch the surface of some of the fundamental issues raised in child safeguarding social work. Intending practitioners will need to incorporate what has been learnt here into their skills development work in carrying out assessments, and may also need to refer to more specialist child care law texts which would provide more detail of the legislation itself and offer guidance in the somewhat complex case law that is relevant to this area. You will find the relevant texts listed below and in the bibliography at the end of the book.

Further reading

For comprehensive overviews of social work law relating to children:

Brammer, A (2015) *Social work law* (4th edn). Part 2. Harlow: Pearson Education.

Brayne, H, Martin, G and Carr, H (2015) *Law for social workers* (13th edn), Chapters 7 and 8. Oxford: Oxford University Press.

Practice-focused textbooks:

Davies, M (ed.) (2012) *Social work with children and families*. Basingstoke: Palgrave.

Jowitt, M and O'Loughlin, S (2012) *Social work practice with children and families* (3rd edn). London: Sage.

Seymour, C and Seymour, R (2013) *Practical child law for social workers*. London: Sage.

Official guidance:

Department for Education (2014) *The Children Act 1989 guidance and regulations. Volume 1: Court orders*. London: Department for Education.

Department for Education (2015a) *Children Act 1989 guidance and regulations. Volume 2: Care planning, placement and case review*. Norwich: The Stationery Office.

Welsh Government (2013b) *Protecting Children in Wales*. Cardiff, Welsh Government.

The child safeguarding system:

Department for Education (2010b) *Munro review of child protection: Part One: A systems analysis*. London: DfE.

Department for Education (2011c) *Munro review of child protection: Final report*. London: DfE.

Useful background reading relating to child safeguarding

Excessive restraint used in residential care:

Brayne, H and Broadbent, G (2002) *Legal materials for social workers*. Oxford: Oxford University Press. Pindown Report extract on pp292–9.

Levy, A and Kahan, B (1991) *The Pindown experience and the protection of children*. Report of the Staffordshire child care inquiry 1990. Stafford: Staffordshire County Council.

Sexual abuse in residential care system in North Wales:

Department of Health (2000) *Lost in Care. Report of the Tribunal of Inquiry into the abuse of children in care in the former county council areas of Gwynedd and Clwyd since 1974*. London: The Stationery Office.

Victoria Climbié case:

Department of Health and Home Office (2003) *The Victoria Climbié Inquiry: Report of an inquiry by Lord Laming*. London: The Stationery Office.

SCIE (Social Care Institute for Excellence):

Bostock, L, Bairstow, S, Fish, S, and Macleod, F (2005) *Managing risk and minimising mistakes in services to children and families*. Bristol: Policy Press.

Peter Connelly case:

Department for Education (2010) Publication of the two serious case reviews – Peter Connelly. Available at: www.education.gov.uk/childrenandyoungpeople/safeguarding

Laird, S (2010) *Practical social work law: Analysing court cases and inquiries*. London: Pearson Education, pp114–35.

Websites

Department for Education: www.gov.uk/government/policies/looked-after-children-and-adoption

All legislation and regulations: www.legislation.gov.uk/ukpga

Measures and regulations specific to Wales: www.legislation.gov.uk/browse/wales

Messages from research: www.gov.uk/government/collections/safeguarding-children

5: Adult Care Services

Achieving a social work degree

This and the next chapter will help you to develop the following capabilities from the **Professional Capabilities Framework:**

2. **Values and ethics**

   Apply social work ethical principles and values to guide professional practice.

4. **Rights, justice and economic well-being**

   Advance human rights and promote social justice and economic well-being.

5. **Knowledge**

   Apply knowledge of social sciences, law and social work practice theory.

7. **Intervention and skills**

   Use judgement and authority to intervene with individuals, families and communities to promote independence, provide support and prevent harm, neglect and abuse.

They are relevant to the following Standards of Proficiency:

1. Be able to practise safely and effectively within their scope of practice.
2. Be able to practise within the legal and ethical boundaries of their profession.
8. Be able to communicate effectively.
10. Be able to maintain records appropriately.

(Continued)

(Continued)

They will also introduce you to the following standards as set out in the 2016 Social Work Subject Benchmark Statement:

5.5 viii   the importance of Social Work's contribution to intervention across service user groups, settings and levels in terms of the profession's focus on social justice, human rights, social cohesion, collective responsibility and respect for diversities;

5.6 vi   the significance of legislative and legal frameworks and service delivery standards, including on core social work values and ethics in the delivery of services which support, enable and empower;

5.3 vi   the complex relationships between justice, care and control in social welfare and the practical and ethical implications of these;

5.6 vi   the significance of legislative and legal frameworks and service delivery standards.

Introduction

Chapters 5 and 6 examine the law as it relates to adult care social work practice. This chapter focuses on care associated with the provision of services for adults, although in practice services are offered only to selected groups. Chapter 6 addresses the law relating to *vulnerable adults*, meaning groups of people who experience disability or long-term illness or frailty that results in an inability to care for themselves, or have insufficient understanding of their own needs to be able to live safely, possibly at immediate danger of exploitation, or in some cases posing a risk to other people.

The list of standards above indicates rightly that at the heart of adult care social work lie the skills of assessment, ability to plan using knowledge of resources to support and empower service users, and a realistic awareness of issues of risk balanced against people's rights of self-determination.

These two chapters together are therefore quite wide-ranging. They cover:

- the assessment of any adult who believes they need care services;
- the provision of services for adults who fall into specific categories;
- support for carers;
- outline of legal provision for safeguarding adults;
- overview of law relating to mental capacity;
- the protection of vulnerable people when at risk of harm to themselves or from others.

What are adult care services?

For some time, adult care was referred to by the term 'community care', which was always a misnomer. Outside the field of health and social care, most people would probably assume that community care refers to services that support people by helping them to stay living in their own homes, in their local communities, for as long as they wish. Community care included residential provision, which in many cases could be quite distant from people's 'home' communities. This was an irony to many social work practitioners, but the law was clear that 'community care' covers all those areas other than hospital in-patient care.

The legacy of this is that identifying adult care services is more complex than you might suppose. You would be perfectly entitled to anticipate at this point a list of services that the social services generally (meaning local authorities, health trusts, independent organisations and voluntary agencies) can offer to people. Given that this is a book about social work law, you would then expect this to be related to rights and duties: the rights of people to have certain kinds of services, and duties laid on statutory agencies to provide them. We are about to prove that life is not so simple.

The kinds of adult care services potentially available to service users depend on the category of person who 'needs' the service. Crude categorisation of people, and assumptions about what groups of people collectively need, appear to run contrary to some core principles of anti-discriminatory practice. Inevitably, people can come under more than one category of need: an older person can have a physical disability and issues with capacity, for example. Yet the law can operate only by specifying which groups of people are entitled to which services. So in order to understand what constitutes adult care services, we need to start with a fundamental question: which groups of adults are identified as requiring services to support them in daily living?

Activity 5.1

If you were a legislator or policymaker, which groups of adults would you identify as being those most likely to need adult care services and why?

Draw up a list, indicating some of the reasons why these groups should be offered services. You may find it easier to start this exercise by drawing up the list first. That should take you about ten minutes or so. Thinking through the reasons will take you longer: perhaps 20-30 minutes.

Comment

Of course, if you have some experience of social work already you will probably have found the first part of this exercise relatively easy, since you are already familiar with which social services are provided and for whom. However, you may not have identified all four of the groups: people with physical disabilities, older people, people with learning disabilities, people who experience mental distress (amplified below). Reflecting about why people need adult care requires broader thinking.

The primary groups for whom adult care services are provided are as follows:

- People with physical disabilities, referred to in the legislation as *disabled persons* – not a term that is generally considered to accord with social work principles of anti-discriminatory practice (Dalrymple and Burke, 2006), but as this is the phrase used in legislation we will of necessity have to keep to it. People can be registered with the local authority as 'disabled' if they wish, and disability is a protected characteristic under the Equality Act 2010.

- Older people: nowhere specifically is the age at which someone becomes *older* defined. It might be reasonable to suppose that this would generally be determined by the statutory retirement age, since allocation of national and local resources reflects this, but even this is not an absolute with retirement ages across Europe beginning to creep up. A common-sense approach would suggest that priority is accorded to people who are frail or who are affected by loss of faculties that impair their ability to care for themselves.

- People with learning disabilities or learning difficulties, whose needs have been specifically highlighted in the government strategy documents *Valuing people* and *Valuing people now* (Department of Health, 2001b; HM Government, 2009) and who have been the subject of a major policy shift in the sense that a number of people in this category have been moved from long-stay hospitals to some kind of community resource (Brown and Smith, 1992; Williams and Evans, 2013).

- People with *mental health problems*, which is a term in social work that refers not just to people with mental 'illness' as such but also extends to people whose ability to function is impaired by various forms of cognitive and behavioural problems. It may be worth noting straight away that the legislation uses the term 'mental disorder' (section 1 Mental Health Act 2007; see discussion in Chapter 6), whereas practice guides prefer the broader approach (HM Government, 2016; Welsh Assembly Government, 2012).

As to the reasons why people should have services, you probably listed several times the expectation that people should be helped to continue living in their own homes. In some cases, this may be part of the process of rehabilitation from hospital; in others, adult social care may prevent people being admitted to hospital. There is much talk about social care services being necessary to avoid 'bed blocking' – that is, people staying in hospital longer than is necessary because of lack of community resources, but this risks moving the focus away from the main purpose of adult care which is to provide a comparatively small amount of additional help for people who can no longer perform basic care functions for themselves. This is the preventative strategy enshrined in the Care Act 2014 (section 1) and Social Services and Well-being (Wales) Act 2014 (section 5).

As far as the legislation is concerned, the key provisions in relation to adult social care services are to be found in the Care Act 2014 (or Social Services and Well-being (Wales) Act 2014).

This was intended as consolidating legislation, bringing together a whole welter of different laws that were previously in force into one unified body. However, small parts of some laws that prevailed prior to the implementation of the Care Act 2014 are still in force – for example, the National Assistance Act 1948, the Health Services and Public Health Act 1968, and the Disabled Persons (Services, Consultation and Representation) Act 1986. Besides services, the other main pieces of legislation relevant to adult care are the Mental Health Acts 1983 and 2007, and the Mental Capacity Act 2005 (all of which are explored in more detail in the next chapter).

When it comes to the provision of services, there are some important underlying principles concerning how local authorities operate to bear in mind. Specifically here four key principles operate.

- Local authorities can do only what the law says they can do – to offer more than this may mean they are acting beyond their powers which would make them liable to legal sanctions such as surcharges.

- Local authorities cannot interfere in people's lives by imposing services on them – there is no such thing as 'knowing what is best' for adults in a way that there is in relation to children, although there is delegated decision-making authority for people who lack capacity to consent (section 5 Mental Capacity Act 2005).

- Services should be offered on the basis of assessed need, and not simply on the grounds of what is available – this is often referred to as the needs-led assessment principle.

- Services are delivered in accordance with general requirements, such as in relation to anti-discriminatory law, as well as specific statutes.

There are some practice implications from this. First and foremost, assessment has to be a first and separate activity conducted before there is a decision about what services are offered. Second, assessment must not be determined by the availability or otherwise of services, although obviously it cannot be conducted entirely in a vacuum. Third, assessment has to centre on what people need, not on what they want.

By now you should be familiar with assessment as a key social work task and in Chapter 4 the importance of this in social work with children was underlined. It is equally important with adult care services, with a number of regulations that need to be complied with as well as the Care Act 2014 itself, principally the Care and Support (Assessment) Regulations 2014, Care and Support (Assessment) (Wales) Regulations 2015 (a list of other regulations will be found in the list of legislation and statutory instruments at the beginning of this book). In addition, there is the Care Act 2014 Guidance (HM Government, 2016) and Social Services and Well-being (Wales) Act 2014 codes of practice and statutory guidance. Further guidance on how to conduct an assessment can be found by accessing the SCIE website which covers such useful matters as *how to conduct an assessment that is appropriate and proportionate* (for their address, see end of chapter). In determining need, you may find it useful to look at the ways in which people have identified different levels or 'hierarchies' of need (see section on Maslow in Parker and Bradley, 2014). The law itself does not define need, but delegates responsibility for determining level of need to social workers, so it is important for you to understand how needs can be assessed and evaluated.

Case study

Jaswinder is finding it increasingly difficult to cope with caring for her ageing mother, Arima, who is 86 and described as 'very frail'. Members of her family and her GP suggest that she might approach the social services department and ask them what kind of services they can offer in order to support the family.

Assessment is the key

Assessment is the starting point. Assessment is fundamental to the provision of adult care services. Except in emergencies, local authorities cannot offer services, or even arrange services for which they pay, without having first carried out a full assessment of need. Assessment is the task around which everything revolves. Indeed, the Care Act 2014 addresses only the provision of information about services, assessment and service delivery principles, saying little about the kinds of services that might be offered, although section 8 does offer generalised examples of what might be provided – accommodation, care and support, counselling and social work, goods and facilities.

Adult care legislation was passed after some considerable deliberation about the role of local authorities in providing adult care services (Cowen, 1999; Lymbery, 2005, 2010). If at all possible, do read about this since it sets into context the ways in which local authority social services are now organised and why the task of assessment has been separated from service provision. As a result of deliberate policy decisions based on the Griffiths Report, *Community care: Agenda for action* (1988), *Our health, our care, our say* (Department of Health, 2006b), *A vision for adult social care* (Department of Health 2010a), the *Adult social care consultation papers* (Law Commission 2010, 2011) and *Caring for our future* (HM Government, 2012), contemporary legislation now centres on the promotion of an individual's well-being, which is the local authority's major responsibility. To this end, specific duties regarding provision of information and assessment are to be found in sections 4 and 8 of Care Act 2014 and Part 3 of Social Services and Well-being (Wales) Act 2014. So Jaswinder should have no difficulty getting information about services, although questions may arise about their suitability for people of different cultural backgrounds; naturally, one would want this information available in the different languages which people speak in the local community. We don't have space to explore this in depth, but this is one area where local authorities can take the lead in providing culturally sensitive services, ensuring that all needs are met in all areas of the community and generally pursuing the principles of anti-discriminatory practice. Of further relevance here may be the general public body duties to promote equality in the Equality Act 2010. These relate not just to race, but also extend to disability, gender, age, sexual orientation, religion or belief, as well as other forms of discrimination. The obligation includes both development of policy and delivery of services (section 149 Equality Act 2010).

The key question, however, is, having obtained the information about services potentially available, how does Jaswinder access them? After all, she is not actually enquiring about services for herself, but rather services for the family and presumably for her mother that, if provided, would relieve her of some of the burden of care. She could, of course, simply approach the service providers themselves direct and arrange help for which she or her mother would then have to pay. That would be an entirely private arrangement and there is absolutely nothing in the legislation that would prevent them doing this. There would simply be an agreement between the service provider and the service user or, in this case, the carer.

If, however, the family wanted the local authority to pay for the provision of services, which is usually the case, there would have to be an assessment of need first. The assessment of need would be an assessment of Arima's needs, which may not necessarily be focused on the support needs of the carer. Because of this, there have been some necessary developments in the law regarding support for carers. The Carers (Recognition and Services) Act 1995 extended the duty of assessment to carers who could then have their needs assessed alongside those of the person for whom they were caring, a duty that was broadened and beefed up by the Carers and Disabled Children Act 2000 and the Carers (Equal Opportunities) Act 2004. This legislation has now been superseded by the more comprehensive duties and obligations towards carers which are to be found in sections 10, 20 and 25 of Care Act 2014 or sections 24 and 40–45 of Social Services and Well-being (Wales) Act 2014. All we need to note for the moment is that in this case Jaswinder does have the right to ask the local authority for an assessment of her needs as carer, and for consideration of ways in which she can be supported in her caring role. In relation to this last point, national carers strategies may also be relevant (Department of Health, 2010b; Welsh Assembly Government, 2013a). It is important to note that the Care Act 2014 and Social Services and Well-being (Wales) Act 2014 place carer support on a parity with services provided directly to service users themselves.

What services can be provided?

Theoretically, anything anyone would like to provide for anyone else for any reason whatsoever can be provided. In a free market, the only real test of the viability of the service is whether there are sufficient customers prepared to pay for it. In adult care, this is more than just theoretical. Service provision is based on the notion that the independent sector, comprising private and voluntary organisations, has a very real role to play and that people are entitled to purchase any services they require in a 'mixed economy' of care. Indeed, section 5 of the Care Act 2014 requires the local authority to *promote the efficient and effective operation of the market* (there is a not dissimilar obligation in section 16 Social Services and Well-being (Wales) Act 2014). The key question that concerns potential service users is, of course, money. How do people access services when they cannot afford to do so? It is precisely for this reason that there is a preliminary assessment of need to determine whether people need services and to what extent. The fundamental question then becomes: what role does the local authority play in the provision of services?

It is very important to keep the sequence right. Assessment comes first. Assessment is an assessment of need; it does not start with services and explore how people might fit into what is available, rather, it starts with an assessment of need and then examines the ways in which needs can be met. This should encourage imaginative planning and service development.

Case study

Mrs Jones lives alone in a house in a tiny village in a rural area. She can just about manage to look after herself except that she can no longer cook. An assessment determines that her only real unmet need is for at least one hot meal a day. Because of the isolation of the village, there is no Meals on Wheels service. Indeed, access to any kind of social services resource is difficult, but there is a pub in the village. The pub provides meals to its customers and is prepared to enter into a contract to provide Mrs Jones with meals on a regular basis.

In this way, Mrs Jones's need is met, although perhaps not quite in the way she may have anticipated. This case study makes the point that there may be a variety of ways of meeting people's needs, and thinking should not be constrained simply by what social services are currently available.

The role of the social worker, then, is to discuss and decide with the service user how their needs can best be met. This means, of course, having a wide knowledge of resources potentially available, but also requires an ability to think laterally and imaginatively. The legislation may help here since it does not impose on the local authority the duty to provide services itself directly, although it does impose a requirement, in cases where the local authority is going to meet need, to prepare a care and support plan (section 24 Care Act 2014; section 54 Social Services and Well-being (Wales) Act 2014). Adding to this the statutory obligation to promote an individual's well-being results in what might be described as an assessment and 'commissioning' role for local authorities.

None of this, of course, stops local authorities from providing services themselves. Acts of Parliament do not actually tell us what services are to be provided. Instead, section 8 of the

Care Act 2014 offers some examples and there is guidance in regulations, codes of practice, or ministerial directions (for explanation of the differences between these ways of implementing legislation, see Chapter 1). The examples are:

- accommodation in a care home or premises of some other type;
- care and support at home or in the community;
- counselling and other types of social work;
- goods and facilities;
- information, advice and advocacy.

Previous legislation included specific services, such as recreational facilities, holidays, meals, telephones, and adaptations; these are now incorporated into the more generic list set out in the Care Act 2014.

Services for people with learning disabilities will be roughly similar to those offered to people who have physical disabilities, since the same legislation now applies. Likewise, services are potentially available to people with mental health problems, if their problems entitle them to be counted as 'mentally disordered' in accordance with section 1 of the Mental Health Act 2007, which broadened the Mental Health Act 1983 definitions with its categorisations of mental illness, mental impairment, severe mental impairment and psychopathy (for further information on this, see Barber *et al.*, 2012). Section 117 of the Mental Health Act 1983 (as amended by section 75 Care Act 2014 and section 53 Social Services and Well-being (Wales) Act 2014) requires social services departments with health trusts to offer aftercare services for certain people who have been compulsorily detained in hospital and are being discharged. A legal anomaly had arisen whereby charges could not be levied for services provided under this section 117 (*R v Manchester City Council, ex parte Stennett* [2002]). This is still the case. Indeed, there are a number of services for which the local authority cannot charge. The Care Act 2014 Guidance (paragraph 8.14) lists these as:

- reablement up to 6 weeks;
- aids and adaptations up to £1,000
- care for people with Creutzfeldt–Jacob Disease;
- continuing healthcare, such as nursing care;
- any service that has to be provided under legislation other than the Care Act 2014.

In addition, the local authority is, naturally, not allowed to charge for the assessment itself.

In passing, it should be noted that the local authority is under an obligation to maintain a register of people who have a disability (section 77 Care Act 2014, section 18 Social Services and Well-being (Wales) Act 2014). Such registration is, of course, voluntary; it is not a prerequisite for service provision. For a definition of disability, this Act adopts the definition in the Equality Act 2010. This, thankfully, replaces the outmoded terms used in the previous prevailing legislation section 29 National Assistance Act 1948 which referred to a 'disabled person' as *blind, deaf* or *dumb* or *substantially and permanently handicapped by illness, injury, or congenital deformity or such other disabilities as may be prescribed by the Minister*. The modern definition is simply that a person has a disability if they have *a physical or mental impairment* and *the impairment has a substantial and long-term adverse effect* on their *ability to carry out normal day-to-day activities* (section 6 Equality Act 2010).

Commissioning services

This section is headed 'Commissioning services' to emphasise that the social worker's key role is to arrange for the provision of services that meet the needs that have been identified.

Case study

Laura has multiple sclerosis. She lives with her partner in a bungalow that generally meets her needs, but in view of a deterioration in her physical condition, she now finds that she needs additional assistance. A full assessment is undertaken and highlights the need for a number of aids and adaptations that would enhance mobility, together with a significant number of hours of home care. The social worker is concerned that if there is a continued deterioration, Laura will get to the position where she needs 24-hour care.

Laura would have clearly been entitled to an assessment, since she *may have need for care and support* (section 9 Care Act 2014; section 19 Social Services and Well-being (Wales) Act 2014), but to what extent is she entitled to services as a result of the assessment? What level of services have to be provided?

The answers lie in the assessment itself and its outcome. The law requires the local authority to assess *whether the adult does have need for care and support* and if they do, they must assess *what those needs are* (section 9 (1) Care Act 2014), which in effect implies that a statement has to be made about how the local authority envisages those assessed needs being met, always bearing in mind the statutory obligation to promote well-being (section 1 Care Act 2014, section 5 Social Services and Well-being (Wales) Act 2014). The obvious first stage in this process is determining the extent to which the local authority is itself planning to meet those needs, and this in turn is determined by eligibility criteria. Under previous legislation, eligibility was determined by reference to government guidance, particularly *Fair Access to Care Services* (Department of Health, 2003b) and by *Prioritising Need in the Context of Putting People First* (Department of Health, 2010b), which set out four categories of need: critical, substantial, moderate and low. Careful phrasing of the law means that the local authority is not automatically directed to meet each and every need it has identified, but it must meet those needs that meet the eligibility criteria (section 18 (1) Care Act 2014; section 32 Social Services and Well-being (Wales) Act 2014). It certainly does not have to meet those needs itself (see discussion above). However, if the local authority is going to meet someone's needs, it is under an obligation to prepare a care and support plan (section 24 Care Act 2014; section 54 Social Services and Well-being (Wales) Act 2014). This plan must include a statement about how the local authority is going to meet the needs it has identified under the eligibility criteria. In drawing up this plan, and indeed throughout the whole assessment process, the local authority must involve people concerned – that is, the individual with the needs, their carer and any other person interested in their welfare. All assessments and plans should be made by agreement wherever possible. To this end, statutory guidance requires local authorities to take steps to aid communication where there are particular difficulties (paragraphs 6.37–6.39 Department of Health, 2016; paragraphs 30–34 Welsh Assembly Government, 2015).

All of this underlines the importance of sharing information with service users – which in any case is a legal obligation under the Data Protection Act 1998 – and being careful and precise as to what is stated about service provision on the basis of the assessment. Once you start practising as a student social worker, it would be well worthwhile asking to see policy statements concerning assessments and expectations of agencies concerning the outcome of those assessments.

Commissioning services obviously presupposes knowledge and awareness of what services are potentially available, and inevitably this will vary from area to area. Clearly, many of these will be drawn from the list that local authorities maintain as part of their adult care plans. One issue of concern to service users will inevitably be finance. The law makes it quite clear that there may be a charge for adult care services with an expectation that service provision will be means tested (section 14 Care Act 2014, paragraph 8.2 Department of Health 2016; Part 5 Social Services and Well-being (Wales) Act 2014). This stands in marked contrast to National Health services which are provided free of charge, and becomes quite problematic when people receive a mixture of medical and social care. It can also encourage redefinition of care so that it becomes medical rather than social. Note, though, that there is provision in the Care Act 2014, and Social Services and Well-being (Wales) Act 2014 for capping costs to the individual; this cap is set by the regulations and adjusted annually (sections 15–16 Care Act 2014; section 61 Social Services and Well-being (Wales) Act 2014). Note also that there cannot be a charge for the assessment itself. Even if the local authority is so short of money that it cannot see a way in which it might be able to finance the provision of services, it is still obligated to carry out an assessment (*R v Bristol City Council, ex parte Penfold* [1998]).

Where the local authority decides to charge the services, those charges must comply with the Care and Support (Charging and Assessment of Resources) Regulations 2014 or the Care and Support and Aftercare (Choice of Accommodation) Regulations 2014 (in Wales, Care and Support (Charging) (Wales) Regulations 2015). Consequently, the scope for local variation in charges levied for services should be minimised, especially given the establishment of a national eligibility framework (Chapter 6, Department of Health, 2016, Care and Support (Eligibility Criteria) Regulations 2015, Care and Support (Eligibility) (Wales) Regulations, 2015). Furthermore, local authorities no longer have the absolute right to insist on the cheapest option. Section 30 of the Care Act 2014 (section 57 Social Services and Well-being (Wales) Act 2014) obliges local authorities to comply with someone's preference for certain accommodation, although, of course, they may have to meet any additional costs.

Indeed, there is a strong desire, reflected in the legislation, that people should commission the services they prefer, and if they exercise their rights to do this, the local authority is obliged to facilitate this. This is in accordance with the principles of personalisation and is put into effect by provisions in the Care Act 2014, especially sections 26 and 31–33. Section 31–33 (in Wales, section 50 Social Services and Well-being (Wales) Act 2014) relates to direct payments, whereby someone who has their needs met at least to some extent by the local authority, and therefore has a personal budget, has the right to administer the money the local authority would pay for those services. In other words, they arrange the provision of services according to their preferences, using the service providers of choice. In the case of someone who lacks capacity, those rights can be exercised by someone who is authorised, such as someone who exercises Lasting Power of Attorney (for an explanation of this, see the next chapter).

What of the quality of the services provided? Commissioners of services undoubtedly have some responsibility for this, but in addition there is provision for inspection and complaints procedures.

Case study

Daphne Meadows is very dissatisfied with Beechwood Lodge where she has been living for the last eight months. Despite the home's claim to offer high-quality care, Daphne feels that it falls short in two respects: there is insufficient staffing and she is still compelled to share a room with another resident despite a promise that she would have a room to herself.

In these circumstances, she can, of course, complain. She can complain direct to the managers of the home and, if the placement was arranged through the local authority social services department, she can complain to them. Local authorities are obliged to have complaints procedures and these must comply with the Local Authority Social Services and National Health Service (England) Complaints Regulations 2009 (sections 113–115 Health and Social Care (Community Health and Standards Act) 2003) or, in Wales, Part 10 Social Services and Well-being (Wales) Act 2014. She can also complain to the Care Quality Commission (England) or the Care and Social Services Inspectorate Wales responsible under the Care Standards Act 2000 (as amended by the Health and Social Care Act 2008, Part 2 Care Act 2014, Part 10 Social Services and Well-being (Wales) Act 2014) for inspecting standards, and taking enforcement action, in residential homes which are required to be registered under the Care Quality Commission (Registration) Regulations 2009 or Regulation and Inspection of Social Care (Wales) Act 2016. The responsibilities of the inspection bodies specifically include management, staffing and facilities, as well as issuing warnings and taking remedial action where these fall short (section 29 Health and Social Care Act 2008 as amended; Regulation and Inspection of Social Care (Wales) Act 2016). For further information, see Chapter 9.

Withdrawing services

Once services are provided, can they be withdrawn?

Naturally, if the service user's needs change, and everyone agrees that they have changed, then withdrawing services is unproblematic. However, consider the following case study which related to an assessment of need under the previous legislation, the NHS and Community Care Act 1990. On this occasion, this is a real case.

Case study

Mr Barry was in his late seventies. He had suffered a stroke and his vision was poor. Gloucestershire social services department had assessed his needs and on this basis provided home care and laundry services. A considerable time after providing the services, the local authority ran into budgetary difficulties and decided to cut adult care services 'across the board', reducing home care and withdrawing the home laundry service. So Mr Barry's level of service provision was reduced considerably. He went to court arguing that the local authority's actions were unreasonable and wrong in that his assessed needs had not changed so how could services be reduced?

(R v Gloucestershire County Council, ex parte Barry [1997])

The courts decided that Mr Barry was right, at least up to a point. He should not have had his services withdrawn since there was no basis on which to change the level of services offered as his assessed needs had not changed. However, and unfortunately for Mr Barry, the court declared that it was open for the local authority to reassess his needs on the basis of the new financial situation in which it found itself. In other words, it could set new eligibility criteria for services, assess Mr Barry by these criteria, and then presumably explain to Mr Barry how he failed to meet them. Nevertheless, the message is loud and clear: services cannot be withdrawn unless there is a reassessment of need, a principle that is restated in the Care Act 2014 and associated statutory guidance (Department of Health, 2016).

What if someone is in residential care and the home closes? Surely that is a withdrawal of service? This is precisely the issue that has occurred in a number of cases, summarised in the next case study.

Case study

Court decisions on residential home closures

- In *R v North East Devon Health Authority ex parte Coughlan* [2000], the courts decided that the decision of the health authority to close a home breached Article 8 of the European Convention.

- In *R v Servite Houses ex parte Goldsmith and Chatting* [2001], it was declared that a housing association is not subject to public law. Likewise, in *R (on the application of Heather and others) v Leonard Cheshire Foundation* [2002], it was decided by the court that a voluntary organisation was not subject to the Human Rights Act 1998. So, in these cases the court had no jurisdiction to review decisions on the grounds of potential breaches of the European Convention on Human Rights.

- In *R (on the application of Madden and others) v Bury Metropolitan Borough Council* [2002], residents of Warthfield residential home persuaded the courts that the authority's decision to close the home was unlawful as the authority owed the claimants a duty to act fairly, and fairness in that case required consultation. In *R (on the application of Goldsmith) v London Borough of Wandsworth* [2004], the decision to move a woman from residential care to nursing care was quashed by the court as the Local Continuing Care panel had failed to produce reasons and failed to consider an adult care assessment. In R (on the Application of S and another) v Leicester City Council [2004], the local authority's decision to move the applicant from her preferred accommodation was quashed as a formal assessment of needs should have been carried out.

- More generally, courts have confirmed that breaches of duty to provide appropriate accommodation under the now superseded section 21 of the National Assistance Act 1948 may possibly be breaches of the European Convention on Human Rights Article 8, as, for example, in *R (Bernard) v Enfield London BC* [2003]. Yet this may not apply if the local authority makes the care arrangement with a private sector provider. In *YL v Birmingham City Council and others* [2008], the House of Lords declared that the Official Solicitor could not bring an action for alleged breach of the European Convention on Human Rights Article 8 against an independent home who wanted to evict an 84-year-old who had Alzheimer's disease.

- However, courts have resisted the argument that closure of a home is life-threatening so could be considered a breach of the right to life under Article 2 of the European Convention on Human Rights. In both *R (on the application of Thomas) v Havering London Borough Council and another [2008]* and *Watts v UK* [2010], it was held that the research evidence was not conclusive in demonstrating this link between closure and potential shortening of life.

You may be wondering why the decisions in these cases vary and what they have to do with the European Convention on Human Rights, particularly Article 8 under which some applications have been successful. If you recall from Chapter 2, Article 8 concerns the right to family life and therefore by implication people's rights to be protected from arbitrary decisions to close the home in which they live. The principle behind this is that residents should have a 'home for life' and should not be required to move without agreement just because public authorities say so. Effectively, what the courts are saying is that decisions to close homes should be taken in consultation with residents and proper notice given. The health authority or social services department should make alternative plans in conjunction with service users and work towards an agreement to move elsewhere.

What if the home is not run by the local authority, but is provided by a voluntary organisation or independent company that decides, for whatever reason, to close the home down? Residents would not be able to appeal to the courts unless the local authority were to some extent providing for their care – for example, by paying all or part of their residential home fees, for reasons stated in the Leonard Cheshire case above. In any case, no court action can be effective if the service provider goes out of business. To address this, the Care Act 2014 includes a number of safeguards, principally under section 48, which obliges local authorities to meet the needs of people where their service providers are *unable to carry on the regulated activity* which provided for their needs (the Welsh equivalent is section 189 Social Services and Well-being (Wales) Act 2014). This obligation extends for as long as is considered necessary by the local authority. A number of other provisions in relation to *provider failure*, *market oversight* and potential failures in the social care market can be found in sections 48–57 of the Care Act 2014. These include the rights of the Care Quality Commission to check on the financial viability of service providers (for provision in Wales, see Regulation and Inspection of Social Care (Wales) Act 2016).

Experiencing adult social care

The Joseph Rowntree Foundation (for their website address, see the end of the chapter) has published a considerable amount of research on adult care, much of it incorporating a carer and user perspective. Some of this has direct relevance to the legally related practice issues examined in this chapter and shown in the following research summary.

Research summary

In 2009, over 200 people were asked about their experience of residential and nursing homes. The principal comment from those who actually lived in residential homes was that they had very little say in what happened to them. Older people who needed substantial support were made to feel a burden. This led the researchers to comment that older people were perceived as commodities, not as consumers or citizens with rights, entitlements or purchasing power.

(Bowers *et al.*, 2009)

Adult social care service users were asked their views on proposals for funding social care in the future. This research found that service users feel that a false divide between social care and health care is perpetuated by conflicting funding arrangements, and that people do not generally want to live in residential care homes, which is often presented as the only option for older people who need support.

(Beresford, 2010)

(Continued)

(Continued)

In 2001, researchers studied older people's experience of home care and community care more generally. Service users valued consistency of support, flexibility in responding to needs and, in the case of ethnic minority groups, culturally sensitive services (for example, specific foods and activities in day-care centres). Service users would welcome regular reviews of the quality of services provided.

(Raynes *et al.*, 2001)

In 2002, researchers asked about advocacy for black and minority ethnic users and carers. This uncovered a great deal of dissatisfaction with mainstream mental health services. There was a lack of awareness of advocacy services, but service users and carers felt most empowered when they had an advocate who reflected their culture, gender and ethnicity.

(Rai-Atkins *et al.*, 2002)

Also in 2002, researchers studied support services for Asian disabled people. Low take-up of adult care services among Asian people was related to a lack of confidence in adult care service providers. The reason for this distrust was clearly connected to a limited understanding of, and response to, cultural and religious differences. Several disabled service users felt discriminated against, pointing to a lack of provision for their religious and cultural needs. The consequence of this was isolation and forced dependency on families.

(Vernon, 2002)

The whole issue of user and carer empowerment is, of course, of great importance (Sharkey, 2006). From the point of view of using the law, three key issues are worth highlighting from this in our conclusion: co-ordination and integration of services, financial arrangements, and empowerment in the context of anti-discriminatory practice.

Integrating health and social care, finance, and empowering service users and carers

A key issue for the future of adult care practice is the move towards greater integration of health and social services. For a long time it has been realised that from a user perspective, the divide between health and social care can appear to be arbitrary – for example, often there is no essential difference between what community psychiatric nurses and mental health social workers do when dealing with people with mental health problems. Yet the financial implications of the difference for some service users are considerable: in England and Wales nursing care is free, but social care has to be paid for and is means tested. Another negative consequence of the divide is lack of co-ordination of services and inconsistencies in assessment. A persistent complaint from carers is that professionals do not know what each other is doing and so service users receive a patchy service, as we saw in the surveys of older people cited above.

To address lack of co-ordination for individual service users, the National Service Frameworks for Older People (Department of Health, 2001a; Welsh Assembly Government, 2006) promoted the notion of *the single assessment process*. This was an important development whereby social work assessments are integrated into an overall assessment that includes health care assessments and therefore builds up one overall, hopefully consistent and integrated, personal assessment. The aim was simple:

> *To ensure that older people are treated as individuals and they receive appropriate and timely packages of care which meet their needs as individuals, regardless of health and social services boundaries.*

> (Department of Health, 2001a, Standard 2)

This objective was to be attained through integrated commissioning arrangements and provision of services, facilitated by changes in funding, organisation and administration contained in the Health Act 1999, the Health and Social Care (Community Health and Standards) Act 2003, and subsequently the National Health Service Act 2006 and the National Health Service (Wales) Act 2006 (Department of Health, 2008). These measures have been further developed and superseded by the establishment of an integration fund, partnership arrangements and associated provisions in Part 4 of the Care Act 2014 and Part 9 of the Social Services and Well-being (Wales) Act 2014.

The thorny question of financing long-term care was examined by a Royal Commission (Sutherland, 1999). This recommended payment of social care services through general taxation after an assessment of need. The report failed to become policy in England and Wales, although the equivalent recommendations for Scotland were implemented through the Adult Support and Protection (Scotland) Act 2007 (for further information and discussion of this legislation, see Pritchard, 2008, Chapter 2). This creates an anomaly and perpetuates a system in England and Wales whereby a fine distinction has to be made between services that are medical, and therefore free, and those that are 'care' and may be chargeable, with some clarification offered by the Health and Social Care Act 2001 and Health and Social Care (Community Health and Standards) Act 2003. The Community Care (Delayed Discharges, etc.) Act 2003 implies an acknowledgement that there is a consequent problem in transferring people to care services, tackling this by introducing a system of charges levied on local authorities where there is a delay in transferring people who are occupying hospital beds (so-called 'bed-blockers'). The Care Act 2014 (section 15) addresses this to some extent by introducing a 'cap' on savings that must be used to finance social care; the equivalent provision for Wales is not so explicit, being relegated to regulations made under section 64 of the Social Services and Well-being (Wales) Act 2014.

The Green Paper issued in 2005 (Department of Health, 2005) set out a number of proposals that moved the whole debate a stage further, with proposals to integrate and co-ordinate voluntary sector services as well as income support, health services and adult social services. To achieve this, there would be a better trained social care workforce, together with an acknowledgement of risks created by greater independence, so that services become person-centred, proactive and seamless. The subsequent White Paper, *Our health, our care, our say* (Department of Health, 2006b), reaffirmed an increased emphasis on service user choice, direct payments and carer support, arguing strongly for better integration of services with comprehensive long-term reform proposals for both health and social care. Much of this centres on selecting services that fit people's needs, the policy of 'personalisation'. There were similar long-term proposals for Wales building on integration underway since 2003 (Welsh Assembly Government, 2003). The 2010 policy document, *A vision for adult social care* (Department of Health, 2010a), tries to marry all of this in a context of significant reductions in public expenditure with a reassertion of the values of freedom, fairness and responsibility, translated into even more emphasis on personalisation and a push towards greater community involvement in provision of support. When translated into legislation, this has resulted in the Care Act 2014 and Social Services and Well-being (Wales) Act 2014, promoting well-being, prevention, personal budgets and individual care and support plans (section 1, sections 24–31 Care Act 2014; section 5, 50–55 Social Services and Well-being (Wales) Act 2014).

As to the specific issue of empowerment and lack of attention to cultural and religious needs, we need to use the law imaginatively and creatively.

Activity 5.2

Given the issues highlighted by the research, in what way can the law potentially be used to promote empowerment and inclusive adult care services?

Write down what legal measures you think can be adopted in order to achieve this aim. Try to keep to procedures and processes that actually exist. You may find it helpful to discuss this issue with others and even to ask service providers what measures they adopt.

Comment

Some suggestions are to be found in Exercise Answers on p189–90, but do note that the law cannot compel people to become good practitioners. All the law can do is facilitate and enhance good practice in ways that you have now explored.

Chapter summary

In this chapter, you were introduced to the concept of adult care and offered an overview of services for adults who might need them. Assessment of need was identified as the central task of social workers. The legal basis for the provision of services was summarised together with the commissioning role of the local authority and service users' rights of redress. At various points reference was made to the key legislation – in England the Care Act 2014 and in Wales the Social Services and Well-being (Wales) Act 2014, both of which were fully implemented in 2016. The chapter then cited some examples from research of service users' and carers' perspectives, and used this as a basis for indicating actual and potential changes in policy and the law. It concluded by inviting you to think about ways in which the law can be used to promote user and carer empowerment in accessing quality services.

In the next chapter, we move on to consider the occasional need to protect vulnerable adults who, for various reasons, are unable to look after themselves. This will include the important topic of safeguarding.

Further reading

Davies, M (ed.) **(2012)** *Social work with adults.* Basingstoke: Palgrave.

Gardner, A (2014) *Personalisation in social work* (2nd edn). Basingstoke: Palgrave.

Johns, R (2011) *Social work, social policy and older people.* London: Sage.

Ray, M and Phillips, J (2012) *Social work with older people* (5th edn). Basingstoke: Palgrave.

For a concise summary of the Law Commission proposals, influential in development of Care Act 2014 and Social Services and Well-being (Wales) Act 2014, written by the person who played a key role in drawing these up:

Spencer-Lane, T (2010) *A statutory framework for safeguarding adults?* The Law Commission's consultation paper on adult social care. *Journal of Adult Protection*, 12(1): 43–9.

Websites

Disability Rights: www.gov.uk/browse/disabilities

Joseph Rowntree Foundation: www.jrf.org.uk/

Legislation: www.legislation.gov.uk

Older People's Commissioner for Wales: www.olderpeoplewales.com/en/Home.aspx

SCIE (Social Care Institute for Excellence): www.scie.org.uk/care-act-2014/assessment-and-eligibility/

6: Vulnerable Adults

Introduction

This chapter is the second of the two-part examination of the law relating to adult care social work. Leading on from the previous chapter's overview of adult care assessments and services, this chapter examines arrangements that may need to be made when adults are unable to look after their own interests. This may be where they are potentially at risk of one of several different kinds of abuse, or where there are doubts about whether they can articulate their own views. In extreme cases, this may mean that action has to be taken to compel someone to receive care. So in this chapter the primary areas of law covered relate to:

- legal provision for safeguarding adults;
- the law relating to mental capacity – that is, people's ability to make decisions for themselves;
- and, more generally, the protection of vulnerable adults both from themselves and from other people.

Chapters 5 and 6 together enable you to attain, in relation to adult care social work law, appropriate standards of the Professional Capabilities Framework and the 2016 Social Work Subject Benchmarks. These were clearly set out and explained in Chapter 5 and so are not repeated here.

The previous chapter also set out the principles that determine when and how services can be provided to support adults in the community and their carers. It is important to remember right through this chapter that nothing takes away people's entitlement to commission services themselves, to request an assessment for the potential provision of adult care services, and to receive services which they or their carers may need. However, on occasion, there may be an impediment that prevents people receiving the care they need. First, they may be in an abusive relationship in which someone else is interfering with their rights to health and well-being. Second, they may not currently have a full or complete understanding of what their needs are due to some cognitive or physical problem.

In legal terms, this translates into:

- legislation or procedures that set out how social workers can help protect someone from abuse;
- what the law says regarding people's ability to make their own decisions and manage their own affairs;
- what can happen when people need protection or care which they are unable to authorise or arrange themselves.

The chapter, therefore, begins with discussion about safeguarding adults. It then moves on to consider the general principles relating to the law concerning the ability to make decisions, or 'mental capacity' as it is referred to in the legislation. There is, then, a summary of the law relating to care that can, in specific circumstances, be arranged even if someone is not able to agree to it. In the final section, we consider the ethical issues that arise from implementing this kind of legislation.

Safeguarding vulnerable adults

Activity 6.1

Consider the following questions:

- In what ways might adults need protection?
- How would you distinguish adults who are vulnerable?

Comment

In considering this question, you probably started by thinking of ways in which adults could be abused by other people and may have therefore started with physical protection. This may have triggered thoughts about how people sometimes need to be protected from themselves, and how sometimes they appear to be in need of removal from a situation which is dangerous to them. Hopefully, it will also have occurred to you that some adults are vulnerable to abuse or exploitation in other ways, especially with regard to their finances.

This chapter considers all of these areas briefly, but we start with a discussion of what constitutes vulnerability.

Elder abuse, as it is sometimes called, is a topic that has attracted an increasing amount of professional attention over recent years (Eastman, 1994; Pritchard, 2008). This interest on the part of social workers was translated into policy and procedures that directed the attention of practitioners to the whole wider issue of the abuse of vulnerable adults (for example, Department of Health, 2000e, National Assembly for Wales, 2000) since abuse is not, of course, confined to older people. So, what is abuse and what constitutes vulnerability?

The Department of Health (2000e) guidelines identified the various forms of abuse as physical, sexual, psychological, financial and neglect. More recent studies, guidance and policies envisage a wider categorisation (for overview, see Brammer, 2014). The Care Act 2014 Guidance (Department of Health, 2016, paragraph 14.17) contains lists of different forms of abuse under each of the following headings:

- physical abuse, which includes misuse of medication;

- domestic violence, which also includes 'honour'-based violence;

- sexual abuse, which includes involvement in pornography;

- psychological abuse, which is wide-ranging but also includes unreasonable and unjustifiable withdrawal of services or support;

- financial abuse, which includes coercion as well as direct theft or fraud;

- modern slavery, which is covered by the Modern Slavery Act 2015;

- various forms of discriminatory behaviour;

- organisational abuse either by individuals within the organisation of the organisation itself;

- neglect and acts of omission, particularly in relation to failing to provide for medical needs;

- self-neglect, which includes neglect her personal hygiene, health or 'surroundings'.

It goes without saying that several of the forms of abuse listed above constitute criminal offences. The law makes it clear that any physical assault is a criminal offence, but the issue for vulnerable adults is that quite often they may have difficulties, because of fear or diminished intellectual abilities, recording precisely what happened and who did what to them. It is for this reason that prosecutions for abuse of older people or people with learning disabilities are extremely rare. The Crown Prosecution Service has to be concerned with the probability of securing a conviction, and vulnerable adults do not make very reliable prosecution witnesses; how can someone with dementia, for example, give evidence when they have significant short-term memory problems? However, there have recently been moves to enhance the potential for vulnerable adults providing credible evidence in court (Ministry of Justice, 2011, 2013a). Most would agree that, in the very small minority of cases where the carer is implicated in the abuse, prosecution is rarely a successful way of addressing abuse, since in many cases the abuser is under stress due to an excess of caring responsibilities.

Safeguarding vulnerable adults is now an important duty of the local authority under the Care Act 2014 (sections 42–46) which elevated the level of responsibility which various agencies share in this area. Every local authority is required under the Care Act 2014 (section 43) to establish a Safeguarding Adults Board through which it establishes local safeguarding arrangements working in conjunction with partners to help and protect adults who fall into one of the ten categories listed above. Such Boards have a strategic role, but the law regarding safeguarding vulnerable adults does not go as far as law relating to children in that there is no equivalent of care proceedings under the Children Act 1989. However, there is now a duty to investigate abuse equivalent to section 47 Children Act 1989. Section 42 of the Care Act 2014 lays on the local authority the duty to make enquiries where there is reasonable cause to suspect abuse or neglect. The purpose of enquiries is *to enable it to decide whether any action should be taken {.} and, if so, what and by whom.*

The SCIE practice guidance on safeguarding adults (for their website, see the end of the chapter) suggests that safeguarding encompasses six key concepts: empowerment, protection, prevention, proportionate responses, partnership and accountability. The Care Act 2014 Guidance (Department of Health, 2016, paragraph 14.13) has a slightly different list of what it calls the 'six key principles' that underpin all adult safeguarding work:

- empowerment, with an emphasis on informed consent;
- prevention, which fits with the principles of the Act itself, especially 'promoting well-being';
- proportionality, clearly relevant in relation to ensuring compliance with European Convention on Human Rights and the Human Rights Act 1998;
- protection, including a participative safeguarding process;
- partnership, involving professional collaboration and involvement in the community;
- accountability which includes transparency.

It is important to discuss empowerment in particular in this context since it would not be good social work practice to assume that everyone needs protection and that, simply because someone becomes vulnerable, they somehow lose the ability to make decisions for themselves. So in the next section we consider what the law says regarding 'mental capacity', mental capacity being the legal shorthand for people's ability to make decisions for themselves in terms of having the physical and mental ability to do so.

Mental capacity and empowerment

For many years, it was a common-law assumption that children had no rights to make decisions for themselves, while adults had absolute rights to make all their own decisions, a right that could only be countermanded in certain specified circumstances. One of these circumstances might be where someone had such a serious mental health issue that they posed a threat to themselves or other people. Other circumstances, such as where someone has lost the ability to manage their financial affairs, or fails to understand when they are putting themselves at risk, presented greater challenges for the legal system. A mishmash of legal measures came to be developed over time, some deriving from common law and others from a medley of statute laws, but thankfully most of these have been brought together by a composite measure – namely, the Mental Capacity Act 2005 (Johns, 2010, pp197–200).

Capacity refers to people's ability to make decisions for themselves. Some people might also refer to competence to make decisions or the physical or mental faculties to do so, but such terms can become problematic. For they might imply that it is legitimate to make some kind of assessment of how competent someone is in terms of the quality of decisions made. That is not, however, the legal consideration. Assessment of how competent someone is simply refers to the degree of disability that prevents them making any kind of rational decision. It does not necessarily refer to how good that decision might be, and indeed, one of the principles made explicit in the Mental Capacity Act 2005 is that someone who does have capacity is under no obligation to make 'wise' decisions (section 1(4) Mental Capacity Act 2005).

Given the assumption that every adult has the right to make their own decisions, how is this translated into legislation? The answer, in short, is by clarifying where someone does not have capacity and what action can be taken where this is the case. So, the Mental Capacity Act 2005 starts from a 'presumption of capacity', and then declares that a person lacks capacity if they are unable to make a decision because of *an impairment of, or a disturbance in the functioning of, the mind or brain* and *it does not matter whether the impairment or disturbance is permanent or temporary* (section 2 Mental Capacity Act 2005). For adults, this in effect means that this usually translates into certain categories of people:

- people of all ages with learning disabilities (note the Mental Capacity Act 2005 has a minimum age of 16 in terms of its applicability);

- people with a 'mental disorder', which means *any disorder or disability of the mind* but excludes *dependence on alcohol or drugs* (section 1 Mental Health Act 1983 as amended by section 1 Mental Health Act 2007);

- people with *functioning impairments* such as dementia or a brain injury;

- and occasionally people with life-threatening conditions when they become unable to communicate.

Note that this does not automatically include older people as such. Indeed, the Mental Capacity Act 2005 is very clear that assumptions should not be made about people's decision-making ability simply on the grounds of their 'age or appearance' (section 2(3)(a) Mental Capacity Act 2005). It may be true that older people might be more vulnerable to certain conditions that affect their capacity but age, of itself, does not determine decision-making ability. A 98-year-old may be as clear thinking and as lucid in their thoughts as someone in their early 20s. Likewise, section 1(3)(d) Care Act 2014 refers to:

> *the need to ensure that decisions about the individual are made having regard to all the individual's circumstances (and are not based only on the individual's age or appearance or any condition of the individual's or aspect of the individual's behaviour which might lead others to make unjustified assumptions about the individual's well-being).*

The Mental Capacity Act 2005 has a useful *Code of Practice* (Department for Constitutional Affairs, 2007) which clarifies what much of the law means in practice. Paragraph 4.4 of that *Code* states that an assessment of someone's capacity *must be based on their ability to make a specific decision at the time it needs to be made, and not their ability to make decisions in general.* Indeed, there are certain other important principles that are relevant here.

Activity 6.2

What do you think the principles should be that underpin any kind of work with people who have lost the ability to make their own decisions?

Comment

One principle that hopefully you might have mentioned straight away is that of advocacy, helping to support people make their own decisions. Another might be that anyone assisting someone else in making decisions, or even making decisions for them, should be entirely guided by what is in that person's best interests.

Reassuringly, both those principles are clearly stated in the Mental Capacity Act 2005 (sections 1–5). Another principle declared in that section of the Act is that when a decision is made on behalf of someone, those who make the decision should always consider the option that is least restrictive of that person's rights and freedom of action.

Section 3 of the Mental Capacity Act 2005 clarifies what it means when we say that someone is unable to make a decision for themselves. The ability to make a decision is impaired if someone is unable to do one or more of the following:

- understand information relevant to a decision;
- retain the information;
- use or weigh that information as part of the process of making the decision;
- communicate that decision (not necessarily orally).

To underline this last point section 3 (2) refers to understanding explanations and communications that are 'appropriate', a point clarified by the *Code of Practice* that suggests this might include simple language, sign language, visual representations, computer-mediated means of communication, visual illustrations, repeating information several times, audiotapes, video or posters (Department for Constitutional Affairs, 2007, paragraph 4.18). The *Code of Practice* also suggests that retaining information is not necessarily affected if someone can only retain information for a comparatively short period (paragraph 4.20). It then suggests (in paragraph 4.36) questions to be addressed if there is doubt about someone's ability to make decisions for themselves.

- Does the person have all relevant information they need to make the decision?
- If they are making a decision that involves choosing between alternatives, do they have information on all the different options?
- Would the person have a better understanding if information was explained or presented in another way?
- Are there times of day when the person's understanding is better?
- Are there locations where they may feel more at ease?
- Can a decision be put off until the circumstances are different and the person concerned may be able to make the decision?
- Can anyone else help the person to make choices or express a view?

All of this applies even if capacity fluctuates, so that occasional short-term memory problems would not of themselves suggest that someone had lost capacity.

In making decisions about what is in someone's best interests, section 4 of the Mental Capacity Act 2005 suggests that practitioners should take into account the person's past and present wishes and feelings, their beliefs and values, together with other factors that a person would be likely to consider if they were in a position to do so (this sounds a bit convoluted, but is in fact is no more than asking the question: what would someone be likely to consider if they did have capacity?). Further guidance and social work principles suggest that, alongside this, what ought to be considered are ways of encouraging someone to participate in the decision-making process, avoiding discrimination of any kind and consulting with people who are significant in that person's life.

Compulsory care or protection?

Given this Mental Capacity Act 2005 context, in which there is a strong emphasis on empowering people to make their own decisions to as full an extent as is possible, it may seem a little odd that the discussion now turns to the specific pieces of legislation that allow the decision about care to be taken out of the service user's own hands. This is not, however, contradictory. If someone loses the ability to make decisions for themselves, it is clearly very much in their interest to ensure that decisions are made on their behalf by others only when absolutely necessary, and that very strict safeguards are in place to ensure that anyone who makes a decision on behalf of someone else does so entirely properly and only with the best interests of that person in mind. Thus, Mental Capacity Act 2005 principles continue to apply even when legislation authorising proxy decision-making (covered in the next part of the chapter) is operationalised.

Case study

Phyllis Philpot has lived on her own for a number of years following the death of her husband. She is now in her mid-80s. Her daughter Janice visits at least once a week but lives in a town some miles away from Phyllis. She and other relatives are seriously concerned about the risk posed to Phyllis by her potential to harm herself accidentally. She does not appear to understand the danger of leaving the gas on in the kitchen, and she does not appear to be eating properly, despite the fact that meals are provided for her at least three times a week. In addition, the house is full of an ever-accumulating pile of rubbish, and Phyllis appears to be making no attempt to attend to her basic hygiene needs. Last week, Janice found Phyllis lying on the floor semi-conscious when she visited; she could give no articulate explanation as to how she came to be there.

The solution suggested by relatives is that Phyllis should go and live with Janice and her family, but she resolutely refuses to leave her home. 'I've lived here for the last 60 years,' says Phyllis, 'and here I stay until the day I die.'

Janice cannot believe that adult care services are telling the truth when they say that they have no powers to compel Phyllis to leave her home and live somewhere safer.

So, the question is, are they telling the truth?

The first consideration would need to be: does Phyllis have the capacity to make the declaration that she intends to stay where she is until she dies? As you now know, her statement has to stand unless it can be refuted on the grounds that she no longer has capacity in relation to this particular decision. Specifically, it would have to be demonstrated that she did not understand the relevant information, could not retain it, evaluate it or communicate it. This seems most unlikely, so in that sense, compelling her to leave her home in order to be safe is not only questionable, it would be illegal.

The only remaining question, then, is whether she qualifies for compulsory intervention through the operation of other legislation that can override her absolute rights to self-determination. The range of such legislation is quite deliberately narrow and specific, being limited to a small range of circumstances. So what provisions are there to compel someone to leave their home when they appear to be at risk to themselves or to other people? In what circumstances might they apply?

The first provision that someone might discover if they looked this up themselves on an out-of-date website is section 47 of the National Assistance Act 1948, which allowed the removal of someone *suffering from grave chronic disease or, being aged, infirm or physically incapacitated {.} living in insanitary conditions* and not receiving *proper care and attention*. This provision was repealed by section 46 Care Act 2014, being widely regarded as an unethical anachronism that constituted a direct contravention of the European Convention on Human Rights (Johns, 2014, Chapter 3).

The second piece of legislation involves the police. There is a general police power that allows officers to enter and search premises if this is necessary in order to save *life and limb* (section 17(1) Police and Criminal Evidence Act 1984). This may be helpful in circumstances where a vulnerable adult is obviously in need of urgent medical attention, perhaps lying on the floor in their locked home. This legislation could be used to enable police to force entry, and common law powers would then enable them to take the vulnerable adult to hospital: this would be seen as a reasonable action that prevents the threat to life, an action authorised by common law. So, in this case, had the police discovered Phyllis lying on the floor, they could have taken action, but this is a very specific and limited legal provision, confined to emergency immediate risk to life and limb situations only.

The third, perhaps better known, piece of legislation that permits compulsory removal is the Mental Health Act 1983. This may directly involve social workers, in this case as Approved Mental Health Professionals who have a special responsibility, after receiving advanced post-qualifying training, for dealing with people with mental 'disorders' (certain other professions are also able to undertake this training). Space does not permit an examination of this Act in detail, but suffice it to say that it does allow for people to be admitted and detained in hospital when they are, or may be, suffering from a mental disorder, and also need to be detained in the interests of their own health or safety or for the protection of other people (sections 2 and 3 Mental Health Act 1983). We explored some of these issues in a human rights context in Chapter 2. It needs to be emphasised, however, that this is a mental health provision – in other words, its purpose is to secure the treatment of people who have mental health needs, and so requires specific statements from medical practitioners that the presenting problems are mental 'disorder' in origin. Furthermore, in the case of the longer term order section 3, following the Mental Health Act 2007 amendments, there is now an explicit requirement that treatment is not only appropriate but 'available' (section 3 (2)(d) Mental Health Act 1983). For further information on this, see the Mental Health Act 1983 *Code of Practice* (Department of Health, 2015) and Barber *et al*. (2012), especially Chapters 4 and 5.

The fourth area of legislation has developed only very recently, and is in response to the 'Bournewood' case which was discussed in Chapter 2 under 'capacity to understand and consent'. The practice issue that often arises with vulnerable adults is that they may not have a mental disorder if 'disorder' is too narrowly defined, and furthermore they may not need treatment for their 'mental disorder' at all, yet do need to be kept in a hospital or care home where they are safe. For this reason, the Mental Health Act 2007 expanded the Mental Health Act 1983 definition of mental disorder deliberately to extend to conditions such as dementia, which formerly failed to qualify since it could not described as a form of mental illness. The Mental Health Act 2007 (section 50) introduced the Deprivation of Liberty Safeguards into the Mental Capacity Act 2005 so that Best Interests Assessors, many of whom will be social workers with advanced post-qualifying training, can authorise the detention of a vulnerable adult in a registered care home or hospital (sections 4A and 4B Mental Capacity Act 2005). Note, however, that the authority of the Best Interest Assessor applies only where someone already is a resident in a care home or an inpatient in a hospital (for further information on this, see Johns (2014), especially Chapter 6).

So, this provision in the amended Mental Capacity Act 2005 cannot apply where someone is still in their own home. In these circumstances, only the Court of Protection could take action. The Court of Protection is a civil court that originated in the Crown's assumed long-standing duty to protect the most vulnerable, and now derives its powers from Part 2 of the Mental Capacity Act 2005. Its jurisdiction relates to interpreting the Mental Capacity Act 2005 regarding who does and does not have capacity to make particular decisions, and it also has a broader remit in relation to protecting property and financial affairs. The Court can appoint a deputy to act on someone's behalf where there is a need to make an ongoing arrangement for day-to-day decision-making. The court has a valuable role in protecting the interests of the most vulnerable where these are not covered by specific statutes. So theoretically, it would have jurisdiction and powers to authorise removal of people from their own homes, but in practice it will only use these in extreme cases, and will always, in any case, be guided by the principles set out in the Mental Capacity Act 2005.

Nevertheless, there are some circumstances in which the courts may decide to use its jurisdiction under common law, in combination with the Mental Capacity Act 2005 and the European Convention, in order to determine what should be done. This might apply in safeguarding cases even if the vulnerable adults concerned still appear to have capacity to make their own decisions, as is now clear from a case that occurred in 2012.

Case study

In *A Local Authority and others v DL* [2012], it was clear that a son's behaviour towards his parents was abusive, yet the parents would not take any legal action themselves, despite having the capacity to do so. The son lived with his parents and there was evidence that he used physical and verbal threats to control his parents, deciding when they should go in and out of their house, and restricting visits from health and social care staff. There were also allegations that he was trying to compel his father into transferring ownership of the house to him.

The Court decided that it did have the authority to put protective measures in place

> *in relation to vulnerable adults who do not fall within the Mental Capacity Act 2005 but who are, or are reasonably believed to be, for some reason deprived of the capacity to make the relevant decision, or disabled from making a free choice, or incapacitated or disabled from giving or expressing a real and genuine consent by reason of such things as constraint, coercion, undue influence or other vitiating factor.*

Comment

Therefore, in this case it would have the right to make appropriate orders if needed.

This case established an important principle – namely, that the Court of Protection will get involved in safeguarding cases even if the vulnerable adults are not deemed to have lost their capacity but feel too disempowered to take action to protect themselves. Here the court is moving beyond the Mental Capacity Act 2005 provisions and using its common law powers to ensure the best outcome.

The case study just highlighted refers, in passing, to financial abuse, so perhaps it would be good to say something more general about this here.

With regard to responsibility for personal financial affairs generally, it is important to note that this needs to be addressed quite separately from adult social care legislation. The law assumes that people are fully entitled to do what they wish with their money and if they choose to give it away, then that is their absolute right. The unscrupulous could potentially easily exploit this situation, for in some cases the vulnerable adult clearly does not have the capacity to understand what they are doing with their money. The two legal processes worth considering here are Lasting Power of Attorney and, again, the Court of Protection.

To explain what a Lasting Power of Attorney is, it is important to begin by drawing a distinction with an ordinary Power of Attorney, which is an authority for one person to ask another to look after their financial affairs. This ordinary Power of Attorney ceases as soon as the person granting authority loses their capacity (as defined in the Mental Capacity Act 2005, see above) to give full consent to the arrangement. To address this, the Enduring Power of Attorney Act 1985 and subsequently the Mental Capacity Act 2005 were introduced.

The 1985 Act allowed someone to declare from the start that they wished the Power of Attorney, which could relate only to property, to continue even when they lose their capacity to consent to it, and the Mental Capacity Act 2005 (section 9) takes this a stage further, allowing the financial powers to be complemented by personal welfare decision-making delegation, thus making the arrangement comprehensive and lasting for the lifetime of the person concerned – hence, the name Lasting Power of Attorney. Note, though, that people have to apply separately for financial and personal welfare Lasting Powers of Attorney as they are different, and sometimes someone will nominate different people to hold them, or might only agree to one of them. Nevertheless, generally, drawing up both kinds of Lasting Powers of Attorney is an excellent course of action to recommend, provided people know in advance that lack of capacity to manage their affairs is likely and are prepared to anticipate this.

In practice, though, more often likely to occur is a situation where someone has already lost their capacity to manage their own financial affairs. Here the only recourse is to the Court of Protection, which will take over people's financial affairs, if necessary, and administer them through a court-appointed deputy. Deputies can take decisions on welfare, health and finance as authorised by the Court, but will not be able to refuse consent to life-sustaining treatment (section 11 Mental Capacity Act 2005). One consideration worth bearing in mind is that, while the court will take over all financial aspects, so effectively barring any possibility of exploitation, there will be fees payable. These could be substantial, being in addition to the deputy's fees and expenses. In terms of day-to-day management in cases involving the Court of Protection, responsibility for oversight lies with the Public Guardian (sections 45–61 Mental Capacity Act 2005).

It may also be worth noting that, in terms of advocacy, the Mental Capacity Act 2005 contains important provisions in that it established the role of Independent Mental Capacity Advocates (IMCAs) who have a responsibility to promote empowerment of vulnerable adults by representing their wishes, feelings, beliefs and values as well as challenging certain kinds of decisions. Examples of such decisions when an IMCA must be appointed, unless there is already an appointed advocate, are where serious medical treatment is proposed, or where there is a plan to provide or change accommodation in hospital or care home (sections 35–41 Mental Capacity Act 2005; see also Brown *et al.* (2009), Chapter 11).

Law and ethics

Activity 6.3

Consider the following question:

What ethical issues arise from using the law to protect vulnerable adults?

(Continued)

(Continued)

Comment

Considering and reflecting on some of the ethical issues that arise when steps are taken to protect vulnerable adults may have triggered a number of thoughts in your mind. These ethical issues will probably relate particularly to self-determination, reliability of vulnerable adults as witnesses, assessment of risk (and risk to whom?) and anti-oppressive practice.

What follows is a summary of some of these issues.

With regard to physical abuse, the principal concern may be the extent to which it is hidden and so, in seeking out potential abuse, the social worker may be violating some key principles. First of these is consent and the rights of an adult to resist an investigation into abuse. It may seem strange that someone would be reluctant to be protected from abuse, but don't forget that there is a possibility that the abuser is a close and normally trusted relative and someone on whom the abused person is utterly dependent. In children's cases, it is clearly legally justified to intervene whether the child consents or not. The issue with adults is quite different. Adults have rights to be informed, an entitlement to have their say as to whether an investigation proceeds and there is no equivalent of care proceedings to impose this. You can doubtless see that in many cases this poses a dilemma, especially where it is debatable whether the older person really understands the situation fully. This is particularly an issue with people with dementia. For further discussion on this, see Johns (2016, Chapter 8).

This leads on to the second ethical issue that concerns the capacity of people to give reliable evidence, which may limit the extent to which abuse can be fully investigated. This does not refer solely to the potential for court proceedings, which are rare, but rather to the wider issue of what steps can be legitimately taken and on what basis.

Extending this to the issue of compulsory intervention, matters become very problematic. Not only is there the whole ethical issue about depriving people of their fundamental rights to self-determination, there is the associated legal issue that this may well infringe their basic rights as enshrined in the European Convention on Human Rights. There is also the very real practice issue that arises in such cases – namely, will any good be achieved by forcibly removing someone from their home? Social workers need to balance the anxiety of leaving people in their own homes against the very real risk of premature death associated with forcible removal from home.

Finally, it may be worth thinking about whether, in the desire to protect vulnerable adults, social workers may inadvertently be acting oppressively. There is an underlying assumption that in pushing for the kinds of procedures outlined by the Department of Health (2016) or the Welsh Assembly Government (2016), this whole area of work is moving towards an approach that is similar to child care social work. Yet the issues are very different. We are here dealing with adults, who have absolute rights to make their own choices (Johns 2014, Chapter 5).

In cases where they are unable to give informed consent, it may not be adequate simply to assume that other people can 'take over'. Rather, what may be needed is greater clarity about the point at which someone becomes incapable of making their own decisions or managing their own affairs, and an acceptance that the extent to which people can give consent may vary.

In this respect, the Mental Capacity Act 2005 may be helpful, for it starts with a presumption that someone has capacity unless proven otherwise; that people must be supported to make their own decisions as far as is practicable; that people are entitled to make unwise decisions; but where someone else makes decisions for vulnerable adults, they must do so in their *best interests* adopting the *least restrictive* option wherever possible (sections 1–4 Mental Capacity Act 2005; Johns, 2007, 2014).

Furthermore, the Mental Capacity Act 2005 (section 37) recognises the need for Independent Mental Capacity Advocates (IMCAs) for people who have no family or friends where serious issues are being decided, which might include provision of community care services. If you practise in this area, you will know that the Act is interpreted by reference to a *Code of Practice* (Department for Constitutional Affairs, 2007); Chapter 10 of this addresses advocacy. This issue of independent advocacy was originally addressed by the Law Commission (1993), but legislation was not immediately forthcoming. Now, however, in addition to the Mental Capacity Act 2005, more comprehensive legislation has been formulated and implemented in the light of the publication of the Law Commission's more general consultation paper on safeguarding adults (Law Commission, 2010, 2011; Spencer-Lane, 2010). This legislation took the form of the Care Act 2014 (in Wales the Social Services and Well-being (Wales) Act 2014). Sections 67 and 68 Care Act 2014 (sections 181–183 Social Services and Well-being (Wales) Act 2014) are of particular relevance, as they stipulate, with certain exceptions, the involvement of independent advocates where someone has difficulty understanding, retaining, evaluating or communicating information in respect of decisions concerning matters such as, to quote the Care Act 2014 list:

- carrying out needs assessments;
- carrying out carer assessments;
- preparing or revising care and support or support plans;
- safeguarding inquiries or reviews.

Chapter summary

This chapter began with the definitions of abuse and vulnerability in the context of safeguarding adults. A distinction was made between the law concerning adult protection and that which pertains to children, although one commonality is that the local authority has a key coordinating role in both. Whereas the local authority

(Continued)

(Continued)

child safeguarding role derives from the Children Act 1989, the current arrangement draws its authority from legislation, namely sections 42-46 Care Act 2014 or Social Services and Well-being (Wales) Act 2014 Part 7, and associated statutory guidance (Department of Health 2016; Welsh Assembly Government 2016).

The chapter then went on to set out the framework for determining the extent to which people could make decisions for themselves. Essentially this is the law relating to mental capacity, where it became clear that the Mental Capacity Act 2005 has enshrined within it the principle that all adults have absolute rights to self-determination except when it can clearly be shown that they lack capacity in relation to particular decisions at particular times.

Adopting these principles and taking them forward when considering the position of adults who appear to need care but are resistant to it (our case study example), the chapter then outlined the quite specific provisions where consent could be overridden. This included a brief look at police powers under the Police and Criminal Evidence Act 1984. There then followed a discussion of mental health legislation, both in the context of authorising compulsory admission and detention of someone in hospital, and also in introducing the Deprivation of Liberty Safeguards (to be found in the amendments to section 4 and Schedule A1 of the Mental Capacity Act 2005) that may apply where someone is compelled to remain in hospital or a care home. The chapter then examined the role of the Court of Protection in protecting the most vulnerable in other circumstances, and this included reference to case law concerning safeguarding adults as well as outlining specific provision in relation to finance. This section concluded with references to some provisions in the Mental Capacity Act 2005 for independent advocacy.

In the final section, you were asked to reflect on the ethical issues that arise from using the law to protect vulnerable adults. A number of these were highlighted, concluding with a reassertion of the importance of the Mental Capacity Act 2005 principles, including the primacy of empowerment which includes rights to independent advocacy. These are bolstered by the provisions in the Care Act 2014 which introduced independent advocacy into a wider range of decision-making by local authorities.

Further reading

Brammer, A (2014) *Safeguarding adults.* Basingstoke: Palgrave.

General guide to social work practice in the areas covered by this and the previous chapter.

Johns, R (2014) *Capacity and autonomy.* Basingstoke: Palgrave.

Guide to social work practice in the areas covered by this chapter and also incorporating issues of capacity and autonomy in relation to children and young people.

Williams, J (2002) Public law protection of vulnerable adults: The debate continues, so does the abuse. *Journal of Social Work*, 2(3): 293–316.

This article argues the case for a new kind of legislation to protect vulnerable adults. It connects this to the Human Rights Act 1998, suggesting that the European Convention on Human Rights poses an obligation on the government to protect vulnerable adults. Includes international comparisons.

Websites

Court of Protection: www.gov.uk/courts-tribunals/court-of-protection

Crown Prosecution Service initiative on vulnerable witnesses and victims of crime: www.cps.gov.uk/victims_witnesses/index.html

Disability Rights: www.direct.gov.uk/en/DisabledPeople/index.htm

Legislation: www.legislation.gov.uk/ukpga

Office of the Public Guardian: www.gov.uk/office-of-public-guardian

SCIE guidance on adult safeguarding: www.scie.org.uk/adults/safeguarding/index.asp

7: Youth Justice

Achieving a social work degree

This chapter will help you to develop the following capabilities from the **Professional Capabilities Framework:**

4. Rights, justice and economic well-being

Advance human rights and promote social justice and economic well-being.

5. Knowledge

Apply knowledge of social sciences, law and social work practice theory.

7. Intervention and skills

Use judgement and authority to intervene with individuals, families and communities to promote independence, provide support and prevent harm, neglect and abuse.

It is relevant to the following Standards of Proficiency:

2.   Be able to practise within the legal and ethical boundaries of their profession.
7.   Be able to maintain confidentiality.
10. Be able to maintain records appropriately.

It will also introduce you to the following standards as set out in the 2016 Social Work Subject Benchmark Statement:

5.5 viii   the importance of Social Work's contribution to intervention across service user groups, settings and levels in terms of the profession's focus on social justice, human rights, social cohesion, collective responsibility and respect for diversities;

5.6 vi	the significance of legislative and legal frameworks and service delivery standards, including on core social work values and ethics in the delivery of services which support, enable and empower;
5.3 vi	the complex relationships between justice, care and control in social welfare and the practical and ethical implications of these;
5.6 vi	the significance of legislative and legal frameworks and service delivery standards.

Introduction

In England and Wales, social workers play an important part in the youth justice system. Many of them are members of multidisciplinary teams, generally called Youth Offending Teams, which have a key role in preventing offences being committed by young people, writing reports on offenders, implementing various court orders, and supervising offenders on their discharge from custody. In Scotland and Northern Ireland, social workers are potentially involved in the entire criminal justice system, including work with adults and adult mentally disordered offenders. The reason for this is historical: there has never been a separate probation service in Scotland, whereas in England and Wales (and Northern Ireland) the probation service has been run as an entirely separate enterprise. Because probation training in England and Wales is now so very different from social work training, it has been decided not to include work with adult offenders in this book. Therefore, the focus in this chapter is exclusively on social work with young people who are likely to commit, or have committed, criminal offences (*offending behaviour*).

The local authority has a key role in youth justice co-ordinating and managing multidisciplinary teams of workers, drawn from the police, probation, education and social work, and these teams are seen as the linchpin of the whole system (section 38 Crime and Disorder Act 1998 as amended by various subsequent Acts including Criminal Justice and Immigration Act 2008, Legal Aid, Sentencing and Punishment of Offenders Act 2012 and Crime and Courts Act 2013). This area of social work attracts people who want to work alongside colleagues from other professions in order to help young people become law-abiding citizens and make a positive contribution to society. Youth justice social workers need the skills and knowledge that enable them to work under the direction of the criminal justice and court system in implementing a whole number of court orders. There are separate National Standards for those who work within the youth justice system issued by the Youth Justice Board (Youth Justice Board, 2013). The principal aim of the youth justice system is to prevent offending by children and young people (Youth Justice Board, 2013, p5). When Youth Offending Teams were first introduced, the national objectives for Youth Offending Teams and the youth justice system generally were declared by the government department then responsible (Home Office, 2001) to be:

- the swift administration of justice so that every young person accused of breaking the law has the matter resolved without delay;

- confronting young offenders with the consequences of their offending for themselves and their family, their victims and the community, and helping them develop a sense of personal responsibility;

- interventions which tackle the particular factors that put a young person at risk of offending and which strengthen 'protective factors';

- punishment proportionate to the seriousness and persistence of offending;

- encouraging reparation to victims by young offenders;

- reinforcing the responsibilities of parents.

Rather than just summarise the way the youth justice system puts these ambitions into effect, this chapter will offer a number of short case scenarios that demonstrate the ways in which youth justice social workers operate under the various pieces of legislation. The chapter addresses the following areas:

- preventing crime;

- arrest and bail;

- dealing with first offenders;

- youth community orders (community sentences);

- special kinds of orders.

The chapter concludes with an invitation for you to research user perspectives on the way the criminal justice system operates.

Preventing crime

Every local authority must work towards the reduction of crime and disorder, and to that end produce an annual youth justice plan (section 40 Crime and Disorder Act 1998). The emphasis on preventing crime is made explicit by section 37 of the Crime and Disorder Act 1998, which talks about preventing *offending by children and young persons*. Yet at the same time courts with whom Youth Offending Teams work must pay attention to the welfare needs of the child (section 44 Children and Young Persons Act 1933). The purpose of sentencing in youth courts is the punishment, reform and rehabilitation of offenders, protection of the public and offenders making reparation (section 9(1) Criminal Justice and Immigration Act 2008).

There is also the requirement to act fairly, which is not just a requirement on the Youth Justice Board, whose task is to oversee the national scheme of Youth Offending Teams, but is also a general duty in relation to race for most public bodies (Equality Act 2010). Section 95 Criminal Justice Act 1991 refers to the duty of those involved in the criminal justice system to avoid discriminating against anyone *on the ground of race or sex or any other improper ground*.

All of this argues powerfully for awareness of equality issues and incorporation of social work's anti-discriminatory practice values into the work of Youth Offending Teams. The inclusion of social workers in Youth Offending Teams is also essential since they provide the link into other areas of local authority social work with children and families, a connection originally strengthened by the Department of Health's Quality Protects Programme (Department of Health, 2000a). This established policy objectives for improving the care of 'looked after' children, including a reduction in their offending rate.

Case study

Family X are generally regarded in their neighbourhood as the 'family from hell'. What particularly irks the neighbours is the fact that the younger children in the family – Terry aged 9 and Jack aged 8 – are often seen engaging in acts of serious vandalism, such as breaking windows in people's homes and throwing stones at passing cars.

Terry and Jack are under the age of criminal responsibility, which in England and Wales is 10. The law assumes that only when children attain this age are they able to distinguish between right and wrong. However, the law now assumes that on their tenth birthdays all children can distinguish between what is lawful and what is criminal (the Crime and Disorder Act 1998 abolished the notion of *doli incapax* whereby the prosecution had to prove that children under 14 knew the difference between right and wrong).

So if they cannot be prosecuted for committing criminal offences, can anything be done? The Crime and Disorder Act 1998 introduced some novel, but so far comparatively rarely used, provisions. Section 11 of the Act refers to child safety orders for which the local authority can apply in the Family Proceedings Courts (different kinds of courts are covered in the next chapter). One of the grounds is that an act has been committed that would have been an offence had the child been ten or over (another is that the child has acted in a manner that caused or was likely to cause harassment, alarm or distress). Note, however, that the civil rather than criminal degree of proof (*balance of probabilities* as opposed to *beyond reasonable doubt*) applies to the offence allegation. The purpose of the child safety order is to enforce supervision for up to 12 months (section 60 Children Act 2004) with requirements such as avoiding certain places or attending special assessment sessions to address offending behaviour.

> ## Case study
>
> It is now two years later. Terry and Jack are therefore aged 11 and 10 respectively. Their behaviour still causes a great deal of concern and anguish.

A number of different courses of action could be taken.

For comparatively low-level anti-social behaviour, an acceptable behaviour contract could be drawn up by the Youth Offending Team, whereby the two boys (and their parents) agreed to stop the nuisance behaviour and address neighbours' concerns. If this failed, or if the anti-social behaviour were more serious, the local council, the police or a housing provider among others could apply for an Injunction for a maximum of 12 months (section 5 Anti-Social Behaviour, Crime and Policing Act 2014). The local youth offending team should be consulted about the intention to apply for such orders (section 14). The grounds for the order centre on actual or likely harassment, alarm or distress, nuisance or annoyance at residential premises, or 'housing-related nuisance or annoyance' (section 1) although clearly it ought not to derive solely from the fact that people have different cultural norms. ASBOs were rarely used when they were first introduced in 1998, and there were doubts as to whether they would conform to the European Convention on Human Rights. However, their operation was recently strengthened by the Anti-Social Behaviour, Crime and Policing Act 2014 which provides for both Injunctions and Criminal Behaviour Orders, the latter applicable where an offender is convicted of an offence and the behaviour *caused or was likely to cause harassment, alarm or distress to any person* (section 22 Anti-Social Behaviour, Crime and Policing Act 2014). Criminal Behaviour Orders last for a minimum of one year and a maximum of three (section 25). Breaching such orders is a criminal offence.

Where children are subject to child safety orders, orders under the Anti-Social Behaviour, Crime and Policing Act 2014 or convicted of an offence, the court may also order parents to attend guidance sessions (maximum 12 months) (parenting orders), providing such sessions exist in their area (section 8 Crime and Disorder Act 1998). Under sections 23–25 of the Police and Justice Act 2006, it is possible for local authorities and registered social landlords to enter into parenting contracts and apply for parenting orders.

If there is a wider problem with the behaviour of children in general in an area that has led to people feeling intimidated, harassed, alarmed or distressed, it is possible for a police officer to order their dispersal and prohibit those who do not live in their area from returning within the following 48 hours (section 35 Anti-Social Behaviour, Crime and Policing Act 2014).

Arrest and bail

Because of the piecemeal development of legislation, these procedures apply mainly to young people under 17, whereas the jurisdiction of the Youth Courts and sentences for young offenders apply up to age 18. However, in 2013 a significant number of provisions that used to apply only to 10- to 16-year-olds were extended to include those aged 17.

Case study

Samantha, aged 15, decides to take the day off school and go shopping or, rather, for the first time in her life, shoplifting. She is caught by a store detective stealing a couple of items of clothing. The police are called. She is arrested and taken to the police station.

When someone like Samantha who is aged 10 to 17 is arrested by the police, the Police and Criminal Evidence Act 1984 Code of Practice (Code C, Home Office, 2014) says they should normally be interviewed about that offence in the presence of an *appropriate adult*. Most often this will be a parent, but where the local authority *accommodates* the young person, it could be their own social worker. In some cases the Youth Offending Team will be asked to perform this function since provision of *appropriate adults* is one of their official functions. There is also a national network of volunteer appropriate adults (see their website at the end of the chapter). The requirements of the role are set out in the Code established by section 66 Police and Criminal Evidence Act 1984 as amended by the Serious Organised Crime and Police Act 2005. Specific training is needed to undertake this task, so it is not covered in detail here (it is comprehensively covered in Brayne *et al.*, 2015, Chapter 10 and Brammer, 2015, Chapter 13). Suffice to say that appropriate adults are not legal advisers, and those arrested have additional rights to have solicitors present when being interviewed.

Once Samantha has been arrested and interviewed in the presence of the appropriate adult, what happens next? Assuming that the police think that there is enough evidence that Samantha committed the offence, they have a number of options.

The police have discretion to caution for an offence that is admitted. This is an official 'Youth Caution' that is recorded (these have now replaced reprimands and warnings under the Crime and Disorder Act 1998). There is no limit to the number of Youth Cautions that can be given, even if the young person has previously been convicted of an offence, although they will automatically be referred to the Youth Offending Team who, in the case of a second Youth Caution, must assess and offer a voluntary rehabilitation programme, unless they consider this inappropriate. Under-17s must receive their Youth Caution in the presence of an appropriate adult (sections 136–8 Legal Aid, Sentencing and Punishment of Offenders Act 2012). Where a young person has previously been convicted of an offence, the police could administer a Youth Conditional Caution which has implications for a court later imposing a conditional discharge for a subsequent offence and for the prosecution to refer to non-co-operation in their trial (section 135).

If the police decide to charge someone with an offence, they then have to decide what should happen before the person appears in court. The Bail Act 1976 (section 4) indicates that there

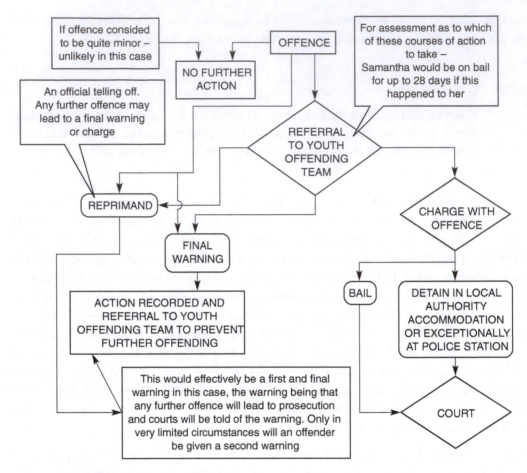

Figure 7.1 What happens after an arrest?

should always be a presumption in favour of someone being bailed rather than held in custody and, naturally, there are additional safeguards in relation to young people. The expectation is that the young person would be bailed unconditionally – that is, simply told to report to the court on a particular date and time without having any specific conditions imposed in the meantime. If it appears likely that a young offender would not do this, or might commit further offences, or interfere with witnesses, or has previously breached bail conditions, or 'needs' protection or welfare, bail can be refused (section 38 Police and Criminal Evidence Act 1984). In these cases young people would generally be remanded to local authority accommodation, thereby becoming a 'looked after' child. Occasionally, the police may detain a young person in their custody overnight, but must then bring them before the next available court and explain their reasons for doing so to the court.

When someone appears in court for the first time, the court must either hear the case or adjourn it until it can be heard. During the adjournment, the offender will usually be bailed, either with or without conditions. Courts have some specific bail options available for young people. They may be so concerned about their welfare that they think that at this stage there should be some support and advice offered, and for this reason one of the functions of the Youth Offending Team is to offer a bail support scheme. These are not always run by the teams themselves, but may be projects run by social workers within a local authority or through voluntary agencies. You may be interested to look at some of the research into Bail Supervision and Support schemes in England and Wales. Here are some very brief key points from the evaluation published by the Youth Justice Board for England and Wales (2005).

Practical example 1

Bail Supervision and Support schemes

Nacro Cymru analysed 11,393 records of young people referred to or receiving services [.]. Of referrals to schemes, 89 per cent were male and 11 per cent female. Seventeen-year-old males made up the biggest single group of young people at 32 per cent, and 79 per cent of referrals were identified as White British.

The length of programmes varied, depending on the seriousness and complications of the case and the working of courts in the area. The majority of bail programmes were for four weeks or less (55 per cent), making any long-term change in the young person's circumstances difficult to achieve.

Some 55 per cent fully complied with their bail supervision programme. These were identified as young people who had not reoffended (measured in terms of arrest and charge) or been reported to the police as being in breach of their bail supervision programme or any other bail condition. In addition, they would have attended all court appearances during the bail supervision period. The main reason for young people not complying was a breach of the requirement to report to a Bail Supervision and Support scheme.

Schemes found that the lack of suitable accommodation was a significant problem, and they made persistent efforts to address the issue.

You might care to reflect on some of these research findings, especially this last point.

Bail Supervision and Support applies to 10- to 17-year-olds. For all those under 18, an alternative would be for the young person to be remanded. Remands would normally be to local authority accommodation although, if the circumstances warrant it, the court could remand to 'youth detention accommodation', the term now used to denote all forms of custody (section 91 Legal Aid, Sentencing and Punishment of Offenders Act 2012). In the case of local authority accommodation, the court decides which local authority is to take responsibility and that local authority must accept the child or young person (section 92) and arrange suitable accommodation as required by section 22C Children Act 1989. The court can forbid the child residing with a named individual and can impose various conditions including electronic monitoring (sections 93–95). In the case of youth detention accommodation, for a first remand there are conditions relating to the offence (violent, sexual or grave crime) and 'necessity' (only adequate means of protecting public from death or serious personal injury or prevent commission of imprisonable offences) (section 98). In the case of a second remand, the offence condition does not apply, but there are conditions in relation to necessity, the real prospect of receiving a custodial sentence, and absconding (section 99).

Not surprisingly, holding young people in this stage in custody before trial is quite controversial. A number of campaigns have been mounted to remove the possibility of under-18s being held in custody at all, with a number of issues raised concerning the use of custody for under-18s, especially children (under-14s).

Practical example 2

In 2009/10 13 per cent of the child custodial population had been imprisoned primarily for breach of a statutory order. For 9 per cent of the children in custody, breach was the only reason. More children and teenagers are imprisoned for breach than for burglary. One in six 10- to 14-year-olds in custody last year was imprisoned primarily for breach. A greater propor-tion of girls and younger children are in custody for breach than older boys, despite the fact that they are less likely to commit breach offences. Nearly three-quarters of 10- to 14-year-olds given an ASBO end up breaching it. In eight of the 32 criminal justice areas that have issued ASBOs to 10- to 11-year-olds, all of them have been breached. Guidance for Youth Offending Team Practitioners states that children and teenagers who miss three appointments should be sent back to court. There is an expectation that all ASBO breaches will be prosecuted, regard-less of the circumstances, and practitioners are not generally aware that there are alternatives.

(Prison Reform Trust extracts from Hart, 2011, ppv–vii)

There must be a concerted effort to reduce the number of children who are remanded to prison. In many cases these young people are very vulnerable and more of a risk to them-selves than the public. What they need is intensive support within clear boundaries to stay out of trouble – not a prison sentence.

Enver Soloman, Children's Society's Director of Policy,
20 January 2011 (Children's Society, 2011)

Dealing with first offenders

More accurately this section should perhaps be entitled 'first-time offenders' or even 'first time in court offenders', for, as has been explained, offences may have already resulted in a reprimand or some other action by the police or Youth Offending Team.

The Powers of Criminal Courts (Sentencing) Act 2000 (section 16) required the Youth Court to make a 'referral order' on first-time offenders who pleaded guilty, but courts now have discretion as an alternative to award a conditional discharge (section 79 Legal Aid, Sentencing and Punishment of Offenders Act 2012). There is no restriction on making further referral orders for subsequent offences, if the court considers this appropriate. The Criminal Justice Act 2003 (Schedule 34 as amended) allows a parenting order to run alongside a referral order where this is appropriate. The referral order system was established by the Youth Justice and Criminal Evidence Act 1999 and implemented nationwide in 2002. This diverts the offender from the court to a youth offender panel which consists of one Youth Offending Team member and two other people drawn from the community, usually volunteers. This panel should negotiate a contract which lasts for as long as is specified by the court, but not less than 3 months and no more than 12. The panel is less formal than the court and aims to discuss in depth with the offender and their family why they are in trouble and what steps can be taken to put right what they did wrong and to prevent further offences. In this process, social worker involvement is important in terms of assessment and putting into effect the panel's decision, but the professional role remains advisory and Youth Offending Team members do not participate in decision-making. There would normally be a minimum of three meetings. The involvement of the victim, if there is one, is expected although whether the victim actually attends the panel is, of course, entirely a matter for them. Reparation is a key consideration and the referral panel system is based on the principles of restorative justice, although not without its critics (see Further reading and References).

Failure to co-operate with the Youth Offender Panel may mean that the matter is referred back to the Youth Court. The Youth Court then has powers to revoke the order if they wish and sentence the young person for the original offence.

After the first offence

If the young person admits the offence, or is found guilty, the court will request a pre-sentence report before deciding what sentence to impose. If they intend to consider only one particular sentence, they may ask for a *specific sentence report* which follows the same format – this procedure is sometimes used for Action Plan Orders or Reparation Orders.

National Standards currently expect the reports to be submitted within 15 working days and to be based on a standard assessment tool (Youth Justice Board, 2013, section 4). The report advises the court about the young person's offending behaviour and action that can be taken to reduce reoffending. The key part of the reports makes a proposal regarding the sentence, or alternatively indicates which sentences would not be suitable. The final decision obviously rests with the court.

Case study

Damien, aged 17, borrowed his mate's moped and rode it on a public road despite the fact that he knew he had no insurance. He had an accident on his fateful journey and damaged both the bike and a neighbour's car. This is his second bike-related offence.

There would be a number of options for the Youth Court to consider in Damien's case. An absolute discharge, which effectively means no penalty and is used for very minor offences, would clearly not be appropriate. Unless certain specified conditions apply (as stipulated in section 135 Legal Aid, Sentencing and Punishment of Offenders Act 2012) the court could make a conditional discharge which simply means that if the offence is committed again within a fixed period of time (up to three years) the offender will be resentenced for the current offence as well as being punished for the new offence. A fine may be imposed – probably a hefty fine in this case as driving without insurance is regarded as a serious offence because of the potential consequences. Fines may be imposed on the parent or young person. Compensation for the damage may be awarded, here presumably for the damage to the neighbour's car, which the offender pays as a penalty. Probably not appropriate in this case, the court may in some circumstances make a reparation order. Exactly what this comprises is determined by the court on the advice of the social worker or Youth Offending Team member, but may not exceed 24 hours and must be completed within three months of making the order (section 74 Powers of Criminal Courts (Sentencing) Act 2000 as amended).

Activity 7.1

Answer the following questions.

- In what kinds of circumstances do you think a reparation order would be appropriate?
- What kinds of things could be done by means of reparation?

Comment

The answer to the first question is for any kind of offence where there is clearly a victim, and where doing something, rather than paying something, seems an appropriate way of making it up to the victim. Appropriate activities might include gardening or household chores, decorating, repair work or anything that is going to be of clear tangible benefit to the victim, but obviously not something that would be exploitative. There are plainly some circumstances where reparation would not be appropriate – for example, where the victim cannot tolerate coming face-to-face with the offender.

Youth rehabilitation orders

Case study

Tom, aged 15, has committed his third offence of taking and driving away. As he is underage, he is charged with the associated offences of driving while disqualified through age and without insurance.

The orders that we have been discussing so far do not require a preliminary assessment of seriousness. However, we are now moving up the scale and in this section consider the key generic measure introduced by the Criminal Justice and Immigration Act 2008, Youth Rehabilitation Orders, which apply where offences are 'serious enough' to merit them (section 1 Criminal Justice and Immigration Act 2008).

Youth Rehabilitation Orders last for a maximum of three years, although they can be extended once for up to six months to allow for completion of the requirements (Schedules 1 and 2 Criminal Justice and Immigration Act 2008 as amended by sections 83–4 Legal Aid, Sentencing and Punishment of Offenders Act 2012). Youth Rehabilitation Orders comprise one or more of the requirements below, but do note that only some combinations make sense. In reality no young offender is going to have all of them imposed, and there are rules about sentences for *two or more associated offences on the same sentencing occasion* to disallow certain combinations and ensure that overall maxima are not exceeded (Youth Justice Board, 2010, p11).

The Youth Rehabilitation Orders requirements, which unless stipulated otherwise can last up to the full duration of the Youth Rehabilitation Order, are as follows.

- *Activity Requirement* It is not actually specified by regulation as to what this might be but can include residential activity. Requirements can be made for any number of days up to an aggregate of 90 (Schedule 1 Part 2 Requirements paragraph 6).

- *Supervision Requirement* Offender has to attend appointments with *responsible officer* or person nominated by *responsible officer* (Schedule 1 Part 2 Requirements paragraph 9).

- *Unpaid Work Requirement* For 16- to 17-year-olds only. Minimum of 40 hours, maximum 240 to be completed within 12-month period (Schedule 1 Part 2 Requirements paragraph 10).

- *Programme Requirement* Very similar to Activity Requirement except that it relates to *a systematic set of activities* which are not actually specified although it is stipulated that they can include residential activities (Schedule 1 Part 2 Requirements paragraph 11).

- *Attendance Centre Requirement* Must attend centre for hours stipulated in order, exact arrangements of those hours decided by the centre. Maximum number depends on age:

12 for under-14s, between 12 and 24 for 14- to 15-year-olds, and 12–36 hours for those aged 16 or above (Schedule 1 Part 2 Requirements paragraph 12).

- *Prohibited Activity Requirement* Offender must *refrain from participating in activities* which may include carrying or possessing firearms (Schedule 1 Part 2 Requirements paragraph 13).

- *Curfew Requirement* This may cover different places and different times each day. The requirement can stipulate up to 16 hours per day for a maximum of 12 months (section 81 Legal Aid, Sentencing and Punishment of Offenders Act 2012).

- *Exclusion Requirement* Prohibits entry to specified place. Requirement can last up to three months (Schedule 1 Part 2 Requirements paragraph 15).

- *Residence Requirement* Can stipulate that young person resides with a specific individual or at a specified place. Applies to offenders aged 16 or above only (Schedule 1 Part 2 Requirements paragraph 16).

- *Local Authority Residence Requirement* Requires residence in local authority accommodation, and can prohibit residence with people specified in order. Maximum six months or until age 18, whichever is the sooner (Schedule 1 Part 2 Requirements paragraph 17).

- *Mental Health Treatment Requirement* Applies only where recommended by doctors and can include in-patient and out-patient treatment and certain other criteria apply such as not qualifying for compulsory admission under the Mental Health Act 1983 (Schedule 1 Part 2 Requirements paragraph 20).

- *Drug Treatment Requirement* Applies only where there is evidence of addiction. Has to be recommended by doctors and can include in-patient and out-patient treatment (Schedule 1 Part 2 Requirements paragraph 22). Offender must consent.

- *Drug Testing Requirement* Can require submission to tests on a regular basis. Order must be quite specific as to numbers of tests and has to run alongside Drug Treatment Requirement (Schedule 1 Part 2 Requirements paragraph 23).

- *Intoxicating Substance Treatment Requirement* Applies only where there is evidence of addiction or misuse of intoxicating substances. Can include in-patient and out-patient treatment (Schedule 1 Part 2 Requirements paragraph 24). Requires offender consent.

- *Education Requirement* Requires compliance with *approved education arrangements* which must include local authority approval. Terminates automatically on attainment of school leaving age (Schedule 1 Part 2 Requirements paragraph 25).

There are certain other requirements that can be made where certain legal criteria are fulfilled (section 1 (4) Criminal Justice and Immigration Act 2008). These further requirements are as follows.

- *Electronic Monitoring* Offender must submit to electronic monitoring which has to be under the supervision of *responsible officer* (Schedule 1 Part 2 Requirements paragraph 26).

- *Intensive Supervision and Surveillance* Includes a *mixture of punishment and opportunities* incorporating education, training or employment, restorative justice, addressing offending behaviour, family support and interpersonal skills development (Youth Justice Board, 2010; Criminal Justice and Immigration Act 2008 Schedule 1 Part 2 Requirements paragraph 3).

- *Intensive Fostering* Requires residence with a local authority foster carer. Lasts maximum of 12 months (Schedule 1 Part 2 Requirements paragraph 18). Note that this is incompatible with Intensive Supervision and Surveillance so cannot run alongside it.

Parenting orders

Courts have powers to make parenting orders in a number of different circumstances. Principally, these are where courts have passed sentences on the young people themselves, but can include cases where students are excluded from school (section 20 Anti-Social Behaviour Act 2003 as amended, section 24 Police and Justice Act 2006), fail to attend school (section 41 Education and Skills Act 2008) or cases where child safety orders have been made (section 8 Crime and Disorder Act 1998 as amended, Schedule 34 Criminal Justice Act 2003). Generally, orders may be made for up to 12 months (section 18 Anti-Social Behaviour Act 2003, section 60 Children Act 2004).

Parenting Orders will normally oblige parents or carers to attend counselling or guidance sessions with the aim of helping parents to improve their child or young person's behaviour, including school attendance. Orders may have conditions included such as attending school meetings, requiring the parent to ensure that their child or young person is at home at particular times, or does not visit certain places unsupervised.

Parenting Orders do not count as criminal convictions against the parent or carer but breaching them is an offence.

Custody

Case study

Neil, aged 16, has just been convicted of his third offence of burglary. He has previous convictions for receiving stolen goods and for robbing another boy of his mobile phone. The present offence was committed with his brother who is aged 22.

First, it may not be the Youth Court that hears his case since, if his offence was committed with an adult, the magistrates' court would have to consider where the case should be heard, bearing in mind that it is never possible for an adult to be tried in a Youth Court. So one outcome may be that the young person is tried in an adult court. Nevertheless, the principle is that the young person's case should be remitted to the Youth Court whenever possible.

In this case, Neil can consider himself very fortunate since if he were an adult and convicted of a third offence of burglary, he would automatically receive a sentence of three years' imprisonment (section 111 Powers of Criminal Courts (Sentencing) Act 2000). As it is, he is at serious risk of receiving a custodial sentence. The Criminal Justice Act 1991 requires courts to decide that such an offence is so serious that only a custodial sentence is appropriate and this is highly likely in this case.

For young people the primary custodial sentence is the Detention and Training Order, for which the minimum age is 12. These orders can only be passed on 12- to 14-year-olds where they are deemed to be persistent young offenders (section 100 Powers of Criminal Courts (Sentencing) Act 2000). Detention and training are intended to run together in the sense that shortly after admission to custody a planning meeting is held. This involves the Youth Offending Team as well as the offender, parents and custodial establishment. Supervision of the training elements then continues in the community, once the offender has served half the period of the order in custody. The orders can be made for specific periods of 4, 6, 8, 10, 12, 18 or 24 months (sections 102–107 Powers of Criminal Courts (Sentencing) Act 2000; section 80 Legal Aid, Sentencing and Punishment of Offenders Act 2012).

For the most serious cases of all, special provision is now made through the Powers of Criminal Courts (Sentencing) Act 2000 and Legal Aid, Sentencing and Punishment of Offenders Act 2012. Young people who commit murder are detained *at Her Majesty's pleasure* (Section 90 Powers of Criminal Courts (Sentencing) Act 2000), meaning for at least a minimum period and then only when the parole board says they can be discharged into the community (under licence). For other *grave* offences, for which an adult could be sent to prison for 14 years or more, the young offender can be detained up to a maximum period laid down for that offence, which might mean life (Section 91). In both cases the young person will be held in a secure unit at the age of 15, being transferred at that age to a Young Offender Institution and then to an adult prison at the age of 18. This is the procedure (under previous legislation) that applied to the young men convicted of the murder of James Bulger in 1993. The Legal Aid, Sentencing and Punishment of Offenders Act 2012 (sections 123–5) replaced provision for public protection detention under the Criminal Justice Act 2003 with 'extended sentences' for certain serious offences (but not those grave offences to which section 91 might apply). These provisions apply where there would be 'serious risk' to the public by further offences being committed and courts want to impose a sentence of four years or more. The young person serves two-thirds of the sentence before being released on extended licence (up to five years for violent offences, eight years for sexual offences).

Special kinds of orders

Just to complete the picture, there are three other kinds of orders that can be made, some of which will apply to young offenders very occasionally (note that drug treatment and testing orders and Intensive Supervision and Surveillance Programmes that used to come into this category have now been incorporated into Youth Rehabilitation Orders).

First, parents of young offenders can be bound over to ensure they comply with community sentences and in order to prevent further offences. Binding over means that parents undertake to exercise proper care and control, and can be required to pay up to £1,000 if there are further offences or failure to comply with the requirements of the community sentences (section 150 Powers of Criminal Court (Sentencing) Act 2000).

Second, a hospital order applies to people who have a form of mental disorder and where the circumstances warrant it (Chapter 6 made reference to the definitions of mental disorder). There is no lower age limit for most disorders, so potentially hospital orders could apply to a young offender. Hence, social workers working in the field of mental health and youth justice would need to know more about this provision and how it relates to supervision in the community after discharge (comprehensively covered in Jones, 2016).

Finally, there is a Sexual Harm Prevention Order, which is not itself a penalty, but can be made by courts where there is reasonable cause to believe that someone (of any age) who has previously been convicted of a sexual offence poses a risk to the public (Part 2 Sexual Offences Act 2003 as amended by Anti-Social Behaviour, Crime and Policing Act 2014). Alongside this preventive measure that applies to convicted offenders, section 113 of the Anti-Social Behaviour, Crime and Policing Act 2014 allows courts to make a civil order, a sexual risk order, against an adult who engages in sexually related activities which, while not themselves being offences, demonstrate that they pose a risk of harm to children. Applications for these orders and their implementation are primarily police matters, but clearly social workers and teachers ought to be aware of these potential ways of protecting children attending schools and organised activities. It may be worth noting in passing that young people who are convicted of certain sexual offences are, like adults, obliged to have their names entered on the sex offenders register, although for half the period of time for which the adult is required to register (section 82 Sexual Offences Act 2003). This register, established by the Sex Offenders Act 1997, is maintained by the police and includes basic information such as name, date of birth and address. Parents of young sex offenders are required to ensure that the offender registers and reports as required (section 89 Sexual Offences Act 2003).

Experiencing the youth justice system

In this section, you are asked to find out about the experience of users of the youth justice system. Here we include victims of crime as well as those who commit offences and are therefore on the 'receiving end' of youth justice.

Activity 7.2

Find out what you can about one of the following topics:

- the experience of young people as victims of crime; or
- young offenders' views of their own experience of youth justice.

Comment

It is up to you to decide how to set about this task, but if you need help there are some suggestions in the Exercise Answers, p190.

It is also up to you to decide how long you want to spend on this exercise. You may even wish to develop it into a mini project if this fits in with the requirements of your social work programme.

Apart from developing your research skills, the purpose of the exercise was to get you in touch with the views, reactions and feelings of people who experience the youth justice system. If you tackled the question on victims, you will no doubt have discovered that little attention, relatively speaking, has been paid to the experience of young people as victims of crime. It sometimes comes as a surprise to older people to discover that young people are disproportionately more likely to be the victims of crime. If you attempted the question on young offenders' experiences, you will have encountered a range of responses, with very varied degrees of acceptance of personal responsibility for offences committed.

On the basis of this research, you may care to consider the implications for practice. Should more attention be paid to the needs of victims of crime, especially younger victims? Should court sentencing pay greater attention to individual differences among offenders? What exactly should the role of the social worker be in the youth justice system and how should they balance the needs of victims and offenders?

Chapter summary

In this chapter, we used a variety of case studies to explain the role of the social worker in the youth justice system. We started with the prevention of crime, the central role of local authorities in running multi-professional Youth Offending Teams, and anti-social behaviour orders as preventative measures. We then went on to look at what happens when an alleged offender is arrested and bailed or detained. This led to a consideration of the first stage of court proceedings when an offender receives their first conviction. We then proceeded through the tariffs for subsequent offences, looking at the various kinds of community sentences and custody, with additional reference to certain kinds of special orders available in particular circumstances. We concluded with a very small-scale research assignment that asked you to investigate either the experience of young people as victims of crime or the experience of young offenders who have experienced the youth justice system at first hand.

Finally, if you decide to work in this area, you will need to keep very alert to new developments as this is one area of social work where there is a great deal of political interest, and where governments are always seeking to make an impact. For example, despite the fact that the Criminal Justice and Immigration Act 2008 was only implemented in late 2009 the government elected in 2010 issued proposals to place much greater emphasis on payback to victims, on payment by results, and on devolving more responsibility to local communities for preventing and tackling youth offending (Ministry of Justice, 2010, p12). These were implemented to a significant extent by the Legal Aid, Sentencing and Punishment of Offenders Act 2012. Thankfully, the original plan to abolish the Youth Justice Board was rescinded, yet there are debates about changes to the way in which youth justice services are delivered in order to move towards local integrated services (Ministry of Justice, 2013b).

Further reading

For the background to youth justice and practice issues not covered in depth here, it would be useful to look at the following.

Home Office (2015) *Guidance on Part 2 of the Sexual Offences Act 2003.* London: The Stationery Office.

Ministry of Justice (2009) *Referral orders and youth offender panels: Guidance for the courts, youth offending teams and youth offender panels.* London: Ministry of Justice.

Pickford, J and Dugmore, P (2012) *Youth justice and social work* (2nd edn). London: Sage.

Stephenson, M, Giller, H and Brown, S (2010) *Effective practice in youth justice* (2nd edn). London: Routledge.

Youth Justice Board (2010) *The youth rehabilitation order and other youth justice provisions of the Criminal Justice and Immigration Act 2008.* London: Youth Justice Board.

Websites

Home Office: www.gov.uk/government/organisations/home-office

Ministry of Justice (which now includes what used to be on the website of the Youth Justice Board aimed at practitioners): www.gov.uk/government/organisations/youth-justice-board-for-england-and-wales

National Appropriate Adult Network: www.appropriateadult.org.uk

For further information on the Children's Society work in youth justice, see: www.childrenssociety.org.uk

8: Ending up in Court

Achieving a social work degree

This chapter will help you to develop the following capabilities from the **Professional Capabilities Framework:**

4. **Rights, justice and economic well-being**

   Advance human rights and promote social justice and economic well-being.

5. **Knowledge**

   Apply knowledge of social sciences, law and social work practice theory.

7. **Critical reflection and analysis**

   Apply critical reflection and analysis to inform and provide a rationale for professional decision-making.

8. **Contexts and organisations**

   Operate effectively within multi-agency and interprofessional settings.

It is relevant to the following Standards of Proficiency:

2. Be able to practise within the legal and ethical boundaries of their profession.
6. Be able to practise in a non-discriminatory manner.
7. Be able to maintain confidentiality.
8. Be able to communicate effectively.
10. Be able to maintain records appropriately.

It will also introduce you to the following standards as set out in the 2016 Social Work Subject Benchmark Statement:

5.3 vi   the complex relationships between justice, care and control in social welfare and the practical and ethical implications of these;

5.6 vi   the significance of legislative and legal frameworks and service delivery standards.

Introduction

This chapter applies the law in a very practical way by looking at what happens when cases end up in court.

The comparatively lengthy list of Standards of Proficiency above indicates how central court working is to some aspects of social work. Social work often involves making major decisions that can have far-reaching consequences for families. It is only right and proper that there should be a strong measure of public accountability – public in this case meaning through the system of public law and procedures authorised by Parliament, not through the press and publicity as such.

Why is the court so important as a forum for decision-making in social work?

Have a go at answering this question yourself.

Activity 8.1

Working on your own or in conjunction with other students or colleagues, what reasons can you suggest as to why it is important for social workers to be accountable to the court? List as many reasons as you can in about ten minutes.

Comment

There are eight reasons highlighted below, but this list is by no means exhaustive and you may have suggested other equally valid reasons not listed here. However, your reasons should have included something on people's rights to have crucial decisions on their lives reviewed by an independent body.

Accountability to the courts is important because:

- The courts are independent of social services departments, children's services authorities and other agencies that employ social workers.

- This offers service users a means of challenging decisions social workers make, and offers social workers an independent view on the appropriateness of their plans.

- Courts bring everything out into the open, and all information has to be shared. This may offer people opportunities to obtain information which they think is important.

- Courts implement the law, and social workers must operate within the law. If necessary, courts can tell social workers that what they are doing is not legally justifiable.

- People are represented in court through solicitors or barristers, and this gives them an opportunity for advocacy through which assessments, plans and decisions can be tested or challenged.

- As a matter of principle, it seems appropriate that major life-changing decisions ought to be confirmed by a credible body that offers independent scrutiny.

- Important decisions about people's lives are shared with other professionals (lawyers) and validated or confirmed by an independent body that concerns itself only with what is lawful and verifiable.

- Courts balance the rights of individuals against the rights of the state, and can also distinguish between the rights and interests of parents as against the rights and interests of children where these differ. The earlier discussion in Chapter 1 concerning the Cleveland Report (DHSS, 1988) is obviously relevant here.

When are social workers likely to end up in court?

As a social worker, when might you be required to attend court in a professional capacity?

Case study

Tom, aged 15, has committed his third offence of taking and driving away. As he is underage, he is charged with the associated offences of driving while disqualified through age and without insurance.

Case study

Mandy (7) and Melissa (5) have been left in their house alone at night on a number of occasions, while their parents have been out visiting friends who are known to be drug users.

→

> Attempts to help the parents understand how dangerous this is have proved fruitless, to the extent that the local authority now believes its only recourse is to institute care proceedings and ask for care orders on both girls.

There are two important areas of social work where practitioners regularly give evidence in court. The first is in relation to youth justice, and this will apply to Tom's case. As we saw in Chapter 7, the general practice is for social workers to combine with professionals from other disciplines in order to form multidisciplinary teams working in the youth justice field. Each member of the team has particular responsibilities, but when it comes to advising courts about possible sentencing outcomes, and reporting to courts on the progress of supervision of young offenders, all members of the team share this responsibility. On occasion, this will include not only writing reports for the court, but also appearing in them. The second area of work is children and families, specifically in cases where care proceedings are instituted, as in the case of Mandy and Melissa. Chapter 4 introduced the grounds for instituting care proceedings, laying emphasis on the notion of *significant harm* (Section 31 Children Act 1989). Significant harm has to be proved in court and to the court's satisfaction. It is in the court that magistrates or judges need to be persuaded of the necessity of making an order, and are advised about the kind of order necessary to secure the best possible future for the child.

There are other instances where courts sometimes hear from social workers. In matters of domestic violence proceedings under the Family Law Act 1996 (as augmented by the Domestic Violence, Crime and Victims Act 2004, Crime and Security Act 2010 and Serious Crime Act 2015), it is possible that social workers might be asked to give evidence in the county court. In criminal cases, social workers have the same responsibilities as every other citizen to give evidence where they have witnessed a crime, but additionally social workers may sometimes be asked to be present when certain people are interviewed at police stations. This is called acting as an *appropriate adult* (section 66 Code of Practice Police and Criminal Evidence Act 1984). This requires the police to have someone present when young people (under 18) or people with mental health problems or learning difficulties are interviewed, although it may be worth noting that this does not necessarily have to be a social worker – in many cases it would be parents or another family member (Mandelstam, 2013; Brammer, 2015, pp382–84, 535–7; Brayne *et al.*, 2015, pp348–59; Staines, 2015). Specialist and non-specialist social workers are sometimes asked to furnish reports to Mental Health Tribunals (technically First-Tier Mental Health Tribunals) and attend their hearings. These reports outline the social circumstances of the patient and the facilities available in the community to offer rehabilitation and supervision if the patient is discharged from hospital. Given the important role of the tribunal in determining whether people who have been compulsorily detained in psychiatric hospitals should be discharged, it is important for such social workers to understand their precise task. Very occasionally, a local authority will be directly involved in cases concerning vulnerable adults who have lost the capacity to make decisions for themselves, especially where there appears to be a need for safeguarding. Such cases are determined by the Court of Protection, which also adjudicates on cases where there is an appeal against the operation of the Deprivation of Liberty Safeguards under the Mental Capacity Act 2005 (for explanation of Deprivation of Liberty Safeguards see Chapter 6). In very rare cases, the High Court may be called upon to adjudicate where a service user alleges that the local authority has acted inappropriately by not interpreting the law correctly. It is just possible that social workers might be called upon to give evidence in such cases (see Chapter 2 for general rights of redress and an overview of how social work agencies are held accountable more widely).

In the first part of this chapter, we will be addressing some of the fears, anxieties and misapprehensions that social workers often share about appearing in court. The aim here is to take away some of the mythology about giving evidence. Courts need not be a stressful experience if practitioners are aware of basic procedures, the principles of giving evidence, and develop a clear idea about what courts expect of them. The second part of the chapter therefore offers an overview of what goes on in courts, distinguishing the different roles people play in Youth Courts, based on criminal law, and Family Proceedings Courts, based on civil law (for an explanation of the differences between criminal and civil law, see Chapter 1). This part of the chapter addresses the specific expectations of the social worker in these courts, with specific references to pre-sentence reports (Youth Court) and statement preparation (Family Proceedings Court). Then follows a section devoted to service users' perspectives, and research and policy debates about court proceedings. This enables the chapter to conclude with reflections on good practice that include preparing service users for court, acting professionally in court, developing skills in synthesising information, and working in a way that incorporates key social work values.

Appearing in court can be fun

It may seem incredible, but that is the view of some practitioners. To them, court is an enjoyable experience because it is challenging: it is good to have one's competence and knowledge tested out, and helps to keep the practitioner focused. It compels them to think clearly about the case and is therefore a stimulating intellectual exercise. Furthermore, from a practice point of view, it is invaluable in clarifying issues that are of concern: young people cannot deny being in difficulties if they are convicted of an offence by a court, parents cannot deny family problems if a court determines that their child is being *significantly harmed*. Thus, court is a cathartic experience: it liberates people to concentrate on the real issues.

For those who are not initially quite so enthusiastic, it is important to remember that appearing in court need not be anxiety provoking. Courts are not set up to catch people out; yet their role is crucial in terms of public accountability for social work. It is in a court that the social worker sometimes has to justify their actions, and certainly has to justify the outcomes of an assessment where it is intended to propose a specific course of action that is opposed by others. The primary purpose of the court is to test the evidence through which people have drawn certain conclusions (Seymour and Seymour, 2011; Foulds, 2009; Association of Directors of Children's Services 2016; Research in Practice 2016; Cooper, 2014). If the children's services authority has concluded that the best interests of the child will be served by placing them with foster carers, and this move is opposed by the parents, it is only right and proper that the parents should have some way of having that conclusion critically scrutinised, or in legal jargon, *cross-examined*. The public needs to be assured that the proposed way of dealing with young offenders is one that minimises the chances of the young person committing a further offence. The sentence should also be justified in terms of being *proportionate* to the seriousness of the offence.

How confident do you feel about appearing in court and giving evidence? The following activity asks you to explore your feelings about giving evidence in a court as a witness. It does not matter, for the purpose of the exercise, whether you imagine this to be a court set up to hear a criminal case, such as the Youth Court, or one that is concerned with civil matters such as care proceedings.

Activity 8.2

Take a blank sheet of paper and draw a line down the middle so that you have two columns.

Fears about court	Impressions I would like to convey

You may like to do this exercise with someone else, working as a pair, or even in a group. Start with the left-hand column and think of how you would feel if someone told you that tomorrow morning you have to go to court to give evidence. Try to be as honest as you can and also try to be as specific as you can. It is important to complete the left-hand column before starting on the positives on the right-hand side. After spending about ten minutes or so on the fears and apprehensions, move on to the impressions you would most like to convey. Do spend the same amount of time on the right-hand column. It may be more difficult to list the impressions you would like to convey, but it will certainly repay you to do so.

Comment

Even the most experienced practitioners have some nervousness about appearing in court. Some of the most common fears and anxieties are:

(Continued)

(Continued)

- fear of the unknown: ignorance of the 'ground rules', not knowing when to do what;
- the physical symptoms of nervousness;
- being afraid that you will forget something vital, such as the case summary;
- worrying that you will be 'tricked' into saying something you don't mean, or will fall into a 'clever' lawyer's trap;
- believing that you are going to make a complete fool of yourself by a combination of all of the above;
- consequently, being left feeling that not only have you let yourself down, you have also betrayed the confidence of the child, family or young person you were meant to be helping.

It is possible to avert most of these fears through careful preparation, prediction of what will happen, practising giving evidence and, above all, by adopting a professional approach.

Preparation

If court procedure is completely new to you, try to spend a day observing what goes on in courts. Magistrates' courts in most large towns or cities sit almost daily, with the public permitted to attend most proceedings. It may be worth a preliminary check with the clerk of the court's office if you are not sure when courts sit, or which will be open to the public. Not all cases are equally interesting, but the purpose of the exercise is for you to see what happens when people are asked to give evidence. While there are some minor differences between courts, general procedures are similar in all courts and at all levels (for an explanation of different kinds of courts, see below).

In all cases, it is important to know the facts about the case and to know how to distinguish between facts, opinion and interpretation. Have the papers in order so the report or case records can be referred to: large documents can be divided into sections that are clearly identifiable. Being familiar with research findings that support the opinions or recommendations offered to the court is to be applauded. Evidence-based practice is more persuasive to courts than opinions simply based on intuition or emotions.

Practice

Go through the evidence in advance, preferably with a colleague who can pick up on points that appear to be unclear or inconsistent. Familiarise yourself with the case to the extent that you become confident about it, so that you really know what information is relevant for the court in its deliberations. As a social worker in care proceedings, you will be attending court in a professional capacity with access to the support and guidance of lawyers who are either employed by the same authority as yourself, or else contracted to provide legal services to your employer. It is therefore highly advisable to contact this lawyer in advance and to run through basic procedures with them. Do not hesitate to explain that this is your first time in court if that is the case. For further guidance, consult resources listed at the end of this chapter.

If nervousness and apprehension are problems, try using relaxation techniques. It does not matter what kind as long as they work for you.

Prediction

It is usually possible to anticipate the kind of questions courts are going to ask. It is rare that people are going to try playing tricks on the social worker by throwing in questions that could not be anticipated so there should be no need to be defensive. It is nearly always possible to predict the areas in which the court is likely to be interested: what would you ask if you were the magistrate or the judge? What are the points at which the service user or family disagree with the social work professionals? In what ways do the grandparents' views, for example, differ from the views of the parents or indeed from those of the social work professionals? Bear in mind, too, the legal issues which the court is bound to consider. In criminal cases the court must weigh up the seriousness of the offence. In care proceedings cases, the court is bound to enquire about the *welfare checklist* (section 1 Children Act 1989; see Chapter 4) and will also be aware of the need not to be discriminatory. For example, regulations require considerations of race, culture and religion to be incorporated into care plans. It is most likely, therefore, that courts will ask detailed questions about the care plan, and specifically about how you plan to meet all the child's needs and comply with all statutory requirements.

Professionalism

Professionalism refers to very practical issues such as observing the dress code and ensuring that one's personal appearance accords the court the respect it thinks it deserves. Dressing appropriately for court is very important since it demonstrates respect, and courts, rightly or wrongly, regard dress that is too casual as an indication that the person is too casual. More importantly, it risks prejudicing the court against the social worker's case and thereby potentially does the child or young person a disservice.

Witnesses should assume that they will be standing to give evidence unless the court makes it clear that people will be sitting throughout, as is now general practice in magistrates' family proceedings courts, or invites the witness to sit. Witnesses should address the 'bench' of magistrates or the judge, not the person who actually asks the question. This is much more difficult than it sounds, for it is natural to look at the person posing questions. One way of overcoming this is to turn one's feet towards the bench or magistrates and so, in that way, addressing the bench or judge becomes more natural.

When answering questions, it is important to speak clearly and concisely, but equally important not to rush into an answer. There is no obligation to answer questions quickly, but there is a duty to answer questions honestly. If, for example, there is a conflict of opinion, it is emphatically not a good idea to try to cover this up. Above all, evidence should be presented using plain English, avoiding the temptation to use jargon. Social work is not exempt from jargon, all professions have their own specific language, but in this context jargon is particularly deplorable since it is not only disrespectful to the court but, more importantly, disempowers families and thereby stops them participating fully in the proceedings.

The final aspect of professionalism is the most important: never take it personally. By this is meant that there should never be a degree of personal and emotional investment or involvement in the case to the extent that the outcome matters if it doesn't go 'your' way. *Stick to what you think is right and what you believe and what you have done*, one family court district judge advises social workers (Roberts, 2011, p12). In the 1960s there was a television series concerning a lawyer called Perry Mason who tirelessly, every week, won every single case while his opponent equally tirelessly lost every case. Life is not like that. No lawyer expects to 'win' every case and no social worker should expect every court to go along precisely with their view. If courts simply rubber-stamped social work decision-making, there would just be no point having a court system, and the consequences for service users would be all too obvious. It is much healthier for social workers to be challenged regularly, for assessments to be scrutinised and for decisions to be tested robustly in the court setting. For social workers, this means inevitably that decisions will not always go 'their' way.

Who's who in the court system?

What can you expect to find when a court is sitting? What roles do the professionals play? Diagrams on the following pages set out some of the differences between the different kinds of court and these are explained more fully below.

Youth Court

A Practice Direction issued by the Lord Chief Justice (Trial of Children and Young Persons in the Crown Court, February 2000) sets out some principles by which criminal courts should organise procedures and settings for cases involving under-18-year-olds. These include:

> *All possible steps should be taken to assist the young defendant to understand and participate in the proceedings (paragraph 3);*
>
> *The trial should, if practicable, be held in a courtroom in which all the participants are on the same or almost the same level (paragraph 9);*

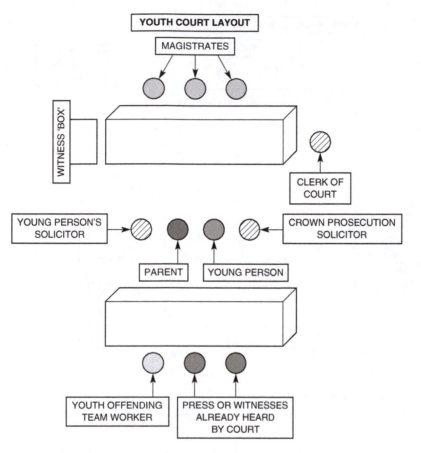

Figure 8.1 Layout of youth court

Note: = legally qualified personnel. Court sits on one level but is stricter on procedure than Family Proceedings Court. People give evidence formally. Young people can choose whether to sit with parent, solicitor, YOT worker or another relative. There may be local variations to this pattern. Not all courts are the same.

> *A young defendant should normally, if he wishes, be free to sit with members of his family or others in a place which permits easy, informal communication with his legal representatives and others {.} (paragraph 11).*

(Practice direction (criminal: consolidated) (2002) 3
All ER 904: 39.3, 39.9, 39.10)

These principles are now codified into *The consolidated criminal practice direction criminal procedure rules* (Ministry of Justice, 2013a) issued to courts and prosecutors.

Family Proceedings Court

Informality is particularly important in family proceedings and it is now virtually standard practice for people to remain seated when they address the magistrates. However, in some courts it is still customary for witnesses to stand while they present their evidence. It is also expected

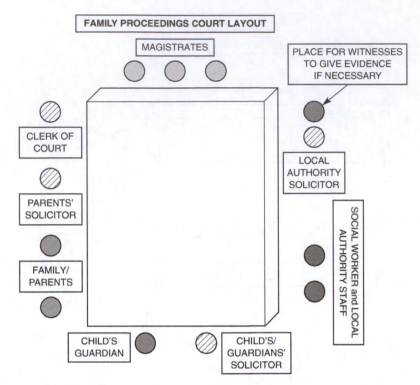

Figure 8.2   Layout of family proceedings court

Note: = legally qualified personnel. Court sits on one level around a table. People address the court and give evidence seated, but there may be local differences in custom and practice. Not all courts are the same.

that parents will sit next to their advocate, while children do not normally attend court. It is assumed that the kind of evidence brought before the court is unsuitable for children to hear and, except in very rare instances, the court will appoint a guardian who speaks for the child and can instruct a solicitor or barrister to advocate for the child's point of view in court.

In general, witnesses should wait outside the court before they are called. This is to prevent them hearing evidence from other witnesses, although sometimes professional witnesses are allowed to stay throughout the whole hearing. Professional witnesses are expected to have written records and documents available to them for reference when giving evidence, but should normally only refer to them with permission of the court. Counsel representing the local authority might ask permission before the social worker presents their evidence (technically the 'examination-in-chief'). Or the social worker may simply ask before opening the file: *May I refer to my notes?*

County Court

It will be seen from this diagram that courts with judges tend to have a more formal arrangement, and this is reflected in their procedures. Witnesses invariably stand throughout

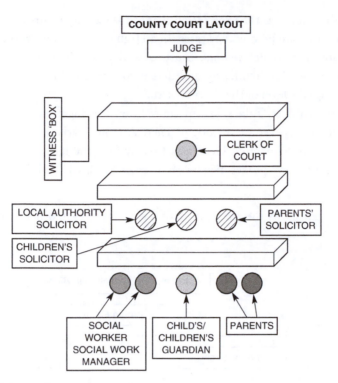

Figure 8.3   Layout of County Court

Note: = legally qualified personnel. Court is on different levels with judge higher than everyone else. Procedure more formal than other courts. People give evidence formally and legal personnel may be wearing robes and gowns. There may be local variations to this pattern. Not all courts are the same.

their evidence. Likewise advocates stand to address the judge and rules of procedure, such as administration of the oath or affirmation, are strictly enforced.

Magistrates and judges

Magistrates are lay people, appointed from the local community, who undergo additional training for a job that is essentially unpaid. There are some specific provisions and qualifications applicable to those appointed to Youth Courts or Family Proceedings Courts. A bench of magistrates is so called because it consists of three (usually) magistrates sitting in a row, although these days not actually on a bench. It is customary for only one magistrate, the chair, to speak for the bench. Very occasionally, there will be one magistrate sitting alone – for example, in criminal cases in very busy areas where the magistrate is legally qualified and full-time and sits as a District Judge (Magistrates' Court). Magistrates are usually addressed as Sir or Madam or, collectively, as Your Worships.

Judges are experienced barristers (normally) or solicitors (occasionally) who hear the more serious criminal cases or the more complex family proceedings cases. Judges sit alone. In family proceedings cases, judges will have been chosen for their experience in cases involving children and families, and it is the expectation that at the County Court level judges will deal with the more difficult care proceedings cases. In a High Court, judges will deal with appeals from the magistrates' Family Proceedings Courts as well as deciding on complex cases, such as those cases which involve children living in different countries or highly contested adoption cases. At the very highest level of the court structure, the Appeal Courts and the ultimate authority the Supreme Court, judges do sometimes hear cases together making a panel of three or five, or sometimes even more, judges. There are some variations as to how judges are addressed depending on their status. Generally, County Court judges are referred to as Your Honour, but in higher courts judges may be My Lord or My Lady – ask legal representatives if you are unsure.

The following diagram shows the relationship of the courts to each other in a form of hierarchy.

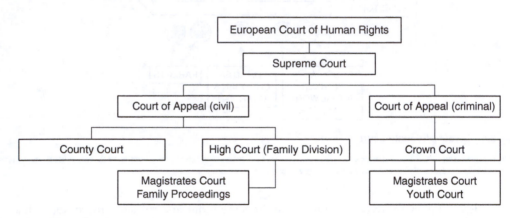

Figure 8.4 Hierarchy of courts

Barristers and solicitors (advocates)

The legal profession is divided into two branches. Barristers, sometimes referred to as 'counsel', are regarded as specialists in advocacy – that is, in presenting cases and speaking on their client's behalf. Solicitors may also be advocates but generally will deal with a wider range of cases than barristers. Barristers cannot take 'instructions' direct from their clients, but usually operate through an 'instructing' solicitor. There are certain rules regarding courts in which solicitors and barristers may appear with the general principle being that only barristers have the right of 'audience' in the very highest courts.

Court clerks and other court officials

As magistrates are lay people, they often need the assistance of someone legally qualified, their clerk. There are restrictions on the powers of magistrates and, in some cases, they are obliged to send (remit) cases to higher courts. The clerk's job is to organise the court and supervise the administration of justice, being responsible for collecting fines, allocating cases, ensuring there are magistrates available, and so on. In care proceedings cases, clerks will also chair the discussion of timetabling and make agreed orders regarding disclosure of documents and evidence ('directions hearings').

In County Courts and High Courts, since the judge is legally qualified, the clerk does not need to be so. Hence, clerks in these cases are most often just that: people who take notes or look up calendars or reference books for the judge.

Ushers are the people who act as receptionists, call cases into court, show people where to go, administer the oath and generally ensure that people are where they should be.

Police and Crown Prosecution Service

The police are not generally involved in family proceedings cases, unless there is a specific reason to call a police officer as a witness. Similarly, the police are not routinely involved in Youth Court cases unless required to give specific evidence since the case is conducted by the Crown Prosecution Service, who will employ a solicitor to present the case. The role of the Crown Prosecution Service is to sift the cases that have been investigated by the police so as to ensure that only those where prosecution is deemed appropriate are taken to court (for their website address, see the end of the chapter).

Guardians

Children's Guardians are social workers who specialise in court work with children in the Family Proceedings Courts, and are appointed to specific cases by the Child and Family Court Advisory and Support Service (CAFCASS or CAFCASS Cymru: for the website addresses, see the end of the chapter). CAFCASS was set up by the Criminal Justice and Court Services Act 2000 with separate arrangements for Wales introduced by sections 35–41 Children Act 2004. Its role is to offer a comprehensive child representation service to the courts (section 12 Criminal Justice and Court Services Act 2000). It took over responsibility from local authorities for the 'guardian ad litem' service, a point worth making since legislation and rules still refer in many cases to the guardian ad litem, although the terminology has now changed. Children's guardians must be independent of the local authority involved in the case, and it is their role to conduct an independent investigation on behalf of the court and to speak for the child. They instruct lawyers to act for the child so as to ensure that the child's perspective, and not just the parents', is conveyed to the court (section 41 Children Act 1989). Guardians have rights of access to local authority documents relating to children (section 42 Children Act 1989) and can call witnesses to court as well as giving independent advice and evidence to courts themselves.

Social workers

Social workers are regarded as professional witnesses – that is, people who are giving evidence by virtue of the position they hold and the role they play in a family's life as an adviser. Hence, the role is unlike that of someone who gives evidence in a criminal case who happens to see a robbery or a road accident. Being a professional witness means the courts can and often do ask for that person's advice and opinion, and expect a professional witness to be able to support their conclusions by reference to research-based evidence as well as by reference to the facts of the case.

Social workers need to be aware that when they are giving evidence they are officers of the court – that is, their first duty is to the court, to tell all that they know and to answer all questions truthfully. There may, on rare occasions, be a conflict of views with their own managers, or with other social workers. The court is entitled to know that there is disagreement; one local authority advises its staff that honesty in these circumstances at least indicates the complexity of the case to the court. While social workers are professionally accountable to their managers, they cannot hide behind someone else's opinion as to what should happen in a particular case. They must present and support their own view. For further discussion of the general issue of accountability, see Chapter 9.

Social workers in the Youth Court need to prepare pre-sentence reports in accordance with national guidelines issued by the Youth Justice Board (Youth Justice Board, 2013).

Social workers in family proceedings play a particular role in collating the background information for the court and putting this together as a chronology (list of events in date order) and statement. Synthesising and analysing information is a key social work skill of particular importance in court work. If this is all new to you, look under Further reading at the end of this chapter for additional sources of advice. If you have the opportunity to work alongside someone in a family proceedings case, it would greatly assist you (and them) to bear in mind the requirements of the *Public Law Outline* (Family Procedure Rules 2014: Practice Direction 12A, 2016). These rules are not always easy to follow, so you may find more user-friendly the recently revised government Children Act 1989 guidance and regulations on court orders and preparing for care and supervision proceedings (Department for Education, 2014). This indicates what should happen both at the pre-court stage and during the court process itself and incorporates the implementation of the *Judicial Proposals for the Modernisation of Family Justice* (Ryder, 2012), as well as sections 14–16 Children and Families Act 2014 regarding time limits and care plans.

Social workers can also be used as independent expert witnesses carrying out instructions for a lawyer. This may happen when someone wants the social work equivalent of a 'second opinion' and the social worker is then called to give evidence on their behalf. Nevertheless, in such situations it still remains the case that the social worker's obligations are to the court and they must give their honest professional opinion.

What happens in court?

How will the courts decide what to do in the cases of Tom Bates, accused of taking and driving away motor vehicles, and Mandy and Melissa Watson, who are too young to be left to look after themselves (see previous case studies)?

Underlying principles that determine what happens in court

The court system is often described as adversarial. The use of this term implies almost continuously hostile conflict, which is rarely the case. Rather, it is a technical term that refers to the system whereby the court itself cannot initiate proceedings, cannot call witnesses and cannot consider anything other than what is presented before it. It is for those bringing the cases, referred to as the *applicants*, to present to the court all the evidence they think they need to 'prove' their case. It is then for the *respondents* (formerly referred to as *defendants*) to present their side of the argument, often refuting or challenging the evidence presented by the applicants.

In criminal cases such as Tom's, the applicant is always the Crown, hence the case would be referred to as *R* (for Regina) *v* (for versus) *Bates*. In civil cases (the differences between civil and criminal law were explained in Chapter 1), the surnames of applicants and respondents are used, or the name of the local authority or organisation concerned. So, in care proceedings, it might be *Anyshire County Council v Watson*, or if it were a dispute between two parents, *Watson v Watson*.

Nevertheless, one principle is common to both criminal and civil cases – namely, that generally they all start in the Magistrates' Courts (one exception is adoption cases, which usually start in the County Court, but note also that there are specialist tribunals and courts for mental health and Mental Capacity Act 2005 cases). Regarding youth justice and care proceedings cases, one would start in the Youth Court branch of the Magistrates' Court, while the other would start in the Magistrates' Family Proceedings Court. This rule applies even though it is intended that the case will be sent to other courts such as the Crown Court for criminal cases and County or High Court for civil cases.

Who starts the proceedings?

Criminal cases are initiated by the police referring the matter to the Crown Prosecution Service who have the ultimate responsibility in deciding whether or not to bring a case before the courts. Care proceedings cases are started by the applicant, usually the local authority, sending a form to the court. This contains some basic information concerning the grounds and is usually prepared by lawyers; for more information, see the Ministry of Justice website (Ministry of Justice, 2014). In urgent cases, care proceedings begin with an Emergency Protection Order (section 44 Children Act 1989), which is immediately referred to the court to decide the next steps. Courts have the authority to adjourn cases for as many times as necessary, although there are rules regarding limits to care proceedings, in particular, the six months' rule introduced by the Children and Families Act 2014 (section 14). Furthermore, there are requirements concerning the duration of, for example, interim care orders; for information on these, look at section 38 Children Act 1989 and the Regulations and Guidance issued, either by the Department for Education (2014), or by the Welsh Assembly Government (2014), depending on where you practise. Serious concern has been expressed about delays in both criminal and civil cases and the youth court is a target for initiatives to reduce delays in offenders coming to court. Family Proceedings Courts operate under the statutory presumption that any delay *is likely to prejudice the welfare of the child* (section 1(2) Children Act 1989), so are charged with making directions, at what are known as *directions hearings*, about the timetabling and progress of cases through, for example, requiring certain documents to be produced by specific dates (Ministry of Justice, 2014). Concern about delays was one of the primary reasons for the introduction of sections 14–16 of the Children and Families Act 2014.

Given the adversarial system whereby one side presents evidence which can then be challenged by the other, the procedure is predictable in that the applicant presents all their evidence first before handing over to the respondents. By this is meant that the applicant calls all their witnesses first, but naturally each witness can be challenged (or technically *cross-examined*) by the 'other side'. The first stage of this evidence is called the *examination in chief* and there are strict rules about the ways in which lawyers can ask questions in this examination. When it comes to cross-examination, questioning can take a different form, including asking what are known as leading questions (questions that imply an answer). Magistrates or judges have the right to ask questions if they wish. It is also possible to re-examine witnesses and occasionally to recall witnesses if an issue comes up which has not been foreseen and it is relevant for the courts to do so, but note there are custom and practice rules about this.

Privacy and confidentiality

Family proceedings by their very nature involve highly personal information about a family being laid out before strangers – magistrates, court clerks, solicitors, social workers. It is essential, in order to preserve privacy and confidentiality, for the hearings to be held in private, so all hearings are generally held *in camera*, although there is now an assumption that some information about the cases should be made public when it is considered that publication would be in the public interest (Munby, 2014, paragraph 16).

In family courts, no one is generally allowed to attend unless they have a clear connection to the case which they can prove to the court's satisfaction, if necessary. By contrast, the media are entitled to attend the Youth Court and may report cases as long as the media do not identify those involved without the court's permission, so Tom's name won't generally appear in the press, although the details of his offences might. Furthermore, the law prohibits the publication of any report or picture which might help reveal the name, address or school of the young person concerned, although it is possible for courts to lift these restrictions if it is in the public interest to do so – such as if the court thinks publicity will help stop them offending (section 49 Children and Young Persons Act 1933, as amended). Furthermore, reporting restrictions are automatically lifted if the Youth Court is considering the breach of Injunctions or Criminal Behaviour Orders (section 30 Anti-Social Behaviour, Crime and Policing Act 2014).

Outcomes

The burden or onus of proof lies always with the person who initiates the proceedings. In Tom's case, he is assumed innocent until proven guilty and the prosecution must prove his guilt to the court. In Mandy and Melissa's case, the local authority has to prove the grounds for care proceedings before the court can contemplate making an order.

The standard of proof is a technical term referring to the test by which the court is guided when it determines a case. The important distinction here is between criminal cases such as Tom's where the court must be convinced *beyond reasonable doubt* that the offender is guilty, whereas in civil cases it is necessary to prove this *on the balance of probabilities*, which is generally regarded as a less stringent test. So, in care proceedings cases like Mandy and Melissa's, it is the second test, the balance of probabilities, that applies.

Courts are required to give a decision in accordance with certain procedures. It is not general practice in criminal cases to explain decisions; they are simply announced. Occasionally, if there is an appeal, magistrates may be asked to provide some kind of explanation to the higher court. However, in family proceedings cases, the court does have to give reasons for their conclusions, and these need to be written down.

What does it feel like to go to court?

Earlier, you were asked about your fears and apprehensions about appearing in court, but how does it feel to go through court as a service user?

Parental perspectives on care proceedings

What follows are some extracts from the key findings of a research summary carried out for the Family Justice Council in 2010. Note that only the findings that are of relevance to social work have been included, incorporating research on the experience of those involved in private family law, usually applications for Children Act 1989 section 8 orders (for what these are, see Chapter 4). If you want to know more, you can access the full research summary online at the address at the end of the chapter and it is well worthwhile doing so.

Research summary

Key messages from research

Key point 2: Parents find the whole experience of going to court traumatic and alienating.

The overriding message is that greater attention needs to be paid to the needs of parents caught up in court proceedings, and most particularly to the needs of especially vulnerable groups such as parents with learning difficulties or mental health problems, women who have experienced domestic violence, and parents from minority ethnic communities. The research indicates that parents want a less intimidating, more personal, and participatory process, preferably with the same judge throughout.

Key point 3: Many parents do not have confidence in the decision-making process.

Parents do not necessarily feel their views are heard and taken into account by CAFCASS or the court. There are criticisms of the quality of the evidence presented, of over-reliance on professional evidence, and about the thoroughness of the CAFCASS investigation. A substantial proportion do not feel that the court, and/or CAFCASS, understood the issues in their case and, in private law, accusations of bias, particularly gender bias, are common.

Key point 4: Parents do not necessarily endorse the settlement-seeking approach of the family justice system and some are critical of how this is operationalised.

Some parents report feeling under pressure to take part in in-court conciliation and while most report that the conciliation session was fair, it is also experienced by some as stressful, rushed, pressurised, not giving parents the opportunity to say what they want, unduly future-focused and resulting in coerced agreements.

Key point 5: Court proceedings do not necessarily make things better for families.

What they do not appear to do {.} is to improve parental relationships and therefore parents' capacity to manage post-separation parenting.

Key point 6: Some groups of parents are more dissatisfied with the family justice system than others.

Two groups of dissatisfied parents particularly stand out. First, non-resident parents in private law proceedings, who are fairly consistently found to be less positive than resident parents about CAFCASS and the courts {.} The second group is mothers who have experienced domestic violence. There is also some evidence in relation to other groups: parents from BME (Black and Minority Ethnic) or traveller communities; parents involved in contact rather than residence proceedings; parents of young children; and parents in cases where either the child or the parent has a special need.

> *Key point 7: While parents' satisfaction with the outcome is related to their views about the system, it is not the only driver and may not be the most important.*
>
> *Most of the research demonstrates that parents who are dissatisfied with the outcome of court proceedings are more likely to be critical of the system than those who were pleased with it. However, the association is far from perfect and studies highlight the importance of process. Hence while it is probably unrealistic to expect that most parents who do not get what they hoped for should nonetheless be positive about the system, it is possible that addressing some of the sources of dissatisfaction could produce a less disgruntled clientele. It is, moreover, concerning that, even where parents achieve a satisfactory outcome, they are not necessarily positive about the outcome.*
>
> (Hunt, 2010)

So much for the general scene, but how does it feel at a personal level? The following is a very articulate personal account from a father whose care case eventually ended up in the High Court.

Facing deportation

> *The main entrance hall of the Royal Courts of Justice is one of those buildings designed, it seems, to make one feel humble. Once through the doorway the roof soars high, footsteps echo from the tiled floor, the benches and arched roof imply that this is a sacred place. The link between justice and divinity is direct and potent. Is this a court or a cathedral? Has one come to stand before a human judge, or to meet one's maker?{.}*
>
> *It did become clear throughout the process that professionals on the whole have very circumscribed choices, and are likely to be very vulnerable themselves if they are seen to get something wrong. The danger here is the potential for professionals becoming interested only in the evidence that will support their view {.} Suddenly, a level of informality and openness I had experienced was ended. I became acutely aware of sources of power available to agencies when the accessibility, informality and the possibility of influence vanished.*
>
> *It was as if I had been semi-hypnotised, watching this machinery working over several years, then awoken suddenly to find myself in its jaws.*
>
> (Tosey, 2000, p16)

Children's perspectives on care proceedings

The next extract summarises some research that centred on children's experiences of care proceedings. When reading this, remember that children do not normally attend court, so the research was especially interested in what happened when children expressed a wish to do so.

Research summary

Thirty-five children reported that they were not consulted about whether they wished to attend court {.} The nine children who were asked all chose to attend. Only one attended the final hearing. She commented that, despite having prior agreement to sit in on the proceedings, when the day arrived she could not bring herself to go any further than the waiting room. The others either attended directions hearings or visited the court building. One child spoke directly with the judge in his chambers {.}

Seventeen of the children interviewed said they would like to have attended court, some because they wished for the opportunity to talk directly with the judiciary, others because they wanted to be more involved. They gave as their reasons, I wanted to see the judges. I don't even know what they look like. I wanted to be there, not in school when they were deciding and if my mum was upset I could tell her I'll still be seeing you (boy, age 8). I would like to see the judge and talk to him and I'll ask him if I can go home to my mum (girl, age 9). I would like to go to the court so I could say my own words (girl age 8). I would like to see it because I have never been before and everyone else went when I had to go to school (girl age 9).

(Ruegger, 2001, pp40–1)

In addition to this, there are a variety of sources that provide first-hand accounts of the experience of care proceedings – for example, on the Research in Practice website (for their address, see the end of the chapter).

Being on the receiving end of the justice system

Finally, what are the issues for people who experience the criminal justice court system at first hand? Once you are in practice as a social worker, there will be no shortage of people who can comment on this. Don't forget that young people also experience the criminal justice system as victims, and indeed there are a number of stakeholders whose views need to be considered (for further discussion on this, see Smith, 2014, Chapter 9). However, with regard to the court process itself, one recurrent theme appears to be the power differential between young people and adults, not just those making decisions in court, but also those who represent them. The introduction of Referral Orders and associated panels has made some difference to this, leading to a feeling among young people that they are more included in the process, and that there is a great opportunity to discuss rather than just being on the 'receiving end' (Botley *et al.*, 2010). Since the publication of *Justice for All* (Home Office, 2002), which was based on both research and consultation with stakeholders, there has been a broad recognition that the youth justice system needs to be more 'user-friendly'. The White Paper recognises that some aspects of courts, *such as formal dress, technical or old-fashioned language and obscure procedures, can make courts appear intimidating and inaccessible to many people,* and that courts need to be *more welcoming* (Home Office, 2002: paragraphs 7.18, 7.21). Subsequently, several measures were introduced to address this – for example, the Courts Act 2003 and, for family proceedings, the Children and Adoption Act 2006 upated by Schedules 9–11 of the Crime and Courts Act 2013. Principal changes have centred on the language used in documents and procedures, formality of the courts, dress code and increased use of modern information technology to speed up procedures.

Making court a positive experience

On the basis of what you have just read, is it possible to suggest ways of making court a positive experience, both for children and parents involved in care proceedings, and for ourselves as social work practitioners in both care and criminal proceedings?

Activity 8.3

Draw up a table with three headings.

What helps make court a positive experience for the following?

Children/young people	Parents	Social workers

Comment

This is essentially a revision exercise: many of the points have been covered in this chapter, and if you encountered any difficulties with the activity, it would be as well to look back over what you have read. To check your answers, refer to Exercise Answers, p190–1.

Chapter summary

This chapter set out a number of reasons why courts are important arenas of accountability for social workers, and by now you should be aware of ways in which courts should be viewed as a positive element of social work practice.

(Continued)

(Continued)

The chapter set out the key ways in which social workers may be directly involved in court, through giving evidence or writing reports for particular cases. Some guidance was offered as to how social workers should prepare themselves for the court process. The roles of key professional personnel were explained, along with an overview of procedures and processes you are likely to encounter as a social worker. These are points to bear in mind particularly when attending court for the first time.

The chapter concluded with a consideration of the needs of service users in the court system. On the basis of this, you were invited to draw up guidelines that will help to make court work as positive an experience as possible for everyone involved.

One final issue you may wish to think about for the future is whether the court system as it currently operates offers the best way of dealing with youth justice and children in need of care. One key issue is whether the adversarial approach that predominates in the court system is appropriate. Hunt (2010) concluded, on the basis of her research summary, that it was hard to find positive messages about the courts from the research on parental perspectives. There is little research on children's perspectives of the court process itself (Ruegger, 2001 is an honourable exception). As we saw in Chapter 7, there is a strong move towards making youth justice less adversarial, at least for first offenders, with the introduction of Referral Orders and a greater emphasis on restorative justice. The Scottish youth justice system has been based since the 1970s on Children's Hearings as distinct from Youth Courts, and this has facilitated open discussions between parents, young people and the courts about reasons for offences being committed (Smith, D, 2000; for broader international comparisons see Hazel, 2008). Likewise, there is a move towards making Family Proceedings Court procedures more informal and less intimidating, with greater emphasis on Family Group Conferencing (Ministry of Justice, 2009a, section 2.5.3) and more flexible forms of procedures that include 'round the table' discussions that may facilitate a more open discussion of a child's needs where professionals are less preoccupied with 'winning' or 'losing' the case.

Further reading

If you are asked to write a pre-sentence report or prepare a statement for court. you must refer to guidelines.

For youth justice these can be found at:

Youth Justice Board (2013) *National standards for youth justice*: www.justice.gov.uk/youth-justice/monitoring-performance/national-standards

For care proceedings the guidelines are:

For England:

Department for Education (2014) *The Children Act 1989 guidance and regulations. Volume 1: Court orders.* London: Department for Education.

Ministry of Justice (2014) *Practice direction 12a — care, supervision and other. Part 4: Proceedings: Guide to case management.* London: Ministry of Justice.

For Wales:

Welsh Assembly Government (2014) *Children Act 1989 guidance and regulations: Volume 1: Court orders.* Cardiff: Welsh Assembly Government.

For more general advice on youth justice, see:

NACRO (2008) *Working in the courts: A good practice guide for practitioners in the youth justice system.* London: NACRO.

Staines, J (2015) *Youth Justice.* Basingstoke: Palgrave.

For more general advice on care proceedings, see:

Cooper, P (2014) *Courts and legal skills.* Basingstoke: Palgrave.

Davis, L (2014) *The social worker's guide to children and families law* (2nd edn). London: Jessica Kingsley.

For general advice on the role and duties of social workers in courts, see:

Seymour, C and Seymour, R (2011) *Courtroom skills for social workers* (2nd edn). London: Sage.

For an excellent summary of research on user perspectives, see:

Hunt, J (2010) *Parental perspectives on the family justice system in England and Wales: A review of research.* London: Family Justice Council, accessible at website listed below.

Websites

Appropriate Adults: www.appropriateadult.org.uk

CAFCASS: www.cafcass.gov.uk

CAFCASS Cymru Wales (CAFCASS Wales): wales.gov.uk/cafcasscymru

Crown Prosecution Service: www.cps.gov.uk

Department of Health: www.gov.uk/government/organisations/department-of-health

Family Justice Council: www.judiciary.gov.uk/about-the-judiciary/advisory-bodies/fjc

Ministry of Justice: www.justice.gov.uk

NACRO: www.nacro.org.uk

Research in Practice: http://coppguidance.rip.org.uk/

9: Providing a Quality Service

Introduction

This final chapter brings together a number of different topics under the heading of providing a quality service in social work. Its primary focus is the ways in which professional standards are promoted and upheld. This draws attention to the legal provisions that govern the regulation of social workers themselves, social work services and standards of care. Included in this are the relationships between social workers and services users, and social workers and their employers, and the broader issue of accountability. It concludes with an examination of the use of law in social work practice, relating this to your own future as a social work practitioner.

This chapter starts with a summary of the law relating to the regulation of the social work and social care workforce. Included in this is reference to ways in which excellence in social work is promoted, since quality assurance is not just about ensuring minimum standards but also about striving for the very best. We then outline ways in which services are regulated, the primary means by which service users are assured that a basic minimum level of service is offered, especially in terms of direct services such as residential care. The focus then moves to service users themselves and issues of accountability and confidentiality. There is a discussion of the relationship between social workers, their employers and the public. The chapter concludes with some reflections on developments in social work law, reminding you of topics not covered in this book, with some suggestions as to what you may need to study in the future in order to complete your professional training and your degree in social work.

Professional standards and promoting sound practice

Are you safe to practise?

Are you honest, trustworthy, reliable and the kind of person in whom service users, especially children, can have confidence?

For the general public to have confidence in social workers, it is essential for them to have affirmative answers to these questions. How is this achieved?

Activity 9.1

How would you set about proving that you were a person worthy to be trusted with the well-being of the most vulnerable members of the community?

(Continued)

(Continued)

Imagine yourself in the position of a service user and ask yourself what expectations you would have of social workers – not what they will do for you, but who they are. What regulations would you expect to be in place to ensure that social workers were trustworthy?

Just spend a few moments thinking about this question. If you already know part of the answer, try to set this aside and think instead of what you would devise if you were to start with a blank sheet of paper.

Comment

Most people undertaking this exercise start with a system of registration of social workers so that people can easily check that anyone who claimed to be a social worker was officially recognised as such. You would then expect registration to involve certain obligations: minimum levels of practice competence, commitment to keep up to date with practice developments, adherence to a professional code of practice, disciplinary procedures for those who failed to meet acceptable standards of probity and competence, and so on. You might also expect some consistency in standards, so that a social worker trained in one country met similar requirements to those trained in another. While you would not expect social workers to be clones, you would most certainly expect them to share in a body of knowledge that was common.

You would also expect a reasonably consistent standard of competence in skills, and might also expect them to adhere to the same principles and values, made explicit perhaps through a code of ethics. These are expectations people rightly have of other professionals such as doctors, lawyers and nurses.

Perhaps surprisingly, this requirement has come rather late into social work. Until the passing of the Care Standards Act 2000, anyone could in effect call themselves a social worker. The prime responsibility for the regulation of the social work and social care workforce in England rested originally with the General Social Care Council, created by that Act, and was then passed to the Health Care Professions Council who also regulate a number of other professions. In 2016 the government announced plans to introduce a bespoke social work regulator (Social Work England) from September 2018. In Wales, regulation was originally the responsibility of the Care Council for Wales (established by section 54(1) Care Standards Act 2000), but in 2017 this became Social Care Wales with a broader remit (Regulation and Inspection of Social Care (Wales) Act 2016). These bodies set regulatory frameworks governing training for professional qualifications in social work, and are also charged with maintaining a national register of social workers. Specific responsibilities include:

- registration of the social care workforce (in England, only registration of social workers is compulsory);

- drawing up codes of practice relating to standards of conduct;

- regulation of professional training: basic qualifying courses, post-qualifying courses and advanced practice awards.

Until 2015, in England alongside the Health Care Professions Council there was the College of Social Work, responsible for overall quality of professional practice, endorsing courses that met certain quality benchmarks. Whereas the Health Care Professions Council lay down minimum standards through its Standards of Proficiency, the College of Social Work promoted high professional standards through its Professional Capabilities Framework which extends from basic qualifying to advanced practice levels. Responsibility for the Professional Capabilities Framework has now been taken over by the British Association of Social Workers (BASW; for their website, see the end of the chapter). In parallel with these organisations, for social care workers in England there is Skills for Care, with a broad remit in relation to the whole social care workforce which it estimates at 1 million, about 5 per cent of the entire working population, of whom 80 per cent have no formal qualifications (see their website at the end of this chapter). It is an employer-led organisation whose mission is to *improve employers' confidence in the competence of their workforce; employees' confidence in their own knowledge and skills; service users' confidence in the quality of service they are receiving.* Social Care Wales incorporates all the functions for Wales of the Health Care Professions Council and Skills for Care, with more besides.

The public needs to be assured that there are no obvious indicators that an intending social worker might pose a risk to vulnerable people. To this end the law makes special provision.

First, the rules regarding the need to declare criminal convictions when applying for a social work post are stricter when this might involve access to vulnerable people. The Rehabilitation of Offenders Act 1974 does not apply: this Act allows people to withhold information on certain 'spent' convictions when they apply for a job. However, social work is exempt from this, so nearly all convictions, no matter of what kind, have to be declared – the only exceptions being old and minor 'filtered' convictions (section 113 Police Act 1997).

Second, the Safeguarding Vulnerable Groups Act 2006 as amended by the Protection of Freedoms Act 2012 sets out specific procedures for disqualifying certain people from working with vulnerable adults or children. The 2006 Act followed the recommendations of the Bichard report, which investigated vetting procedures following the Soham murders, and was highly critical of the previous system whereby there were two overlapping lists of people deemed unsuitable to work with children. Yet the 2006 Act replicated this division by having two 'barring' mechanisms, the Independent Safeguarding Authority and the Criminal Records Bureau. However, these functions have now been combined with the creation of the Disclosure and Barring Service (section 87 Protection of Freedoms Act 2012), although there are still two 'barred lists'– one for adults and one for children. The basic principle is that anyone who works with either children or vulnerable adults will be subject to scrutiny, whether they are paid professionals or volunteers. The degree of scrutiny depends on what the person is doing, in particular whether they are engaged in a 'regulated activity' since it is a criminal offence to seek work in a regulated activity from which a person is barred. Likewise, it is an offence for employers or voluntary organisations to appoint barred people to work in regulated activities. In effect, 'regulated' comprises frontline work which involves significant direct contact with vulnerable people, excluding activities as a member of a family. For adults, the Department of Health (2011) guidance states that this includes:

- healthcare, including psychotherapy and counselling and first aid in some circumstances;
- personal care;
- social work;
- assisting with certain household matters – for example, shopping for someone;
- assisting with managing affairs – for example, under a Lasting Power of Attorney;
- conveying someone somewhere for healthcare, personal care or social work purposes.

For children, the definition is quite wide-ranging and will in practice cover not only social work, but also foster care, childminding, teaching, healthcare, counselling, and even moderating internet chatrooms or driving school buses (Department for Education 2012; for legal definitions, see Schedule 4 Safeguarding Vulnerable Groups Act 2006 (as amended by Protection of Freedoms Act 2012). However, someone who carries out these activities under supervision is not necessarily engaged in 'regulated' activities. The secondary category of 'controlled activity', which used to refer to where someone has indirect contact with children or vulnerable adults, for example someone who is an administrator who can access records, has now been abolished.

There are clearly some circumstances in which people will automatically be barred from working with vulnerable groups. In addition, there are requirements on employers and others to report any incidents that give rise to the potential need to bar someone (Safeguarding Vulnerable Groups (Miscellaneous Provisions) Regulations 2012). These are in addition to any other procedures they may need to instigate, such as applying to the professional regulatory body to remove someone from the professional register. Also, predictably, there are rights to make representations about decisions to bar, and to appeal, given that someone who is barred will not be able to secure any kind of employment in social work and, of course, would be dismissed if they were already in employment.

It is also worth noting some specific aspects of legislation that recognise the need to enhance protection for the vulnerable – for example, the creation of the offence of abuse of trust in the Sexual Offences Act 2003 (sections 16–19), and the provisions for a penalty of up to five years' imprisonment for ill-treatment or neglect of people who lack capacity (section 44 Mental Capacity Act 2005).

Now to the more positive side: the promotion of excellence. To achieve this, the government established the Social Care Institute for Excellence as part of its Best Value strategy (Department of Health, 2000). The purpose of the Institute is to promote quality and continuous improvement in social care through research, evidence-based knowledge primarily based on the views and experience of users, together with analyses from the Care Quality Commission and its predecessor Commission for Social Care Inspection. It is essentially an organisation dedicated to dissemination of information, but also has a role in commissioning research, which has included an analysis of teaching social work law that you may find particularly interesting (Braye *et al.*, 2005).

Quality assurance of services and standards of care

Case study

The Fitzsimons family are looking for a residential home for Shelagh who is in her early nineties and finding it increasingly difficult to cope on her own. Shelagh was widowed two years ago and is still finding it strange to be alone and would welcome some company. The family want to know how they can be assured of the quality of the residential home. How do they know it will be well run? How do they know that the residents will be treated with respect? How do they know that the home will provide the special diet Shelagh needs and also respect her desire to attend the local Roman Catholic church regularly?

The quality of residential care is overseen by the Care Quality Commission, a non-departmental public body, part central-government financed and part funded by registration fees, created by the Health and Social Care Act 2008. In Wales, these functions are performed by the Care and Social Services Inspectorate Wales, which now has a wider remit under the Regulation and Inspection of Social Care (Wales) Act 2016. These inspectorates cover both social care and health establishments and agencies. The Care Quality Commission will be the organisation of greatest direct interest to the Fitzsimons family since a primary objective is to regulate the quality of care and provision in individual homes and through individual organisations. It is the regulatory body charged with inspection, enforcing minimum national standards and investigating specific complaints where these arise. Reports on routine inspections of individual establishments are openly accessible online (see their website addresses at the end of the chapter).

Generally speaking, both inspectorates are responsible for registration and inspection of care services for adults in all sectors and settings, including the private and voluntary sectors.

In addition, the Welsh body is responsible for care services to children, while in England these responsibilities have now been incorporated into the work of Ofsted, the Office for Standards in Education, Children's Services and Skills (Part 8 Education and Inspections Act 2006). Specifically, Ofsted (and the Social Services Inspectorate Wales) are responsible for the overall level of services for children in local authority areas, plus the work of CAFCASS (Children and Family Courts Advisory Service) and CAFCASS Cymru, together with inspection of childminders, day care, and adoption and fostering agencies. In Wales, the Health Care Inspectorate for Wales is additionally responsible for the inspection of standards and enforcement in relation to healthcare providers.

The work of the Mental Health Act Commission, which was responsible for certain aspects of mental health care, was transferred to the Care Quality Commission and the Health Care Inspectorate for Wales by the Health and Social Care Act 2008.

What aspects of the legislation would be particularly relevant in Shelagh's case?

As with a great deal of health and social care legislation, the precise way in which the law is to be effected is governed through schedules, regulations and nowadays also through national minimum standards. Here, however, of greatest relevance would be the care homes provisions in the Health and Social Care Act 2008, the Health and Social Care (Safety and Quality) Act 2015, and associated regulations. These include such issues as:

- the suitability of the managers, employees and premises;
- the quality of provision for welfare, management and operational procedures;
- ensuring there are sufficient staff with a minimal level of training;
- oversight of financial aspects.

Regulations cover the kinds of issues more likely to be of day-to-day concern to residents and their families, such as healthcare, medication, privacy, meals, social activities, washing facilities, heating, furniture and fittings, and dealing with residents' money. Under these broad headings will come specific issues such as respecting Shelagh's desire to practise her religion; this is in effect covered by the dignity and respect Regulation 10 of the Health and Social Care Act 2008 (Regulated Activities) Regulations 2014. At a much broader level, the family might be interested in the national work of the Care Quality Commission, Ofsted, and Care and Social Services Inspectorate Wales, since these inspectorates check the overall quality of services offered throughout the social care system, and sometimes evaluate social care providers. They have an important role in advising the central government or Welsh Assembly ministers, and also in providing readily accessible information to service users and policy-makers. They are also required to produce annual reports which are available on their respective websites (for website addresses, see the end of the chapter).

Social workers and service users

Here we are focusing on two specific issues concerning the relationship between social workers and service users in the context of responsibility for the quality of service. The first issue is accountability, especially when things appear to be going wrong; the second is confidentiality and the extent to which social workers are under an obligation to respect this.

Accountability

Activity 9.2

Imagine you are a residential social worker working in a home that offers long-term support to adults with learning disabilities in care. You become aware that some of the residents are frightened of one particular member of staff, but will not tell you what it is that is making them frightened. Your attempts to raise this with the senior management of the establishment are frustrated. You are told that you are imagining the problem and appearing frightened is a ploy to get your attention. Totally dissatisfied with this ludicrous response, you consider finding yourself another job but realise that you are under an obligation to do something.

What would you do?

Comment

You as a social worker will clearly be torn several ways. First, you will want to do something for the service user who is in distress. Second, you realise that the senior managers are in effect your employers and they are the ones with the power. They are, of course, themselves accountable so you may have to consider going above them to the trustees if it is a voluntary organisation, to the owners if it is a private organisation, or to the members (councillors) if it is a local authority. Third, you are under a professional obligation not to walk out on service users in need. There is clearly a strong ethical requirement for you to do something.

The whole notion of accountability is by no means straightforward (Braye and Preston-Shoot, 2016, Chapter 6; Welbourne, 2010). The ultimate question for social workers is: accountability to whom? Certainly social workers would want to consider themselves accountable to service users for the quality of services they offer. Yet social workers are clearly accountable to their employers who pay their salaries and lay down policies and procedures that they expect employees to follow. This is as true of a voluntary organisation as it is of a local authority. A third dimension to accountability is responsibility to professional bodies and codes of ethics. The British Association of Social Workers has a published codes of ethics, which runs in parallel with the Health and Care Professions Council's Standards of Conduct, Performance and Ethics that apply to all 16 of the professions that it covers (see the website list at end of chapter to access these codes). In Wales, there is a code of ethics as well as National Occupational Standards for all social care workers, including social workers, published online by Social Care Wales.

As far as service users are concerned, there are two ways of looking at the issue of accountability. One is simply to argue that service users are consumers and therefore if they are dissatisfied with the quality of service, they will presumably go elsewhere. This was a strong driving force behind the privatisation of much residential care for adults in the 1980s, but one objection to this is that it fails to recognise the relative powerlessness of service users. In the free market, it may be difficult for those who cannot speak for themselves and lack effective advocates. Another approach is to say that social work promotes a participative approach that sees service users as partners – hence the notion of partnership is a key principle underpinning the operation of the Children Act 1989. Again, though, it could be argued that this fails fully to recognise the power imbalance between social workers and service users and sometimes, as we saw in Chapter 4, there is an underlying question as to who is the person in most need and who exactly should be the partners.

What does the law say? First and foremost, the law draws a distinction between the needs of adults and children. In the case of children it is assumed that parents, or people acting in a parental capacity, will have the right to 'speak for' children. Therefore, in the case scenario described, had the home catered for children rather than adults, there would have been a much stronger obligation on the social worker to act to prevent abuse. In the case of a local authority this would have connected to their obligations under section 47 Children Act 1989 (see Chapter 4). In the case of adults, their vulnerability is not explicitly recognised, as we saw in Chapter 6. There is a common law obligation to prevent people coming to serious harm, but this really relates to extreme circumstances – the danger of accidental death or suicide, for example.

What does the law say regarding an organisation running the home that fails to take complaints of possible ill-treatment seriously? The answer to this has already been covered in this chapter: reference needs to be made to the commission charged with implementing the regulatory law (Care Standards Act 2000, Health and Social Care Act 2008 and associated regulations), and the obligations to have procedures to address possible abuse (Health and Social Care Act 2008 (Regulated Activities) Regulations 2014). However, you will no doubt realise that 'blowing the whistle' on what is going on in any organisation is a dangerous business. There is a very real risk of repercussions for the social worker themselves. Here the Public Interest Disclosure Act 1999 may help. The need for this legislation was recognised as a result of the Waterhouse Inquiry (Department of Health, 2000c) which acknowledged the very important role of Alison Taylor, the care worker who tried repeatedly to report the systematic sexual abuse of boys in care to the authorities (Ells and Dehn, 2001). The Act sets out a clear framework for protecting workers who raise issues of concern within their organisations, and also offers protection for wider public disclosures where initial attempts to raise issues have been thwarted.

The whole notion of professional accountability in social work was strengthened by the introduction, in April 2005, of a professional register that attempts to put social work on the same footing as the medical and healthcare professions. One clear expectation is that social workers will not tolerate abuse and will report their concerns promptly and appropriately. It is not sufficient for social workers simply to say that they are 'just' employees or that it is 'more than their job's worth' to highlight malpractice. So, in the case scenario you were given, the social worker should proceed up through the management structure of the organisation and keep going until the matter is investigated properly.

Confidentiality

One important feature of a quality service is the extent to which it honours the principle of confidentiality. Most people are aware of the confidentiality of their relationship with their GP, and many would expect a similar relationship with a social worker. However, we need to be careful since there are clear limitations on the extent of confidentiality. Naturally, social work is committed to the principle that information between social worker and service user can be shared only by agreement, but there are occasions when information must be shared regardless of objections. What are the exceptions to this principle that information may be shared only by agreement?

First, the principle would clearly not apply where the service user is a child and not yet able to give informed consent about disclosure of information. It is a clear principle in law that information may be disclosed if it is necessary to protect the child's health or well-being, and must be disclosed to other agencies where necessary to protect the child (HM Government, 2015). In this sense, disclosure is in the interests of the service user if we accept the child as the service user – and the overriding message from review of child abuse inquiries is that we must (Department of Health, 1991a).

There may be other circumstances where there is a risk of harm to others – for example, where someone has a serious mental health problem and endangers the safety of others. In one case, *W v Edgell* [1989], the court ordered the disclosure of a psychiatric report despite objections in these circumstances. Where social workers have a statutory duty to assess likely harm to the public, as is the case of Approved Mental Health Professionals considering compulsory admission under the Mental Health Act 1983, of necessity they are going to breach some aspects of the confidentiality principle, but nevertheless must still be careful about the extent to which they disclose information.

There has been a number of other cases involving disclosures of information in court cases, particularly in relation to child abuse. These generally have followed the line that disclosure of confidential information will be tolerated if necessary to protect the interests of children, but only insofar as it is truly necessary to reveal it (for a full discussion, see Brayne *et al.*, 2015, Chapter 4).

With regard to the disclosure of information, two Acts of Parliament are now relevant.

The Data Protection Act 1998, as implemented for social work in the Data Protection (Subject Access Modification) (Social Work) Order 2000 and Data Protection (Subject Access Modification) (Social Work) (Amendment) Order 2011, accords service users rights to access information about themselves. The guidelines issued by the Information Commissioner point out that, with a few exceptions, people are entitled to access information about themselves, either held in conventional files or electronically, but only about themselves (Information Commissioner's Office, 2014). The Department of Health guidelines point out that local authorities have a general duty in common law to safeguard the confidentiality of personal information. Disclosing information without consent is permissible only where this is *reasonable in all circumstances*. Local authorities are obliged to consider requests from children and young people for access to their own files, and where they consider that the child or young person has sufficient understanding, they must accede to this request (Department of Health, 2000b, 6.2, 5.8).

The other relevant Act is the Freedom of Information Act 2000. This Act gives a general right to information held by public authorities: central government, local authorities, the NHS, the police and schools. However, this is not to be used for obtaining information about other people, but can be used to access documents which public authorities have relied on to carry out their responsibilities. Its purpose is to create openness to information and to enhance public accountability (for further information, see the Information Commissioner's website at the end of this chapter).

Social workers, their employers and the public

To what extent are social workers accountable to the public at large and how should social workers and their employers interpret their mutual obligations?

In the case of local authority social workers, lines of accountability are fairly clear. Social workers often work in teams and therefore the person responsible for day-to-day oversight of the quality of social work will be a team manager. Above the team manager will be more senior managers, headed by a Director of Social Services or Director of Children's Services. Local authorities are obliged by law to appoint these chief officers or equivalents (section 6 Local Authority Social Services Act 1970, section 18 Children Act 2004). The Director in turn is responsible to a committee, cabinet or lead member of the local authority and at this level those who hold ultimate power and responsibility will be elected members. This is important since it provides the crucial element of democratic accountability on which local government relies. We might also note that this differentiates social work, locally responsible to elected councillors, from the health service whose employees are locally responsible to NHS Trusts.

In the case of voluntary or private organisations, lines of accountability may be somewhat different. It is generally held that both kinds of organisations tend to have a 'flatter' hierarchy than local authorities. In private organisations accountability will be to an owner or company board. In voluntary organisations there may be boards, councils, trustees or management committees, almost replicating the local authority structure (Harris, 2001). Whatever the organisation, as an employer it is entitled to expect certain standards of work from its employees and may take disciplinary action where this is not the case. In cases of professional misjudgements, perhaps more to be feared are the consequences of ending up in front of some kind of judicial inquiry, as has happened to social workers in the Cleveland and Climbié Inquiries (DHSS, 1988; Department of Health and Home Office, 2003). The other potential consequence is to be sued by the service user for compensation although in reality it is more likely that someone would successfully sue the employer – they are more likely to be able to pay. As we saw in the Bedfordshire case, Z and others *v* the United Kingdom, because of the consequences of implementing the Human Rights Act 1998 the courts can no longer grant local authorities immunity to legal action for persistent failure to carry out their duties.

If social workers are asked to act in some kind of court capacity, writing a report to court, advising the court or giving evidence to it, they must understand that their first duty then is to the court. They are under an obligation to give full and complete information to the court, even if this conflicts with the interests of service users or the interests of their employers. Written records may have to be made available to others despite the usual rules of confidentiality. Answers have to be given to questions (even if the social worker would prefer not to) and must be truthful, otherwise the social worker will be committing perjury. Once written evidence is submitted to court, it becomes the property of the court, and may not be disclosed for other purposes without permission from the court.

What are the employers' duties and obligations to their social workers? First, along with all employers they have a duty of care to their employees. In an important test case for social work, *Walker v Northumberland County Council* [1995], the court awarded substantial compensation to a social worker who suffered serious psychiatric consequences as a result of work-related stress. Compensation has been awarded where social workers have demonstrated that their employer knew of the excessive degree of stress they were suffering, that there was something they could have done about it, but failed to do so.

Social work and the law

In Chapter 1 we set out a number of ways in which the law is a key component in social work practice. It was explained that the law informs social workers about what their powers, duties and responsibilities are. We have now seen that in the field of child care especially, the law is quite extensive. It relates not just to Acts of Parliament themselves, but also to regulations, codes of guidance and circulars. In the field of adult care in particular we need to keep a sharp eye on the distinction between duties, that is the law that says what we must do, and permissive powers which set out what local authorities may do. As we saw in Chapters 5 and 6 there is not a great deal of adult care law that is actually mandatory, which contrasts quite markedly with the position in child care law covered in Chapters 3 and 4. It is also in this field that the law has intervened most, setting out lines of accountability, and in Chapter 8 we focused on the courts which in the UK, perhaps more than in any other country, play a key role in setting out the boundaries between the state, parents and child. Social workers in Britain maintain a high level of accountability to the courts, which offer an ultimate avenue of appeal when service users feel that they have been dealt with unfairly or unjustly. In areas such as mental health, the law helps to demarcate that fine line between the individual's right to self-determination and the duty of social workers to intervene to protect others (Chapter 6, protecting vulnerable adults). In child safeguarding cases the courts endorse or reject decisions made by social work agencies. Summarising all of this, we can see that in all areas, the courts are invaluable in offering a neutral, independent and authoritative venue where social work decisions can be tested and social workers publicly held to account. This may not be terribly comfortable at the time, but it is an important safeguard in any system where social workers still work primarily in the state sector and therefore have considerable power.

Inevitably, the law has greatest impact on local authority social workers, but social workers in all spheres, employed by a whole variety of different kinds of organisations, need to know the basics of how the law regulates social work. By now, you should be well aware of how the law serves to set the boundaries within which social work operates. It is hoped that you can also now see how the law can be used positively in order to promote people's rights, to protect them from infringements of their basic freedoms and to further their interests. The book was deliberately entitled *Using the law in social work*, and it is hoped that by this point you begin to see how law can be used in order to empower social work service users and how it is a positive tool in social work practice.

So, what's next?

Review and the future: what next?

The law that has been covered here should be more than adequate for the attainment of relevant Professional Capabilities Framework expectations or Welsh National Occupational

Standards. Academically, the book was geared to the QAA Subject Benchmarks for Social Work at Levels One and Two of the BA, and equivalent level of the MA. At higher levels you may require more specialist information about the law and how it operates in social work so in this section there is a brief overview of areas of law that we have not examined in detail, followed by an exposition of potential future changes which will incorporate some suggestions for further study.

To remind you, at the outset it was declared that the book would not examine welfare benefits law, although this will be an important area if you intend to work as a social worker in some kind of advocacy role. Allied with this is the law relating to asylum seekers and refugees. This is a specialist area in social work of particular importance in relation to unaccompanied children and young people, but unfortunately beyond the scope of this book. Key legislation here is the Immigration and Asylum Act 1999, the Nationality, Immigration and Asylum Act 2002, the Asylum and Immigration (Treatment of Claimants, etc.) Act 2004, the Immigration, Asylum and Nationality Act 2006 and the Criminal Justice and Immigration Act 2008 (for further information, see Brammer, 2015, Chapter 20).

We have also not covered housing law, either in terms of homelessness, tenancy protection or issues that arise when people wish to live together as a unit (the most relevant legislation in these areas being the Housing Act 1996, the Homelessness Act 2002, the Civil Partnership Act 2004 and the Housing and Regeneration Act 2008). If you are engaged in advocacy or advice work concerning the break-up of relationships, you may wish to know more about the law regarding domestic violence than is contained in this book – for example, we have not addressed the detailed procedures under the Family Law Act 1996 as amended and extended by the Domestic Violence, Crime and Victims Act 2004 for obtaining occupation orders and non-molestation orders or the implications of non-compliance with injunctions. Nor has the book covered domestic violence protection orders (sections 24–33 Crime and Security Act 2010), provisions relating to forced marriage (Forced Marriage (Civil Protection) Act 2007), or offences labelled 'coercive or controlling behaviour' (section 76 Serious Crime Act 2015).

In Chapter 6 there was brief reference to the Mental Health Act 1983 in the context of protecting vulnerable adults, but mental health legislation has a number of other facets. Social workers with post-qualifying experience sometimes opt to become Approved Mental Health Professionals, who have the power and authority to arrange compulsory admissions under the Mental Health Act 1983. Suffice it to say that this requires much more detailed knowledge and practice experience than would be expected at this stage, including attendance at a post-qualifying Health and Care Professions Council or Social Care Wales approved training course. Also under mental health law, we have not examined guardianship, a form of supervision of people with *mental disorders*, or the law relating to tribunals and their expectations of social workers, although this was mentioned in passing. If you work with vulnerable adults, you may want to find out more about the Mental Capacity Act 2005 regarding capacity to consent and managing one's own affairs, especially if you are considering eventually becoming a Best Interest Assessor under the Deprivation of Liberty Safeguards since this too involves attending a post-qualifying course.

While Chapter 7 covered youth justice, this book has made no attempt to cover adult criminal law as this is outside the area of responsibility of social workers in England and Wales. However, if you intend to practise in Scotland or Northern Ireland, the situation is quite different. Scottish social workers in particular do need to know about the provisions of the adult criminal justice system. Although there was some reference to the police powers in criminal investigations in Chapter 7 regarding the role of social workers acting as *appropriate adults*, it was not really feasible to cover the rules governing police procedures. These are mainly to be found in the Police and Criminal Evidence Act 1984 (PACE), as amended by the Police and Justice Act 2006 and Crime and Security Act 2010, and as implemented by the regularly updated Codes of Practice associated with PACE, particularly Code C (Home Office, 2014).

Two other areas have not been covered. Access to financial support for service users involved in court cases, either as litigants or as victims, has not featured in this book. For this reference needs to be made to legal aid provision, for which the Legal Aid Agency is responsible, and to the criminal injury compensation scheme, for which the Criminal Injury Compensation Authority is responsible (website addresses can be found at the end of the chapter). Nor has there been detailed consideration of anti-discrimination legislation for reasons that were explained in Chapter 1, although there have been references to the Equality Act 2010, with its requirement that local authorities and other public bodies take a proactive stance in relation to discrimination, the public sector Equality Duty.

Now to possible future developments.

Chapter 2 looked at the importance of the European Convention on Human Rights in UK law. Some politicians have expressed frustration that their powers are apparently fettered by interpretation of the European Convention on Human Rights by a court outside the UK, with a serious move in some quarters to propose the repeal of the Human Rights Act 1998. A Bill to this effect was proposed in Parliament in February 2013 but subsequently withdrawn. In the light of plans to withdraw the UK from the European Union, plans to repeal the Human Rights Act 1998 have been resurrected, with suggestions that the European Convention on Human Rights could be replaced for Britain by some kind of constitutional Bill of Rights interpreted solely by UK courts. It does not, of course, follow automatically that withdrawal from the EU necessarily entails withdrawing from the European Convention on Human Rights; the only formal link is that new EU members are required to abide by it. In Chapters 3 and 4, we looked at the extensive field of child care law where there are a number of issues. The Children Act 2004 is key here. The Act had a major impact on the organisation of social services, with a clear demarcation emerging between adults' services and children's services.

Likewise, the Adoption and Children Act 2002 is of significance, but this Act has been only partially explored here. So, if you intend to engage in permanency planning for children work, especially if you are involved in adoptions, you will need to learn more about this legislation and its implications for practice. You should also keep an eye on new legislation since the government has regularly tried to increase the number of adoptions through various policy initiatives (Department for Education, 2013). In 2016, the government announced its intention to introduce an additional number of 'pro-adoption' measures in the Children and Social Work Bill, building on the Children and Families Act 2014. While there are no plans declared for changing the basic provisions of the Children Act 1989, the Children and Young Persons Act 2008 extended the 1989 Act by introducing a raft of additional responsibilities for local authorities and Ofsted. These include securing sufficient appropriate accommodation for children in local authority care (section 9), certain measures to enhance support for looked-after children (sections 15–19), a duty on state schools to designate a member of staff to promote the educational achievement of children in care (section 20), and a wider local authority duty to assist young people who have been through the care system to pursue education and training (section 22). Duties in relation to educational achievement of looked-after children were enhanced in the Children and Families Act 2014 (section 99), which also introduced (in section 14) a time limit of 26 weeks for care proceedings. Other measures in this Act range from speeding up adoptions (sections 1–7) to extending statements of special needs to age 25 or even beyond (section 46), and improvements in child care and more flexible arrangements for parental leave after the birth of a child (sections 117–25). In child safeguarding, apart from a statutory time limitation on care proceedings, major legislative changes are not envisaged in England, but social work practice continues to be scrutinised following the Munro Review of practice published in 2011 (Department for Education, 2010b, 2011c). In 2016 the government announced plans to make changes to assessment in child safeguarding alongside changes in social work education. These were to run alongside planned legislative changes to the way that children's services are delivered, although to what extent these will come to fruition remains to be seen.

In Wales, significant changes are afoot in that, following implementation of the Social Services and Well-being (Wales) Act 2014, further guidance and regulations will be introduced in order to offer a comprehensive legislative framework for provision of social services to children and adults. These are likely to relate both to Part 6 of the Act, the law relating to looked-after children, and Part 7 covering safeguarding (elsewhere in the Act there are the various provisions for assessment, meeting need, finance, reviews, complaints and advocacy).

The field of adult care law has been crying out for a long time for legal reform, and, as explained in Chapters 5 and 6, there has been a pressing need for codification of the law regarding service provision and informed consent. This was partly remedied with the implementation of the Mental Capacity Act 2005, which sets out a single clear test for determining whether someone 'lacks capacity'. There have also been changes in mental health legislation so as to broaden its scope and potentially bring people with personality disorders within the remit of compulsory control. The Mental Health Act 2007 introduced deprivation of liberty safeguards into the Mental Capacity Act 2005 to legitimise legal authority over people who are deemed to need supervision rather than treatment, thereby responding to the European Court's judgement in the Bournewood case (outlined in Chapter 2). Nevertheless, there are as yet no plans to try to create a charter of rights of entitlement to services for people with mental health problems, and you will undoubtedly have noticed the strong contrast between the lack of real substantive rights for vulnerable adults compared with the entitlement to services of children in need. In 2011, the Law Commission drew up proposals for new legislation and codes of practice that would help create a coherent social care system and put adult safeguarding on a proper legal footing (Law Commission, 2011). The majority of these were incorporated into the Care Act 2014 and the Social Services and Well-being (Wales) Act 2014, both of which are now fully implemented and provide the bedrock for adult social care legislation; note also that the Welsh law also provides a foundation for social work law relating to children – an opportunity lost in England?

The field of youth justice (Chapter 7) is always politically sensitive. The Criminal Justice and Immigration Act 2008 with its extensive list of 'requirements' that substitute for the previous range of orders (see Chapter 7 for the full list) has now been fully implemented, but there are already hints of amendments being considered. Significantly, the Youth Justice Board's responsibilities have been transferred to the Ministry of Justice, thus bringing youth justice under the direct control of a government minister. The anti-social behaviour provisions of the Crime and Disorder Act 1998 were not widely used when first introduced, but courts were encouraged to use them more frequently and more widely, aided by the passing of the Anti-Social Behaviour Act 2003. Again, there was virulent opposition to this in some quarters for these orders were not made as a result of proven criminal acts but were civil measures taken where the courts were persuaded on the balance of probabilities that there was a likelihood of committing offences. There may even be some doubt as to whether anti-social behaviour orders conformed to the European Convention on Human Rights. In February 2011, the government announced plans to abolish Anti-Social Behaviour Orders as such and replace them with new provisions, but with a similar aim in mind. The Anti-Social Behaviour, Crime and Policing Act 2014 implemented a number of changes including, in Part 1 of that Act, Injunctions and Criminal Behaviour Orders, as explained in Chapter 7.

Looking at court work, the subject of Chapter 8, major recent developments have related to the organisation and administration of the courts themselves following implementation of Crime and Courts Act 2013. The Courts Act 2003 Act led to the establishment of a unified national courts administration service, facilitating attempts to make the court system more responsive to users' needs. Section 17 of the 2013 Act relaunched the Family Court; it is hoped that this, alongside other developments such as updating protocols and procedures, will help to implement the speeded-up care proceedings made mandatory by the Children and Families Act 2014 and Family Procedure Rules 2014 Practice Direction 12A (the Public Law Outline). The 2009 rationalisation of the court system that created the Supreme Court to replace the House of Lords as the final court of appeal in the UK is now complete, although cases can still sometimes be taken on to the European Court of Human Rights in Strasbourg if need be. Further information on what the Supreme Court does and decisions they have made can be found on their website (their address can be found at the end of the chapter).

In this chapter, we noted developments in relation to the Inspectorates, who appear to be broadening their scope and now comment both on social care policy implementation and quality of standards in individual establishments and organisations. We also noted other measures designed to protect service users and promote professional standards. This brings us, finally, to the area that has most direct immediate impact on you – the Care Standards Act 2000 together with the Health and Social Care Act 2012 with their professional registration requirements for social work practitioners. For student social workers in England, reference should be made to the requirements of the HCPC Guidance on Conduct and Ethics for Students Health and Care Professions Council (Health and Care Professions Council, 2010). Students in Wales will need to be registered with Social Care Wales and agree to abide by its Code of Practice and conform to its registration rules. In addition, you are subject to the requirements of the Disclosure and Barring Scheme (Safeguarding Vulnerable Groups Act 2006, Protection of Freedoms Act 2012), so you will need to know what these provisions are. If you are in any doubt as to what is expected of you, please put down this book now and go on to the relevant council's website immediately.

Further reading

For further discussion of the role of law in social work, see:

Braye, S and Preston-Shoot, M (2016) *Practising social work law* (4th edn). Basingstoke: Palgrave.

Johns, R (2016) *Ethics and law for social workers*. Sage: London.

Websites

BASW for Code of Ethics: www.basw.co.uk

BASW for Professional Capabilities Framework: www.basw.co.uk/pcf/

Care Quality Commission: www.cqc.org.uk

Care and Social Services Inspectorate Wales: http://cssiw.org.uk

Criminal Injuries Compensation Authority: www.gov.uk/government/organisations/criminal-injuries-compensation-authority

Department for Education: www.gov.uk/government/organisations/department-for-education

Department of Health: www.gov.uk/government/organisations/department-of-health

Health Care Professions Council: www.hpc-uk.org

Information Commissioner: https://ico.org.uk/

Legal Aid Agency: www.gov.uk/government/organisations/legal-aid-agency

Office for Standards in Education (Ofsted): www.gov.uk/government/organisations/ofsted

Skills for Care: www.skillsforcare.org.uk

Social Care Institute for Excellence (SCIE): www.scie.org.uk

Social Care Wales: www.ccwales.org.uk

Supreme Court: www.supremecourt.uk/

Exercise Answers

Chapter 1

Activity 1.3

	Statute law	Common law
Criminal law	Crime and Disorder Act 1998 Theft Act 1968 Sexual Offences Act 2003	Once found not guilty of an offence by the court a defendant cannot usually be retried People who are accused of crimes are assumed innocent until found guilty Actively assisting someone to commit suicide is murder
Civil law	Failing to pay a TV licence fee Children Act 1989 Care Act 2014 All employees must be provided with a contract of employment Family Law Act 1996 *Care Quality Commission (Registration) Regulations 2009*	Failing to pay rent An employer's duty of care to employees Spending money on a service which a local authority does not have statutory authority to provide means it is acting ultra vires

Chapter 2

Activity 2.2

European Convention on Human Rights

Article 1	The convention applies to everyone.
Article 2	Right to life. Some exemptions: • execution as court sentence • use of force in defence of someone subject to unlawful violence • lawful arrest or prevention of escape from custody • to quell a riot or insurrection.
Article 3	No one shall be subjected to torture or to inhuman or degrading treatment or punishment.
Article 4	No slavery or forced labour. Limited exemptions for prisoners, military service, time of war.
Article 5	Right to *liberty and security* of person. Exceptions: (a) detention following conviction by court; (b) arrest and detention for non-compliance with law; (c) arrest or detention in order to bring before court on suspicion of committing offence; (d) detention of young people in relation to education;

(Continued)

(Continued)

Article 5	(e) the lawful detention of persons for the prevention of the spreading of infectious diseases, of persons of unsound mind, alcoholics or drug addicts, or vagrants;
	(f) arrest in relation to deportation or extradition.
	There are additional provisions in relation to arrest. Some of these are referred to later in the chapter. Note especially (e) above.
Article 6	Right to trial. Innocent until proven guilty. List of minimum rights set out in relation to people charged with criminal offences.
Article 7	No retrospective convictions, i.e. cannot be prosecuted for an action that was lawful at the time it was committed.
Article 8	Everyone has the right to respect for his private and family life, his home and his correspondence.
	There shall be no interference by public authority with the exercise of this right except such as is in accordance with the law and is necessary in a democratic society in the interests of national security, public safety or the economic well-being of the country, for the prevention of disorder or crime, for the protection of health or morals, or for the protection of the rights and freedoms of others.
Article 9	Right to *freedom of thought, conscience and religion*. This includes right to change religions and the freedom to manifest religion or belief in worship, teaching, practice and observance. Exceptions must be in the interests of public safety or protection of public order, health or morals or protection of the rights and freedoms of others.
Article 10	Rights of freedom of expression. Several exemptions acknowledging that this carries duties and responsibilities: underlying criterion here is necessary in a democratic society.
Article 11	Rights of assembly and association. Again exemptions as are necessary in a democratic society.
Article 12	Right to marry and *found a family*.
Article 13	Rights to an effective remedy for violation of Convention.
Article 14	No discrimination in applying Convention rights.

NB The above table is a summary with partial quotations. For complete European Convention on Human Rights see: **www.echr.coe.int/Convention/webConvenENG.pdf**

Potential relevance of Convention to social work and service users

Of the Articles of the Convention, those which appear to be particularly relevant to social work are (in Convention order, not necessarily potential order of importance):

Article 2	euthanasia, abortion (although European court has tried to steer clear of this one), medical decision-making and capacity to make informed medical choices
Article 3	failure to protect from harm (Bedfordshire case – see below), physical punishment of children, standards of care in homes, treatment in psychiatric hospitals and prisons
Article 5	detention of people with mental disorder, capacity to consent to hospital admission
	asylum seekers
	political interference in court sentences
Article 6	arrest rights
	right to fair trial

	discharge from prison
	discharge from secure hospitals
Article 8	routine checking of correspondence: prisons, hospitals
	surveillance equipment
	rights of patients and service users to nominate nearest relative
Article 10	confidentiality
	press coverage of particular cases
Article 12	position of transsexuals
	changing birth data
Article 13	denying children access to remedies (Bedfordshire case)

Chapter 3

Activity 3.3

The government schemes originally introduced since 1997 but reformulated in 2004 and 2011 are (in brief) as follows.

Sure Start

The Sure Start programme brought together early education, health and family support in order to address disadvantage and social exclusion. Its aim was to promote universal early education and improved child care, through, for example, children's centres and specific local programmes. Its principles are very similar to those undergirding the Children Act 1989: working in partnership with parents; services offered according to need; flexibility; responsiveness to what parents want, together with an emphasis on community links and simpler funding mechanisms. Provision continues in some areas (www.gov.uk/find-sure-start-childrens-centre) where local authorities use the Early Intervention Grant (see below).

Children's centres

Local authorities have duties under the Childcare Act 2006 to secure sufficient provision to meet local need so far as is reasonably practicable. To this end they must specifically consider the needs of younger children (Childcare Act 2006 section 3).

The Early Intervention Grant

This is a general grant to local authorities to make provision to support the development of children and young people. It is not ring-fenced or tied to specific projects and there are no rules as to how local authorities use the funding. However, there is a general government expectation that funding will be used to support:

- Sure Start children's centres;
- free early education places for disadvantaged two-year-olds;
- short breaks for disabled children;
- targeted support for vulnerable young people;
- targeted mental health in schools;
- targeted support for families with multiple problems.

Chapter 4

Activity 4.2

In the first scenario, it is very likely that you concluded that children of this age are terrified at being left alone even for a short time, although clearly you would want to know more about the circumstances. However, the question also arises what kind of abuse would this be potentially? No direct physical harm is caused, so you might conclude that this is neglect.

Scenario 2 is more problematic since many would consider the parents' expectations quite reasonable, and therefore not abusive. However, if this were to be considered abuse, what kind of abuse would it be? It is not neglect, but it could be argued that excessive demands on children impede their intellectual or emotional development (although unlikely in this case).

Most people would conclude that scenario 3 is highly abusive since, although not directly physically harmful, it is quite terrifying to children to be locked in a confined space even for a short time.

Scenario 4 appears to be a clear-cut case of physical abuse but one might want to know how the injuries were caused – or perhaps you wouldn't: does it matter if it's a dog bite or the consequences of being bitten by another child?

Scenario 5 raises the issue of sexual abuse but also the possibility of the need to take into account both children as victims and abusers.

The final scenario would now be considered an obvious case of physical abuse, although relatively common standard child care practice until fairly recently. Indeed beating children with an implement now appears to be a direct contravention of the European Convention on Human Rights (see cases summarised in Chapter 2).

Chapter 5

Activity 5.2

There are no specific *legal measures* that promote empowerment as such, but there are various pieces of legislation that promote rights to advocacy and representation and choice, together with anti-discrimination legislation. You could have referred to some of the following:

Information regarding availability of services and entitlements	Section 4 Care Act 2014 or section 17 Social Services and Well-being (Wales) Act 2014
	Section 18 Care Act 2014 or section 32 Social Services and Well-being (Wales) Act 2014
	Care Act 2014 Statutory Guidance (Department of Health 2016); for Wales Social Services and Well-being (Wales) Act 2014 guidance (http://www.ccwales.org.uk/codes-of-practice-and-statutory-guidance)
Advocacy and rights to be represented and involved in decision-making	Carer rights especially section 10 Care Act 2014 or section 24 Social Services and Well-being (Wales) Act 2014
	Section 11 Care Act 2014 (section 20 Social Services and Well-being (Wales) Act 2014) covers assessment refusal due to lack of capacity
Communication facilitation	Care Act 2014 and Social Services and Well-being (Wales) Act 2014 statutory guidance
Choice of service provider, choice of accommodation	Direct payments: sections 31-33 Care Act 2014 or section 50 Social Services and Well-being (Wales) Act 2014
	Choice of accommodation: section 30 Care Act 2014 or section 57 Social Services and Well-being (Wales) Act 2014
Independence and right to make own decisions and to secure services of own service providers	Direct payments (see above)
	Personal budget section 26 Care Act 2014 (not applicable in Wales)
	Care and support plan section 27 Care Act 2014 or section 54 Social Services and Well-being (Wales) Act 2014
Anti-discrimination provisions	Equality Act 2010
Appeal rights and access to complaints procedures	Complaints: Local Authority Social Services and National Health Service (England) Complaints Regulations 2009 or Part 10 Social Services and Well-being (Wales) Act 2014; Care Standards Act 2000 as amended
	Appeals: some specific rights under, for example, Mental Heath Act 1983
Judicial review and right to challenge decisions on human rights grounds	Common law rights to challenge decisions made by public bodies
	Human Rights Act 1998: various rights from European Convention on Human Rights incorporated into UK law

In terms of service provision, you may have referred to the regulatory duties of inspection (these are covered in detail in Chapter 9). Relevant here would be the Care Standards Act 2000. Also relevant would be:

- regulations: for example, regarding assessment, eligibility, charges, choice of accommodation;

- local authority circulars (LACs): for example, regarding finance and organisation of services;

- Codes of Practice: regarding sensitive practice in matters such as mental health;
- National Service Frameworks: for older people, mental health and White Paper on Learning Disabilities all set out ways of achieving good practice but these do not themselves have the full force of law. They set standards by which central government makes judgements about the quality of services so may carry financial rather than legal weight.

For a full discussion of the status and standing of Regulations, Circulars and Codes of Practice, see Chapter 1.

Chapter 7

Activity 7.2

Sources of possible avenues for research:

- books, not just textbooks but also biographical and autobiographical accounts;
- articles in refereed journals (possibly accessed through databases);
- articles in professional journals;
- articles in newspapers – do be careful here, given the media tendency to sensationalise;
- service users themselves, obviously, although do pay close attention to issues such as sensitivity and confidentiality;
- practitioners in the youth justice field, although be careful about how much time you take up;
- information from research bodies such as the Joseph Rowntree Trust or RPS Rayner (these are only two examples, there are plenty of others);
- information from groups representing the interests of users such as victim support groups, either published information or personal visits – but again do be careful how much time you take up if you visit them;
- internet sources: although again pay great attention to the reliability and authenticity of the websites you use.

Chapter 8

Activity 8.3

Answers to Activity 8.3 ought to have included at least the following:

The key issues for children/young people are:

- keeping them aware of what is happening;
- presenting information in a way that they can understand;
- clarifying their wishes and feelings;
- ensuring that wishes and feelings are properly conveyed to the court.

The key issues for parents are:

- understanding what is happening to them;
- obtaining sound legal advice and assistance;
- openness and transparency;
- social workers being honest about issues.

The key issues for social workers are:

- being straight with people about issues involved;
- continuing to work in partnership with parents;
- proper preparation of cases for court;
- testing out evidence, being clear about the difference between facts, interpretation of facts, and opinion;
- maintaining objectivity and impartiality.

Appendix 1

Professional Capabilities Framework (2015)

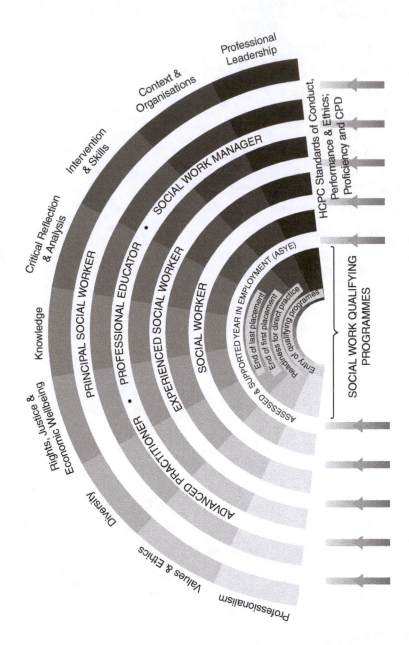

Professional Capabilities Framework diagram reproduced with permission of The College of Social Work.

HCPC Standards of Proficiency

Registrant social workers must:

1. be able to practise safely and effectively within their scope of practice;

2. be able to practise within the legal and ethical boundaries of their profession;

3. be able to maintain fitness to practice;

4. be able to practise as an autonomous professional, exercising their own professional judgement;

5. be aware of the impact of culture, equality and diversity on practice;

6. be able to practise in a non-discriminatory manner;

7. be able to maintain confidentiality;

8. be able to communicate effectively;

9. be able to work appropriately with others;

10. be able to maintain records appropriately;

11. be able to reflect on and review practice;

12. be able to assure the quality of their practice;

13. understand the key concepts of the knowledge base relevant to their profession;

14. be able to draw on appropriate knowledge and skills to inform practice;

15. be able to establish and maintain a safe practice environment.

Professional Capabilities Framework (2015)

1. **Professionalism: Identify and behave as a professional social worker, committed to professional development**

Social workers are members of an internationally recognised profession, a title protected in UK law. Social workers demonstrate professional commitment by taking responsibility for their conduct, practice and learning, with support through supervision. As representatives of the social work profession they safeguard its reputation and are accountable to the professional regulator.

- Demonstrates an initial understanding of the role of the social worker.

- Demonstrates motivation and commitment to qualify and practice as a social worker.

- Identifies own potential strengths and weaknesses in relation to the role of social worker.

- Demonstrates an initial understanding of the importance of personal resilience and adaptability in social work.

- Demonstrates the ability to take responsibility for own learning and development.

2. **Values and Ethics: Apply social work ethical principles and values to guide professional practice**

Social workers have an obligation to conduct themselves ethically and to engage in ethical decision-making, including through partnership with people who use their services. Social workers are knowledgeable about the value base of their profession, its ethical standards and relevant law.

- Recognises the impact their own values and attitudes can have on relationships with others.

- Understands the importance of seeking the perspectives and views of service users and carers.

- Recognises that social workers will need to deal with conflict and use the authority invested in their role.

3. **Diversity: Recognise diversity and apply anti-discriminatory and anti-oppressive principles in practice**

Social workers understand that diversity characterises and shapes human experience and is critical to the formation of identity. Diversity is multi-dimensional and includes race, disability, class, economic status, age, sexuality, gender and transgender, faith and belief. Social workers appreciate that, as a consequence of difference, a person's life experience may include oppression, marginalisation and alienation as well as privilege, power and acclaim, and are able to challenge appropriately.

- Demonstrates an initial understanding of difference and diversity within society and the implications of this for social work practice.

- Is receptive to the views of others.

4. Rights, Justice and Economic Well-being: Advance human rights and promote social justice and economic well-being

Social workers recognise the fundamental principles of human rights and equality, and that these are protected in national and international law, conventions and policies. They ensure these principles underpin their practice. Social workers understand the importance of using and contributing to case law and applying these rights in their own practice. They understand the effects of oppression, discrimination and poverty.

- Recognises the contribution of social work to promoting social justice, inclusion and equality.

- Is receptive to the idea that there may be conflicts in the social work role between promoting rights and enforcing responsibilities.

5. Knowledge: Apply knowledge of social sciences, law and social work practice theory

Social workers understand psychological, social, cultural, spiritual and physical influences on people; human development throughout the life span and the legal framework for practice. They apply this knowledge in their work with individuals, families and communities. They know and use theories and methods of social work practice.

- Identify how own learning (formal, informal and experiential) contributes to understanding the social work role.

6. Critical Reflection and Analysis: Apply critical reflection and analysis to inform and provide a rationale for professional decision-making

Social workers are knowledgeable about and apply the principles of critical thinking and reasoned discernment. They identify, distinguish, evaluate and integrate multiple sources of knowledge and evidence. These include practice evidence, their own practice experience, service user and carer experience together with research-based, organisational, policy and legal knowledge. They use critical thinking augmented by creativity and curiosity.

- Demonstrates an ability to reflect on and analyse own experience (educational, personal, formal and informal).

- Demonstrates curiosity and critical thinking about social issues.

7. **Intervention and Skills: Use judgement and authority to intervene with individuals, families and communities to promote independence, provide support and prevent harm, neglect and abuse**

Social workers engage with individuals, families, groups and communities, working alongside people to assess and intervene. They enable effective relationships and are effective communicators, using appropriate skills. Using their professional judgement, they employ a range of interventions: promoting independence, providing support and protection, taking preventative action and ensuring safety while balancing rights and risks. They understand and take account of differentials in power, and are able to use authority appropriately. They evaluate their own practice and the outcomes for those they work with.

- Communicates clearly, accurately and appropriately to the level of training applied for, in verbal and written forms.

- Demonstrates an ability to engage with people with empathy.

8. **Contexts and Organisations: Engage with, inform, and adapt to changing contexts that shape practice. Operate effectively within own organisational frameworks and contribute to the development of services and organisations. Operate effectively within multi-agency and inter-professional partnerships and settings**

Social workers are informed about and pro-actively responsive to the challenges and opportunities that come with changing social contexts and constructs. They fulfil this responsibility in accordance with their professional values and ethics, both as individual professionals and as members of the organisation in which they work. They collaborate, inform and are informed by their work with others, inter-professionally and with communities.

- Demonstrates understanding of importance of working as a member of a team and an organisation.

9. **Professional Leadership: Take responsibility for the professional learning and development of others through supervision, mentoring, assessing, research, teaching, leadership and management**

The social work profession evolves through the contribution of its members in activities such as practice research, supervision, assessment of practice, teaching and management. An individual's contribution will gain influence when undertaken as part of a learning, practice-focused organisation. Learning may be facilitated with a wide range of people including social work colleagues, service users and carers, volunteers, foster carers and other professionals.

- Recognises how own learning, behaviour and ideas can influence and benefit others.

Appendix 2

Subject Benchmark for Social Work (2016): Extracts

4 Defining concepts and principles

4.7 The expectation that social workers are able to act effectively in such complex circumstances requires that qualifying degree programmes in Social Work are designed to help students learn to become accountable, reflective, critical and evaluative.
This involves learning to:

> think critically about the complex social, legal, economic, political, cultural, theoretical and research contexts in which Social Work practice is located

> work in a transparent and responsible way, balancing autonomy with complex, multiple and sometimes contradictory accountabilities (for example, to different service users, employing agencies, professional bodies and the wider society)

> exercise authority constructively within complex frameworks of accountability and ethical and legal boundaries

> understand the complexity of Social Work practice recognising the need for identified knowledge, skills and values which reflect the life course of individuals, families and communities

> acquire and apply the skills of critical reflection, self-evaluation and consultation and use opportunities for professional supervision

> make appropriate use of research in decision making and professional judgement about practice and in the evaluation of outcomes.

5 Knowledge, understanding and skills

5.2 Social Work theory, which includes:

i   critical explanations from Social Work theory and other subjects which contribute to the knowledge base of Social Work

ii an understanding of Social Work's rich and contested history from both a UK and comparative perspective

iii   the relevance of sociological and applied psychological perspectives to understanding societal and structural influences on human behaviour at individual, group and community levels, and the relevance of sociological theorisation to a deeper understanding of adaptation and change

iv   the relevance of psychological, physical and physiological perspectives to understanding human, personal and social development, well-being and risk

v   social science theories explaining and exploring group and organisational behaviour

vi   the range of theories and research informed evidence that informs understanding of the child, adult, family or community and of the range of assessment and interventions which can be used

vii   the theory, models and methods of assessment, factors underpinning the selection and testing of relevant information, knowledge and critical appraisal of relevant social science and other research and evaluation methodologies, and the evidence base for Social Work

viii   the nature of analysis and professional judgement and the processes of risk assessment and decision making, including the theory of risk informed decisions and the balance of choice and control, rights and protection in decision making

ix   approaches, methods and theories of intervention in working with a diverse population within a wide range of settings, including factors guiding the choice and critical evaluation of these, and user-led perspectives.

5.3 Values and ethics, which include:

i   the nature, historical evolution, political context and application of professional Social Work values, informed by national and international definitions and ethical statements, and their relation to personal values, identities, influences and ideologies

ii   the ethical concepts of rights, responsibility, freedom, authority and power inherent in the practice of social workers as agents with statutory powers in different situations

iii   aspects of philosophical ethics relevant to the understanding and resolution of value dilemmas and conflicts in both interpersonal and professional contexts

iv   understanding of, and adherence to, the ethical foundations of empirical and conceptual research, as both consumers and producers of social science research

v   the relationship between human rights enshrined in law and the moral and ethical rights determined theoretically, philosophically and by contemporary society

vi   the complex relationships between justice, care and control in social welfare and the practical and ethical implications of these, including their expression in roles as statutory agents in diverse practice settings and in upholding the law in respect of challenging discrimination and inequalities

vii   the conceptual links between codes defining ethical practice and the regulation of professional conduct

viii   the professional and ethical management of potential conflicts generated by codes of practice held by different professional groups

ix   the ethical management of professional dilemmas and conflicts in balancing the perspectives of individuals who need care and support and professional decision making at points of risk, care and protection

x   the constructive challenging of individuals and organisations where there may be conflicts with Social Work values, ethics and codes of practice

xi   the professional responsibility to be open and honest if things go wrong (the duty of candour about own practice) and to act on concerns about poor or unlawful practice by any person or organisation

xii   continuous professional development as a reflective, informed and skilled practitioner, including the constructive use of professional supervision.

5.4 Service users and carers, which include:

i   the factors which contribute to the health and well-being of individuals, families and communities, including promoting dignity, choice and independence for people who need care and support

ii   the underpinning perspectives that determine explanations of the characteristics and circumstances of people who need care and support, with critical evaluation drawing on research, practice experience and the experience and expertise of people who use services

iii   the social and psychological processes associated with, for example, poverty, migration, unemployment, trauma, poor health, disability, lack of education and other sources of disadvantage and how they affect well-being, how they interact and may lead to marginalisation, isolation and exclusion, and demand for Social Work services

iv   explanations of the links between the factors contributing to social differences and identities (for example, social class, gender, ethnic differences, age, sexuality and religious belief) and the structural consequences of inequality and differential need faced by service users

v   the nature and function of Social Work in a diverse and increasingly global society (with particular reference to prejudice, interpersonal relations, discrimination, empowerment and anti-discriminatory practices).

5.5 The nature of Social Work practice, in the UK and more widely, which includes:

i   the place of theoretical perspectives and evidence from European and international research in assessment and decision-making processes

ii   the integration of theoretical perspectives and evidence from European and international research into the design and implementation of effective Social Work intervention with a wide range of service users, carers and communities

iii   the knowledge and skills which underpin effective practice, with a range of service-users and in a variety of settings

iv   the processes that facilitate and support service user and citizen rights, choice, co-production, self-governance, well-being and independence

v   the importance of interventions that promote social justice, human rights, social cohesion, collective responsibility and respect for diversity and tackle inequalities

vi   its delivery in a range of community-based and organisational settings spanning the statutory, voluntary and private sectors, and the changing nature of these service contexts

vii   the factors and processes that facilitate effective interdisciplinary, interprofessional and interagency collaboration and partnership across a plurality of settings and disciplines

viii   the importance of Social Work's contribution to intervention across service user groups, settings and levels in terms of the profession's focus on social justice, human rights, social cohesion, collective responsibility and respect for diversities

ix   the processes of reflection and reflexivity as well as approaches for evaluating service and welfare outcomes for vulnerable people, and their significance for the development of practice and the practitioner.

5.6 The leadership, organisation and delivery of Social Work services, which includes:

i   the location of contemporary Social Work within historical, comparative and global perspectives, including in the devolved nations of the UK and wider European and international contexts

ii   how the service delivery context is portrayed to service users, carers, families and communities

iii   the changing demography and cultures of communities, including European and international contexts, in which social workers practise

iv   the complex relationships between public, private, social and political philosophies, policies and priorities and the organisation and practice of social work, including the contested nature of these

   v   the issues and trends in modern public and social policy and their relationship to contemporary practice, service delivery and leadership in Social Work

   vi   the significance of legislative and legal frameworks and service delivery standards, including on core social work values and ethics in the delivery of services which support, enable and empower

   vii   the current range and appropriateness of statutory, voluntary and private agencies providing services and the organisational systems inherent within these

   viii   development of new ways of working and delivery, for example the development of social enterprises, integrated multi-professional teams and independent Social Work provision

   ix   the significance of professional and organisational relationships with other related services, including housing, health, education, police, employment, fire, income maintenance and criminal justice

   x   the importance and complexities of the way agencies work together to provide care, the relationships between agency policies, legal requirements and professional boundaries in shaping the nature of services provided in integrated and interdisciplinary contexts

   xi   the contribution of different approaches to management and leadership within different settings, and the impact on professional practice and on quality of care management and leadership in public and human services

   xii   the development of person-centred services, personalised care, individual budgets and direct payments all focusing upon the human and legal rights of the service user for control, power and self determination

   xiii   the implications of modern information and communications technology for both the provision and receipt of services, use of technologically enabled support and the use of social media as a process and forum for vulnerable people, families and communities, and communities of professional practice.

5.11 Managing problem-solving activities: graduates in Social Work are able to:

   i   think logically, systematically, creatively, critically and reflectively, in order to carry out a holistic assessment;

   ii   apply ethical principles and practices critically in planning problem-solving activities;

   iii   plan a sequence of actions to achieve specified objectives, making use of research, theory and other forms of evidence;

   iv   manage processes of change, drawing on research, theory and other forms of evidence.

5.12 Gathering information: graduates in Social Work are able to:

i demonstrate persistence in gathering information from a wide range of sources and using a variety of methods, for a range of purposes. These methods include electronic searches, reviews of relevant literature, policy and procedures, face-to-face interviews, and written and telephone contact with individuals and groups;

ii take into account differences of viewpoint in gathering information and critically assess the reliability and relevance of the information gathered;

iii assimilate and disseminate relevant information in reports and case records.

5.13 Analysis and synthesis: graduates in Social Work are able to analyse and synthesise knowledge gathered for problem-solving purposes, in order to:

i assess human situations, taking into account a variety of factors (including the views of participants, theoretical concepts, research evidence, legislation and organisational policies and procedures);

ii analyse and synthesise information gathered, weighing competing evidence and modifying their viewpoint in the light of new information, then relate this information to a particular task, situation or problem;

iii balance specific factors relevant to Social Work practice (such as risk, rights, cultural differences and language needs and preferences, responsibilities to protect vulnerable individuals and legal obligations);

iv assess the merits of contrasting theories, explanations, research, policies and procedures and use the information to develop and sustain reasoned arguments;

v employ a critical understanding of factors that support or inhibit problem solving including societal, organisational and community issues as well as individual relationships;

vi critically analyse and take account of the impact of inequality and discrimination in working with people who use Social Work services.

5.14 Intervention and evaluation: graduates in Social Work are able to use their knowledge of a range of interventions and evaluation processes creatively and selectively to:

i build and sustain purposeful relationships with people and organisations in communities and interprofessional contexts;

ii make decisions based on evidence, set goals and construct specific plans to achieve outcomes, taking into account relevant information including ethical guidelines;

iii negotiate goals and plans with others, analysing and addressing in a creative and flexible manner individual, cultural and structural impediments to change;

iv   implement plans through a variety of systematic processes that include working in partnership;

v   practice in a manner that promotes well-being, protects safety and resolves conflict;

vi   act as a navigator, advocate and support to assist people who need care and support to take decisions and access services;

vii   manage the complex dynamics of dependency and, in some settings, provide direct care and personal support to assist people in their everyday lives;

viii meet deadlines and comply with external requirements of a task;

ix   plan, implement and critically monitor and review processes and outcomes;

x   bring work to an effective conclusion, taking into account the implications for all involved;

xi   use and evaluate methods of intervention critically and reflectively.

5.15 Graduates in Social Work are able to communicate clearly, sensitively and effectively (using appropriate methods which may include working with interpreters) with individuals and groups of different ages and abilities in a range of formal and informal situations, in order to:

i   engage individuals and organisations, who may be unwilling, by verbal, paper-based and electronic means to achieve a range of objectives, including changing behaviour;

ii   use verbal and non-verbal cues to guide and inform conversations and interpretation of information;

iii   negotiate and where necessary redefine the purpose of interactions with individuals and organisations and the boundaries of their involvement;

iv   listen actively and empathetically to others, taking into account their specific needs and life experiences;

v   engage appropriately with the life experiences of service users, to understand accurately their viewpoint, overcome personal prejudices and respond appropriately to a range of complex personal and interpersonal situations;

vi   make evidence informed arguments drawing from theory, research and practice wisdom including the viewpoints of service users and/or others;

vii   write accurately and clearly in styles adapted to the audience, purpose and context of the communication;

viii use advocacy skills to promote others' rights, interests and needs;

ix   present conclusions verbally and on paper, in a structured form, appropriate to the audience for which these have been prepared;

x   make effective preparation for, and lead, meetings in a productive way.

5.16 Graduates in Social Work are able to build relationships and work effectively with others, in order to:

   i   involve users of Social Work services in ways that increase their resources, capacity and power to influence factors affecting their lives;

  ii   engage service users and carers and wider community networks in active consultation;

 iii   respect and manage differences such as organisational and professional boundaries and differences of identity and/or language;

  iv   develop effective helping relationships and partnerships that facilitate change for individuals, groups and organisations while maintaining appropriate personal and professional boundaries;

   v   demonstrate interpersonal skills and emotional intelligence that creates and develops relationships based on openness, transparency and empathy;

  vi   increase social justice by identifying and responding to prejudice, institutional discrimination and structural inequality;

 vii   operate within a framework of multiple accountability (for example, to agencies, the public, service users, carers and others);

viii   observe the limits of professional and organisational responsibility, using supervision appropriately and referring to others when required;

  ix   provide reasoned, informed arguments to challenge others as necessary, in ways that are most likely to produce positive outcomes.

5.17 Graduates in Social Work are able to:

   i   work at all times in accordance with codes of professional conduct and ethics;

  ii   advance their own learning and understanding with a degree of independence and use supervision as a tool to aid professional development;

 iii   develop their professional identity, recognise their own professional limitations and accountability, and know how and when to seek advice from a range of sources including professional supervision;

  iv   use support networks and professional supervision to manage uncertainty, change and stress in work situations while maintaining resilience in self and others;

   v   handle conflict between others and internally when personal views may conflict with a course of action necessitated by the Social Work role;

  vi   provide reasoned, informed arguments to challenge unacceptable practices in a responsible manner and raise concerns about wrongdoing in the workplace;

 vii   be open and honest with people if things go wrong;

viii   understand the difference between theory, research, evidence and expertise and the role of professional judgement.

5.18 Graduates in Social Work are able to use information and communication technology effectively and appropriately for:

i   professional communication, data storage and retrieval and information searching;

ii   accessing and assimilating information to inform working with people who use services;

iii data analysis to enable effective use of research in practice;

iv   enhancing skills in problem-solving;

v   applying numerical skills to financial and budgetary responsibilities;

vi   understanding the social impact of technology, including the constraints of confidentiality and an awareness of the impact of the 'digital divide'.

7 Subject-specific and other skills

7.4 On graduating with an honours degree in Social Work, students must be able to demonstrate a developed capacity to:

i   apply creatively a repertoire of core skills as detailed in Section 5;

ii   communicate effectively with service users and carers, and with other professionals;

iii integrate clear understanding of ethical issues and relevant codes or standards of ethics, conduct and practice with their interventions in specific situations;

iv   consistently exercise an appropriate level of autonomy and initiative in individual decision-making within the context of supervisory, collaborative, ethical and organisational requirements;

v   embed skills of critical reflection on their performance and take responsibility for modifying action and learning in light of this, drawing on appropriate support mechanisms where necessary.

References

Adams, R (2002) *Social policy for social work*. Basingstoke: Palgrave.

Alcock, P, Erskine, A and May, M (eds) (2008) *The student's companion to social policy* (3rd edn). Chichester: Wiley.

Aldgate, J (2001) *The Children Act now: Messages from research*. London: The Stationery Office.

Ariès, P (1979) *Centuries of childhood*. Harmondsworth: Penguin.

Association of Directors of Children's Services (2016) Social work evidence template. Available online at: http://adcs.org.uk/care/article/SWET

Barber, P, Brown, R and Martin, D (2012) *Mental health law in England and Wales* (2nd edn). London: Sage.

Beresford, P (2010) *Funding social care: What service users say*. York: Joseph Rowntree Foundation.

Bhabra, S, Ghate, D and Brazier, L (2002) *Raising the educational attainment of children in care*. London: Policy Research Bureau.

Bochel, H and Daly, G (2014) *Social policy* (3rd edn). London: Routledge.

Bostock, L, Bairstow, S, Fish, S and Macleod, F (2005) *Managing risk and minimizing mistakes in services to children and families*. Bristol: Policy Press for SCIE (Social Care Institute for Excellence).

Botley, M, Jinks, B and Metson, C (2010) *Young people's views and experiences of the youth justice system*. Leeds: Children's Workforce Development Council.

Bowers, H et al. (2009) *Older people's vision for long term care*. York: Joseph Rowntree Foundation.

Brammer, A (2014) *Safeguarding adults*. Basingstoke: Palgrave.

Brammer, A (2015) *Social work law* (4th edn). London: Pearson.

Braye, S and Preston-Shoot, M (2016) *Practising social work law* (4th edn). Basingstoke: Palgrave.

Braye, S and Preston-Shoot, M, with Cull, L-A, Johns, R and Roche, J (2005) *Teaching, learning and assessment of law in social work education*. London: Social Care Institute for Excellence/Policy Press.

Brayne, H and Broadbent, G (2002) *Legal materials for social workers*. Oxford: Oxford University Press.

Brayne, H, Carr, H and Goosey, D (2015) *Law for social workers* (13th edn). Oxford: Oxford University Press.

British Association of Social Workers (online) *Professional Capabilities Framework for social work in England.* Birmingham: BASW.

Brown, H and Smith, H (eds) (1992) *Normalisation: A reader for the nineties.* London: Tavistock/Routledge.

Brown, K (ed.) (2011) *Vulnerable adults and community care* (2nd edn). London: Sage.

Brown, R, Barber, P and Martin, D (2009) *The Mental Capacity Act 2005: A guide for practice* (2nd edn). London: Sage.

Care Council for Wales (2013) *Professionalising the social care workforce and protecting the public.* Cardiff: Care Council for Wales.

Children's Society (2011) *Our response to 2009/10 youth justice statistics.* Children's Society. Available at: www.childrenssociety.org.uk/news-views/press-release/our-response-200910-youth-justice-statistics (accessed 25 March 2011).

Clarke, J (1993) *A crisis in care: Challenges to social work.* London: Sage.

Clements, L (2007) *Community care and the law* (4th edn). London: Legal Action Group.

Cooper, P (2014) *Court and Legal Skills.* Basingstoke: Palgrave.

Corker, M and Davis, JM (2000) Disabled children (still) invisible under the law, in Cooper, J (ed.) *Law, rights and disability.* London: Jessica Kingsley.

Cossar, J, Brandon, M and Jordan, P (2014) 'You've got to trust her and she's got to trust you': children's views on participation in the child protection system. *Child and Family Social Work* 21(1): 103–12.

Cowen, H (1999) *Community care, ideology and social policy.* Hemel Hempstead: Prentice-Hall.

Crawford, K and Walker, J (2008) *Social work with older people* (2nd edn). London: Sage.

Cunningham, J and Cunningham, S (2012) *Social policy and social work: An introduction.* London: Sage.

Dalrymple, J and Burke, B (2006) *Anti-oppressive practice social care and the law* (2nd edn). Buckingham: Open University Press.

Davies, L and Duckett, N (2008) *Proactive child protection and social work.* London: Sage.

Davies, M (ed.) (2012a) *Social work with adults.* Basingstoke: Palgrave.

Davies, M (ed.) (2012b) *Social work with children and families.* Basingstoke: Palgrave.

Davis, L (2007) *See you in court: A social worker's guide to presenting evidence in care proceedings.* London: Jessica Kingsley.

Department for Children, Schools and Families (2010) *Promoting educational attainment of looked after children.* Nottingham: DCSF Publications.

Department for Constitutional Affairs (2007) *Mental Capacity Act 2005 code of practice.* London: The Stationery Office.

Department for Education (2010a) *Children Act 1989 guidance and regulations volume 3: Planning transition to adulthood for care leavers.* Norwich: The Stationery Office.

Department for Education (2010b) *Munro Review of Child Protection: Part One: A systems analysis.* London: Department for Education.

Department for Education (2011a) *Children Act 1989 guidance and regulations: Volume 4: Fostering services.* Norwich: The Stationery Office.

Department for Education (2011b) *Children Act 1989 guidance and regulations: Volume 5: Children's homes.* Norwich: The Stationery Office.

Department for Education (2011c) *The Munro review of child protection: Final report.* London: Department for Education.

Department for Education (2011d) *Developing quality tuition effective practice in schools: Looked after children.* London: Department for Education.

Department for Education (2014) *The Children Act 1989 guidance and regulations: Volume 1: Court orders.* London: Department for Education.

Department for Education (2012) *Regulated activity in relation to children: Scope.* London: Department for Education.

Department for Education (2013) Further action on adoption: Finding more loving homes. London: Department for Education.

Department for Education (2015a) *Children Act 1989 guidance and regulations. Volume 2: Care planning, placement and case review.* London: Department for Education.

Department for Education (2015b) *Children Act 1989 guidance and regulations. Volume 3: Planning transition.* London: Department for Education.

Department for Education and Skills (2004) *Every child matters: Change for children.* London: The Stationery Office.

Department for Education and Skills (2005) *Statutory guidance on the duty on local authorities to promote the educational achievement of looked after children under section 52 of the Children Act 2004.* Nottingham: DfES Publications.

Department for Education and Skills (2006a) *Care matters: Transforming the lives of children and young people in care.* Norwich: The Stationery Office.

Department for Education and Skills (2006b) *The Children Act 1989 report 2004 and 2005.* Nottingham: DfES Publications.

Department of Health (1989) *An introduction to the Children Act 1989.* London: HMSO.

Department of Health (1991a) *Child abuse: A study of inquiry reports 1981–1989.* London: HMSO.

Department of Health (1991b) *Children Act 1989 guidance and regulations*. London: HMSO.

Department of Health *Public health outcomes framework*. London: Department of Health. Available at: www.phoutcomes.info/

Department of Health (2000a) *A quality strategy for social care*. London: The Stationery Office.

Department of Health (2000b) *Data Protection Act 1998 guidance to social services*. London: The Stationery Office.

Department of Health (2000c) *Lost in care – Report of the tribunal of inquiry into the abuse of children in care in the former County Council areas of Gwynedd and Clwyd since 1974*. London: The Stationery Office.

Department of Health (2001a) *National service framework for older people*. London: Department of Health.

Department of Health (2001b) *Valuing people: A new strategy for learning disability for the 21st century*. London: The Stationery Office.

Department of Health (2002) *Requirements for social work training*. London: Department of Health.

Department of Health (2003a) *Care homes for older people*. London: The Stationery Office.

Department of Health (2003b) *Fair access to care services LAC 2002(13)*. London: Department of Health.

Department of Health (2004a) *Mental Health Bill 2004*. London: The Stationery Office.

Department of Health (2004b) *National service framework for children, young people and maternity services*. London: The Stationery Office.

Department of Health (2005) *Independence, well-being and choice: Our vision for the future of social care for adults in England*. London: The Stationery Office.

Department of Health (2006a) *Mental Health Bill 2006*. Norwich: The Stationery Office.

Department of Health (2006b) *Our health, our care, our say: A new direction for community services*. Norwich: The Stationery Office.

Department of Health (2008) *Putting people first*. London: Department of Health.

Department of Health (2009a) *Guidance on direct payments for community care, services for carers and children's services*. London: Department of Health.

Department of Health (2009b) *New horizons: A shared vision for mental health*. London: Department of Health.

Department of Health (2010a) *A vision for adult social care: Capable communities and active citizens*. London: Department of Health.

Department of Health (2010b) *Prioritising need in the context of Putting People First: A whole system approach to eligibility for social care – guidance on eligibility criteria for adult social care*. London: Department of Health.

Department of Health (2010c) *Recognised, valued and supported: Next steps for the Carers Strategy.* London: Department of Health.

Department of Health (2011) *Regulated activity (adults): The definition of 'regulated activity' (adults) as defined by the Safeguarding Vulnerable Groups Act 2006 from 10th September 2012.* London: Department of Health.

Department of Health (2015) Mental Health Act 1983 Code of Practice. Norwich: The Stationery Office.

Department of Health (2016) *Care and support statutory guidance.* Available at: www.gov.uk/government/publications/care-act-statutory-guidance/care-and-support-statutory-guidance

Department of Health and Home Office (2003) *The Victoria Climbié Inquiry: Report of an inquiry by Lord Laming.* London: The Stationery Office.

DHSS (Department of Health and Social Security) (1974) *Report of the Committee of Inquiry into the care and supervision provided in relation to Maria Colwell.* London: HMSO.

DHSS (Department of Health and Social Security) (1988) *The report of the inquiry into child abuse in Cleveland 1987 (Butler-Sloss Inquiry).* London: HMSO.

Dugmore, P, Pickford, J and Angus, S (2012) *Youth justice and social work* (2nd edn). London: Sage.

Eastman, M (1994) *Old age abuse: A new perspective.* London: Chapman & Hall.

Ells, P and Dehn, G (2001) Whistleblowing: Public concern at work, in Cull, L and Roche, J (eds) *The law and social work.* Basingstoke: Palgrave.

Fennell, P (1999) The third way in mental health policy: Negative rights, positive rights and the convention. *Journal of Law and Society*, 26: 103–27.

Foulds, J (2009) Coping with court. *Professional Social Work*, February: 12–14.

Fox Harding, L (1997) *Perspectives in child care policy* (2nd revised edn). London: Longman.

Freeman, P and Hunt, J (1998) *Parental perspectives on care proceedings.* London: HMSO.

Gardener, A (2014) *Personalisation in social work* (2nd edn). London: Sage.

General Social Care Council/TOPSS (2002) *National occupational standards for social work.* Leeds: Training Organisation for the Personal Social Services.

Goldson, B (2002) *Vulnerable inside: Children in secure and penal settings.* London: Children's Society.

Goldson, B and Muncie, J (2006) *Youth crime and justice.* London: Sage.

Griffiths, R (1988) *Community care: Agenda for action.* London: HMSO.

Harris, M (2001) Boards: Just subsidiaries of the state?, in Harris M and Rochester, C (eds) *Voluntary organisations and social policy in Britain.* Basingstoke: Palgrave.

Hart, D (2011) *Into the breach: The enforcement of statutory orders in the youth justice system.* London: Prison Reform Trust.

Hazel, N (2008) *Cross-national comparison of youth Justice.* London: Youth Justice Board.

Health and Care Professions Council (HCPC) (2010) *Guidance on conduct and ethics for students.* London: Health and Care Professions Council.

Health and Care Professions Council (HCPC) (2012) *Standards of proficiency: Social workers in England.* London: Health and Care Professions Council.

Hill, A (2010) *Working in statutory contexts.* Cambridge: Polity Press.

HM Government (2007) *Putting people first: A shared vision and commitment to the transformation of adult social care.* London: Department of Health.

HM Government (2009) *Valuing people now: A new three-year strategy for people with learning disabilities.* London: Department of Health.

HM Government (2015) *Working together to safeguard children: A guide to inter-agency working to safeguard and promote the welfare of children.* Norwich: The Stationery Office.

HM Government (2016) *Care Act Statutory Guidance.* Department of Health. Available at: https://www.gov.uk/government/publications/care-act-statutory-guidance/care-and-support-statutory-guidance#using-the-care-act-guidance

Home Office (2001) *Youth justice: The statutory principal aim of preventing offending by children and young people.* London: Home Office.

Home Office (2002) *Justice for all.* London: HMSO.

Home Office (2003) *Youth justice next steps.* London: HMSO.

Home Office (2014) *Police and Criminal Evidence Act 1984 Revised Code of Practice for the detention, treatment and questioning of persons by police officers police and Criminal Evidence Act 1984 (Pace) – Code C.* London: The Stationery Office.

Home Office (2015) *Guidance on Part 2 of the Sexual Offences Act 2003.* London: The Stationery Office.

Hunt, J (2010) *Parental perspectives on the family justice system in England and Wales: A review of research.* London: Family Justice Council. Available at: www.family-justice-council.org.uk

Hunt, J, Macleod, A and Thomas, C (1999) *The last resort: Child protection, the courts and the 1989 Children Act.* London: HMSO.

Information Commissioner's Office (2014) Data Protection: Subject access code of practice. Wilmslow: Information Commissioner's Office.

International Federation of Social Workers (IFSW) (2014) Global definition of social work. IFSW. Available at: @ ifsw.org/get-involved/global-definition-of-social-work

Johns, R (2005) Of unsound mind? Mental health social work and the European Convention on Human Rights. *Practice,* 16(4): 247–59.

Johns, R (2007) Who decides now? Protecting and empowering vulnerable adults who lose the capacity to make decisions for themselves. *British Journal of Social Work,* 37(3): 557–64.

Johns, R (2010) Vulnerability, autonomy, capacity and consent, Chapter 11 in Long, L, Roche, J and Stringer, D *The law and social work* (2nd edn). Basingstoke: Palgrave.

Johns, R (2011) *Social work, social policy and older people.* London: Sage.

Johns, R (2014) *Capacity and autonomy.* Basingstoke: Palgrave.

Johns, R (2016) *Ethics and law for social workers.* Sage: London.

Jones, R (2016) *Mental Health Act manual* (19th edn). London: Sweet & Maxwell.

Jowitt, M and O'Loughlin, S (2012) *Social work with children and families* (3rd edn). London: Sage.

Laird, S (2010) *Practical social work law: Analysing court cases and inquiries.* London: Pearson.

Lavalette, M and Pratt, A (2005) *Social policy: A conceptual and theoretical introduction* (2nd edn). London: Sage.

Law Commission (1993) *Mentally incapacitated adults and decision-making: A new jurisdiction.* London: HMSO.

Law Commission (2010) *Adult social care: A consultation paper.* London: Law Commission.

Law Commission (2011) *Adult social care.* London: Law Commission.

Levy, A and Kahan, B (1991) *The pindown experience and the protection of children – Report of the Staffordshire Child Care Inquiry 1990.* Stafford: Staffordshire County Council.

Long, L, Roche, J and Stringer, D (eds) (2010) *The law and social work* (2nd edn). Basingstoke: Palgrave.

Lymbery, M (2005) *Social work with older people.* London: Sage.

Lymbery, M (2010) A new vision for adult social care? Continuities and change in the care of older people. *Critical Social Policy*, 3(1): 5–26.

Mandelstam, M (2011) *Safeguarding adults at risk of harm: A legal guide for practitioners.* London: SCIE (Social Care Institute for Excellence).

Mandelstam, M (2013) *Safeguarding vulnerable adults and the law* (2nd edn). London: Jessica Kingsley.

Ministry of Justice (2008) *Mental Capacity Act 2005 deprivation of liberty safeguards.* Norwich: The Stationery Office.

Ministry of Justice (2009a) *Preparing for care and supervision proceedings.* London: Ministry of Justice.

Ministry of Justice (2009b) *Referral orders and youth offender panels: Guidance for the courts, youth offending teams and youth offender panels.* London: Ministry of Justice.

Ministry of Justice (2010) *Breaking the cycle: Effective punishment, rehabilitation and sentencing of offenders.* London: Ministry of Justice.

Ministry of Justice (2011) *Achieving best evidence in criminal proceedings: Guidance on interviewing victims and witnesses, and guidance on using special measures*. London: Ministry of Justice.

Ministry of Justice (2013a) *Consolidated criminal practice direction criminal procedure rules*. London: Ministry of Justice.

Ministry of Justice (2013b) *Modern youth offending partnerships*. London: Youth Justice Board for England and Wales.

Ministry of Justice (2014) *Practice direction 12a — care, supervision and other Part 4 proceedings: Guide to case management*. London: Ministry of Justice.

Munby, J (2014) *Transparency in the family courts: Publication of judgments practice guidance*. London: Judiciary of England and Wales. Available at: www.judiciary.gov.uk (accessed 19 February 2014).

NACRO (2008) *Working in the courts: A good practice guide for practitioners in the youth justice system*. London: NACRO.

National Assembly for Wales (2000) *In safe hands*. Cardiff: Welsh Assembly Government.

National Assembly for Wales (2005a) *Raising the standard: The revised adult mental health National Service Framework and an action plan for Wales*. Cardiff: Welsh Assembly Government.

National Assembly for Wales (2005b) *The strategy for older people in Wales*. Cardiff: Welsh Assembly Government.

Office of the Public Guardian (2008) *Mental Capacity Act 2005 deprivation of liberty safeguards*. Norwich: The Stationery Office.

Ofsted, Healthcare Commission, HM Inspector of Constabulary (2008) *Review of services for children and young people, with particular reference to safeguarding*. Available at: www.ofsted.gov.uk/oxcare_providers/la_view/(leaid)/309 (accessed 2 February 2009).

Packman, J (1975) *The child's generation*. Oxford: Blackwell.

Parker, J and Bradley, G (2014) *Social work practice: Assessment, planning, intervention and review* (4th edn). London: Sage.

Parton, N (1985) *The politics of child abuse*. Basingstoke: Macmillan.

Parton, N (2014) *The politics of child protection: Contemporary developments and future directions*. London: Palgrave Macmillan.

Prior, PM (2001) Protective Europe: Does it exist for people with mental disorders? *Journal of European Social Policy*, 11(1): 25–38.

Pritchard, J (ed.) (2008) *Good practice in the law and safeguarding adults*. London: Jessica Kingsley.

QAA (Quality Assurance Agency for Higher Education) (2016) *Social work subject benchmark statements*. London: QAA.

Rai-Atkins, A, Ali-Jama, A, Wright, N, Scott, V, Coy, J, Craig, G and Katbanma, S (2002) *Best practice in mental health: Advocacy for African, Caribbean and South Asian communities.* Bristol: Policy Press.

Ray, M and Phillips, J (2012) *Social work with older people.* Basingstoke: Palgrave.

Raynes, N, Temple, B, Glenister, C and Coulthard, L (2001) *Quality at home for older people: Involving service users in defining home care specifications.* Bristol: Policy Press.

Research in Practice (2014) Court orders and pre-proceedings. Available at: http:// coppguidance.rip.org.uk/

Richardson, G (2008) Coercion and human rights: A European perspective. *Journal of Mental Health*, 17(3): 245–54.

Roberts, L (2011) Courting appeal. *PSW Professional Social Work,* April: 12–13.

Ruegger, M (2001) *Hearing the voice of the child.* Lyme Regis: Russell House.

Ryder, J (2012) *The family justice modernisation programme: Final report.* Available at: www. judiciary.gov.uk/publications/family-modernisation-final-report/ (accessed 4 June 2014).

Seebohm (1968) *Report of the committee on local authority and allied personal social services.* London: HMSO.

Seymour, C and Seymour, R (2011) *Courtroom and report writing skills for social workers* (2nd edn). London: Sage.

Seymour, C and Seymour, R (2013) *Practical child law for social workers.* London: Sage.

Sharkey, P (2006) *The essentials of community care: A guide for practitioners* (2nd edn). Basingstoke: Macmillan.

Smith, D (2000) Learning from the Scottish Juvenile Justice System. *Probation Journal*, 47(1): 13–17.

Smith, F (2000) *Looking after children: Good parenting, good outcomes.* London: Children Act Enterprises.

Smith, R (2014) *Youth justice: Ideas, policy, practice.* London: Routledge.

Spencer-Lane, T (2010) A statutory framework for safeguarding adults? The Law Commission's consultation paper on adult social care. *Journal of Adult Protection*, 12(1): 43–9.

Spray, C and Jowett, B (2012) *Social work practice with children and families.* London: Sage.

Staines, J (2015) *Youth justice.* Basingstoke: Palgrave.

Stephenson, M, Giller, H and Brown, S (2011) *Effective practice in youth justice* (2nd edn). London: Routledge.

Sutherland, S (1999) *With respect to old age: Long term care – Rights and responsibilities: A report by The Royal Commission on Long Term Care.* London: The Stationery Office.

Thompson, N (2012) *Anti-discriminatory practice* (5th edn). Basingstoke: Palgrave.

Tosey, P (2000) Making sense of interventions, in Wheal, A (ed.) *Working with parents: Learning from other people's experience.* Lyme Regis: Russell House.

Vernon, A (2002) *User-defined outcomes of community care for Asian disabled people.* Bristol: Policy Press.

Welbourne, P (2010) Accountability, Chapter 6 in Long, L, Roche, J and Stringer, D (eds) *The law and social work* (2nd edn). Basingstoke: Palgrave.

Welsh Assembly Government (2000) *In safe hands.* Cardiff: Welsh Assembly Government.

Welsh Assembly Government (2002) *Health and social care for adults: Creating a unified and fair system for assessing and managing care.* Cardiff: Welsh Assembly Government.

Welsh Assembly Government (2003) *Health, social care and well-being strategies: Policy guidance.* Cardiff: Welsh Assembly Government.

Welsh Assembly Government (2010) *Community care, services for carers and children's services (direct payments) (Wales) regulations.* Cardiff: Welsh Assembly Government.

Welsh Assembly Government (2012) *Together for mental health: A strategy for mental health and wellbeing in Wales.* Cardiff: Welsh Assembly Government.

Welsh Assembly Government (2013a) *Carers strategy for Wales 2013.* Cardiff: Welsh Assembly Government.

Welsh Assembly Government (2013b) *Protecting Children in Wales.* Cardiff: Welsh Assembly Government.

Welsh Assembly Government (2014) *Children Act 1989 guidance and regulations: Vol. 1 Court orders.* Cardiff: Welsh Assembly Government.

Welsh Assembly Government (2015) *Social Services and Well-being (Wales) Act 2014 Part 3 Code of Practice (assessing the needs of individuals).* Cardiff: Welsh Assembly Government.

Welsh Assembly Government (2016a) *Social Services and Well-being (Wales) Act 2014. Working together to safeguard people. Volume 4.* Cardiff: Welsh Assembly Government.

Welsh Assembly Government (2016b) Together for mental health delivery plan. Cardiff: Welsh Assembly Government. Available at: http://gov.wales/docs/dhss/publications/121203planen.pdf

White, R, Carr, P and Lowe, N (2002) *The Children Act in practice* (3rd edn). London: Butterworths.

White, R, Carr, P and Lowe, N (2008) *The Children Act in practice* (4th edn). London: Butterworths.

Williams, J (2002) Public law protection of vulnerable adults: The debate continues, so does the abuse. *Journal of Social Work*, 2(3): 293–316.

Williams, J (2008) *Child law for social work* (2nd edn). London: Sage.

Williams, P and Evans, M (2013) *Social work with people with learning difficulties* (3rd edn). London: Sage.

Wilson, J (2001) *A guide to interviewing children*. London: Routledge.

Wilson, K, Ruch, G, Lymbery, M and Cooper, A (2008) *Social work: An introduction to contemporary practice*. London: Pearson.

Youth Justice Board for England and Wales (2005) *National evaluation of the bail supervision and support schemes.* London: Youth Justice Board for England and Wales.

Youth Justice Board for England and Wales (2010) *The Youth Rehabilitation Order and other youth justice provisions of the Criminal Justice and Immigration Act 2008*. London: Youth Justice Board.

Youth Justice Board for England and Wales (2013) *National standards for youth justice*. London: Youth Justice Board.

Index

Locators shown in *italics* refer to figures and tables.